THE OTHERNESS WITHIN

THE OTHERNESS
WITHIN *Gnostic Readings*

in Marcel Proust, Flannery O'Connor,

and François Villon

JEFFERSON HUMPHRIES

Louisiana State University Press

Baton Rouge and London

Designer: Albert Crochet
Typeface: Linotron Galliard
Typesetter: Graphic Composition, Inc.
Printer: Thomson-Shore, Inc.
Binder: John H. Dekker & Sons, Inc.

LIBRARY OF CONGRESS CATALOGING IN PUBLICATION DATA

Humphries, Jefferson, 1955–
   The otherness within.

   Bibliography: p.
   Includes index.
   1. Gnosticism in literature. 2. Psychoanalysis and literature. 3. Proust, Marcel,
1871–1922—Criticism and interpretation. 4. O'Connor, Flannery—Criticism and
interpretation. 5. Villon, François, b. 1431—Criticism and interpretation. I. Title.
PN49.H85 1983   809'.9338   82–22856
ISBN 0–8071–1089–2

Acknowledgment is made to the following publishers for permission to quote
from these works: "The Alchemist," in *Permanent Errors*, copyright © 1970 by
Reynolds Price, reprinted with the permission of Atheneum Publishers; foreign
rights by permission of Harriet Wasserman Literary Agency. *The Poems of François
Villon*, translated by Galway Kinnell, copyright © 1965 by Galway Kinnell,
reprinted by permission of Houghton Mifflin Company. *Everything That Rises Must
Converge*, copyright © 1958, 1965 by the Estate of Mary Flannery O'Connor.
Mystery and Manners, copyright © 1969 by the Estate of Mary Flannery
O'Connor. *The Habit of Being*, copyright © 1979 by Regina O'Connor. These
three works by Flannery O'Connor are used by permission of Farrar, Straus &
Giroux, Inc.; foreign rights by permission of Harold Matson Company, Inc. *A
Good Man Is Hard to Find*, by Flannery O'Connor, copyright © 1976 by Regina
O'Connor, used by permission of Harcourt Brace Jovanovich, Inc.; foreign rights
by permission of Harold Matson Company, Inc.

Publication of this book has been assisted by a grant from the Andrew W. Mellon
Foundation.

In Memory of
Ellen Gray Banks Humphries
   for
Sara Aduston Meriwether Humphries
   for
William Washington Humphries

The Alchemist

Laughing, the chemist set the hot alembic
Where it could cool, fuming at his grin.
Now he knew what—simply—he would need
To force the thing he coveted to come—

Mind as girdling as the zodiac,
Free and sovereign but fiercely ruled,
Glomerate with power as the sea;
Eons for seething down this crystal crib.

—In which the monster of his yearning lay
(Got now, blind, by him on this blind night),
Prima materia—rose past him to God;

While babbling like a drunk, he lay among
His magic set, his priceless brittle gear,
And craved the crumb of gold he'd just now had.

                          —Reynolds Price, after Rilke

Chaque jour j'attache moins de prix à l'intelligence.

                          —Marcel Proust

Contents

Acknowledgments

I would like to thank Wallace Fowlie, who introduced me to the work of Proust when I was an undergraduate at Duke University; Joseph Halpern, whose encouragement and criticism have been absolutely indispensable; Barbara Guetti, without whose advice this study would be much the poorer; Paul de Man, who at a crucial time recognized what some could not, that whatever merit and usefulness this volume may have lie in its eccentricity and showed me how to let it be as perverse as it could be; Jacques Guicharnaud, who waded through early drafts and was generous with advice; Reynolds Price, who read an early version of the section on Proust and inspired me by his example and kind words, and by the challenge and provocation of his own ideas about Proust and O'Connor (very different from my own); Fredric Jameson and Jeffrey Kittay, both of whom encouraged me at a time when I badly needed it; my friends Thomas Fay, Christopher Miller, and Michèle Cone, who have in just the right proportion teased, cajoled, mocked, criticized, amended, and encouraged the ideas contained herein; the participants in the first Winthrop Symposium on Modern Continental Writers, who gave some of these ideas their first public hearing; Beverly Jarrett, Executive Editor at LSU Press, for shepherding my manuscript so graciously and kindly through the labyrinth of stages which lead to final publication; my copy editor, Marie Blanchard, for her sympathetic meticulousness; and finally Mary Christoforo, who typed and retyped the manuscript with heroic patience and good humor.

THE OTHERNESS WITHIN

Introduction

It is better to fail in teaching what should not be taught than to succeed in teaching what is not true.
—Paul de Man

I. Gnosis and Literature

This began as a study of Proust. The more I read him, however, the more I came to suspect that I had stumbled onto something which could not be confined to a monograph: a kind of literariness which by its nature is not accessible to the more traditional scholarly apparatus, which could only be intimated, glimpsed, through an eclectic application of some of the most recent critical strategies. I decided to undertake something less tidy than a monograph, which might have remained safely over the net of scholarly convention and observed the unities of critical orthodoxy: exhaustiveness and methodological purity. According to the traditional criteria, there is an arbitrariness here, in method and in the choice of texts. I invite the reader to consider that this arbitrariness is calculated. I am trying to observe a rigor of heresy.

Paul Zweig has written of the way in which gnostic redemption is inseparable from a narcissistic introspectiveness, and an antipathy for the things and ways of orthodoxy and community. Each human being, in gnostic theology, contains an occulted, imprisoned bit of divinity, and to discover and free it entails an uncompromising rejection of the world and a descent into the depths of self. Salvation, escape from an evil world, can only be reached by turning inward. This has meant that "the Gnostic imagination is powerfully subversive. Nothing in the world claimed their allegiance if not that concealed fragment of their being which they were taught to cultivate."[1] Because this fragment is occluded by the dross of flesh, each individual repeats in microcosm the corruptedness, the mediatedness, the "createdness" of the universe, which came into being when the all-encompassing Light permitted Darkness to arise within it. From that darkness issued the physis or female principle of nature. Then the Word of God, the Logos of the Light, entered into the dark, humid physis and bestowed order upon its chaos. From this contamination of Light with Dark, Dark with Light, the cosmos arose, as an ordered disorder. All of this is described in the visionary *Poimandres* of Hermes Trismegestus:

> Everything opened up before me and I saw a boundless vista.
> Everything became a bright and cheerful light; I was enraptured by the sight. After a while, a fearful and terrifying darkness gradually appeared, forcing its way down, rolling and twisting so that I compared it with a snake. Then the darkness was changed into a kind of moist Physis, and fell into inextricable confusion, exuding smoke as if from a fire, and emitting an indescribable voice as if in lament.
> Then it let out an inarticulate cry that sounded like the voice of fire.
> From the light however. . . . (lacuna) a Holy Logos came over the Physis, and unmixed fire leaped out of the moist Physis and strove up towards height. The fire was fleeting and violent, and at the same time active, and the air, which is light, followed the Pneuma as it rose from the earth and water to the fire, so that it seemed to be suspended from the fire. The earth and water remained mixed with each other, however, so that the earth could not be seen for water.
> These (elements) were kept in motion by the pneumatic Logos, which hovered (cf. Gen. 1,2) (over them), so that a sound became audible.[2]

<hr/>

1. Paul Zweig, *The Heresy of Self-Love* (2nd ed.; Princeton, 1980), 6.
2. "Poimandres," in *Gnosis: Character and Testimony*, ed. Robert Haardt, trans. J. F. Hendry (Leiden, 1971), 168. See also Hans Jonas, *The Gnostic Religion* (Boston, 1958), 48–96, 147–73. *Poimandres* is the first of the so-called *Corpus Hermeticum*, supposed to have been composed by the god Hermes Trismegistus. It is believed to date from the first three centuries, A.D. The entire *Corpus* is not homogeneously gnostic but is heavily larded with commonplaces of gnostic belief, especially here, in the *Poimandres*. There are extremely few genuine gnostic texts available to us today, due to the early church's strenuous efforts to stamp out the heresy. Some of the most valuable sources in such a vacuum have become the attacks on gnostic doctrine by such spokesmen as Hippolytus of Rome (165–235 A.D.) whose *Philosophumena* sought to discredit contemporary gnostic sects. As for gnosticism itself, the term is misleading, for it implies a unified body of thought and a group of individuals tightly bound together by adherence to such a gospel. The actual gnostics comprised many diverse sects, only a few of whom actually called themselves by

The Light or intellect of the deity then created the demiurge, god of fire, and his seven helpers, the archons of time and space, to rule over the cosmos. The demiurge, by the will of the Light, "encloses the spheres and whirls them tumultuously around . . . and has them circulate from an undefined point of departure to a goal in the infinite; for the revolution begins where it ends."[3] This downward whirling brings forth all of the fragmentary variety of natural phenomena.

Man comes into being in a more specific way. Motivated by the wish to contemplate his own perfection, the Godhead creates primal man, Anthropos, as his duplicate, a mirror image of his own androgynous totality, so that in man, he may love, and yet love himself. God is desire; man comes into being as both object and expression of desire which is wholly reflexive and self-sufficient. "The Intellect, however, the Father of all, being life and light, gave birth to a being like himself; he loved him as his own child; for the Man (Anthropos) was very beautiful, bearing in him the image of his Father. For God was truly pleased with the form that was his own and he delivered to him (i.e. Anthropos) all his creatures."[4] The creation, and man in particular, multiplies and divides God, so that he may contemplate himself and take pleasure in all the shapes of his perfection, remaining the totality of all, desire desiring desire.

Primal man is empowered to rule over the cosmos along with the demiurge. All of the eight "Administrators were pleased with him and each gave him a share of his own area." Man, however, seems to forget his dependence on the Light, and repeats the latter's self-absorption, as though he too could encompass his desire and its object, attain self-sufficient unity. This mimesis of the divine doubling is the cause of man's fall.

---

that name. The first gnostics may have been contemporaries of Christ. They reached the height of their power and influence during the second century of the Christian era, when Valentinus, perhaps the most remembered of all the gnostic theologians, lived. But gnosticism survived in such later avatars as Manicheanism for a few more centuries. The most valuable body of primary sources available was discovered at Nag Hammadi in Egypt in December 1945—the buried library of some fifth century gnostic(s). Even in this case, the texts have no common author or date of composition and do not represent anything like a unified theology. What all of the various gnostic sects have in common is a belief in the identity of knowledge—an alien knowledge, a knowledge of otherness within the self—and salvation.

3. "Poimandres," in *Gnosis*, ed. Haardt, 169.
4. *Ibid.*, 170.

Thus Anthropos, who possessed complete authority over the world of mortal creatures and unreasoning animals leaned out of the world of the spheres and so broke through their outer shell and showed the beautiful form of God to the lower Physis. When it saw that he possessed in himself the inexhaustible beauty and all the strength of the administrators, together with the form of God, Physis smiled on him with love, for it had seen the image of the wonderfully beauteous form of Anthropos reflected in the water and his shadow on earth. He saw in it the form similar to his own, reflected in the water, loved it and desired to live in it. This desire was at once fulfilled, and so he began to dwell in the unreasoning form. Physis had now received the form it loved, embraced it and they were united, since they loved each other.

For this reason, man, unlike all other creatures on earth, is dual in nature: mortal in the body, but immortal through the real Anthropos. Though he is immortal and possesses authority over all things, he undergoes the fate of mortals in being subject to Destiny. Though above the world of the spheres, yet he has become a slave within that world: male and female generated from the bisexual Father, sleepless since he derives from a sleepless creature, nevertheless he is vanquished by love and sleep.[5]

Man's embracement of physis vitiates both because it is mediated, misdirected. It is *the* primal irony, misunderstood by all but the hypothetical Light: nature loves God, knowing him only through his image, man, and man loves himself in his own image, which nature reflects. Each seeks in the other something which is not there.

The *Hypostasis of the Archons* gives a different account of the fall, in which man is created by the archons in the image of the deity, which is mediated through a female principle called "Incorruptibility," in order to lure part of it down into their dominion.

> As Incorruptibility looked down into the region of the Waters, her Image appeared in the Waters; and the Authorities of the Darkness became enamored of her. But they could not lay hold of that Image, which had appeared to them in the Waters, because of their weakness—since beings that merely possess a soul cannot lay hold of those that possess a Spirit—; for they were from Below, while it was from Above.
>
> This is the reason why "Incorruptibility looked down into the region (etc.)": so that, by the Father's will, she might bring the Entirety into union with the Light. The Rulers (Archons) laid plans and said, "Come, let us create a man

5. *Ibid.*, 170–71.

that will be soil from the earth." They modelled their creature as one wholly
of the earth.

. . . .

They took some [soil] from the earth and modelled their [Man], after their
body and [after the Image] of God that had appeared [to them] in the Waters.

. . . .

They said, "[Come, let] us lay hold of it by means of the form that we have
modelled."[6]

This version, despite the permutations worked on other aspects of the
myth, emphasizes the role of the specular image in the creation and sub-
sequent fall just as strongly as *Poimandres.*

It is within the image of Light, which the self is, that man must find
his way back to the Light, even if that image is occluded by the dross of
flesh, *of cosmogonic irony,* of misdirected desire. By discovering the fragment of pure Light lost in the self, one intimates the real, primal identity
with God, who wants to help man back to Him because He loves Himself. As man's sense of identity with the divine principle, the first cause,
is aroused, the self's sense of estrangement from the world and all its
trappings becomes greater, even as its own powers of creation are in-
creasing.

In all of these myths there is a paradigm of artistic creation. Language
is a medium in which man may reenact the self-contemplation and self-
desire which brought about his being and his fall. Though words are
mediated, vitiated, by nature ironic, like man's lust for himself, he may
see in them his own error, the miscarriage of his own unity with Light.
In the error of words, he glimpses—as the antithesis of their mediatedness and indirection—the totality of the Word, as antinomial, absolute
otherness. In literature, fallen man may learn of the loss which has constituted him, his language and his desire, as mediation, heteronomy, contamination of light by dark. The mediation of literature, its projection of
a ghostly space in which lies are truth and pleasure is entirely in being
misled, by radicalizing the sense of lostness, reflecting the spectral irony
and mendacity of all human knowledge, the absence of the totality of

6. "The Hypostasis of the Archons," in *The Nag Hammadi Library,* ed. James M.
Robinson (San Francisco, 1977), 153.

Light, plunges every "Anthropos" deeper into himself, into the negative, antithetical lostness of the Light within him.

> This is the one who is a Father and the one whom they are not able to speak about, and the one of whom they do not conceive; he is the one who first exists.
>
> It is impossible for anyone to conceive of him or think of him. Who can approach there, toward the exalted one, toward the preexistent in the proper sense? But all the names conceived or spoken about him are produced for an honor, as a trace of him, according to the power of each of those who glorify him. Now he who arose from him stretches himself out for begetting and for knowledge on the part of the Totalities. He [also], without falsification, is all of the names, and he is, in the proper sense, the sole first one, [the] man of the Father. He it is whom I call the form of the formless,
>> the body of the bodiless,
>> the face of the invisible,
>> the word of [the] unutterable,
>> the mind of the inconceivable,
>> the fountain which flows from him,
>> the root of those who are planted,
>> and the god of those who exist,
>> the light of those whom he illuminates,
>> the love of those whom he loved,
>> the providence of those for whom he providentially cares,
>> the wisdom of those whom he made wise,
>> the power of those to whom he gives power,
>> the assembly of those whom he assembles,
>> the revelation of the things which are sought after,
>> the eyes of those who see,
>> the breath of those who breathe,
>> the life of those who live,
>> the unity of those who are mixed with the Totalities.
>
> . . . .
>
> The prayer of the Totality helped him to return to himself and (to) the Totality, for it caused him to remember those who have existed from the first, and them to remember him. This is the thought which calls out from afar, bringing him back.[7]

Language, as Saussure and Derrida have taught us to consider, comprising signifier, signified, and referent, signifying differentially, by virtue

7. "The Tripartite Tractate," *ibid.*, 63–64, 71.

of the non-integrity, heteronomy, mutual contamination of all its parts, each sign defined not absolutely but relative to all the others, is the perfect analogue, speculum, for the state of fallen man. Literature, insofar as it is private and self-directed, the instrument of a self-contemplation, is necessarily "gnostic," in the most associative and circumstantial way. This would perhaps exclude theater and oral poetry, though not necessarily.[8] It is quite arguable that, though experienced in the presence of others, the experience itself is quite individual. Furthermore, the charge of solipsism, once made of recluses, has a way of spreading to taint gossips, party-goers, politicians, the very public egotists who accused the private ones.

The heresy of "private" literatures is belied by the "moral" pretensions of many critics and scholars, not to mention novelists and poets, those steeped in the Anglo-American tradition of historical and empirical, "pragmatic" criticism. Such critical discourses subordinate literature to the greater good of communities, families, individuals as responsible members of collectivities. But there are writers, and critics, whose "moral" pretensions, if they claim any, are expressly individual and asocietal, conceiving themselves, if not in opposition to communal, moral orthodoxies, in contempt or disregard of them. It is those critics and those writers who might be said, in a metaphorical sense, to descend from the heresy of gnosticism.

They exploit qualities acknowledged to be innate in language since Plato: "No man of sense will like to put himself or the education of his mind in the power of names."[9] To put oneself in the power of names, of language, as we self-consciously do when we experience literature, when we read, is to experience the untrustworthiness and the fictiveness of linguistic knowledge, the mediatedness of the language by which we know ourselves, each other, and all the things we do and think—for, as phenomenology and psychology have taught us to consider, we can only conceive our own selves as an otherness, as though we were an other

---

8. See for instance Arthur F. Lord, *The Singer of Tales* (New York, 1965).

9. Plato, *Collected Dialogues*, ed. Edith Hamilton and Huntingdon Cairns (Princeton, 1961), 474. The discussion of love in "The Symposium," in the same volume, is highly relevant and decidedly "gnostic" in character.

subject and object at once.[10] Art—whether language of words or of images—is the self-conscious experience of that differential otherness. We take a pleasure in suspending disbelief and losing ourselves in words. Like the hero of the gnostic *Hymn of the Pearl*, returning to the house of his father and finding there his robe of many colors, we find in a made thing some intimation of misplaced totality:

> And though I had forgot its majesty—
> Having left my father's house in childhood—
> Suddenly as I saw it before me
> It became a reflection of myself.
> I saw its entirety in myself,
> And saw myself in it, there, facing me,
> For we were two in our diversity
> Yet one in similarity again.[11]

Thus, whenever we take pleasure in literature, we reenact the gnostic fable of creation, and of fallenness. Through the bits and pieces of language, we strain towards an antithetical unity of lost knowledge, of ourselves, of the truth—of gnosis.

Edgar Allan Poe, in his *Eureka*, described knowledge and being as entropic: "In the original unity of the first thing lies the secondary cause of all things, with the germ of their inevitable annihilation."[12] Paul Valéry, writing about this work of Poe, elaborates its gnostic message:

> The cosmogonic form . . . comprises sacred books, admirable poems, excessively bizarre stories, full of beauty and nonsense, physico-mathematical researches of a profundity sometimes worthy of an object less insignificant than the universe. But it is the glory of man to be able to spend himself on the void; and it is not only his glory. Lunatic researches are akin to unforeseen discoveries. The role of the nonexistent exists; the function of the imaginary is real; and pure logic teaches us that *the false implies the true*. It seems then

10. See Jacques Lacan, "Le stade du miroir comme formateur de la fonction du Je," *Ecrits I* (Paris, 1966); René Girard, *Violence and the Sacred* (Baltimore, 1977), 143–68.

11. "The Hymn of the Pearl," in *Gnosis*, ed. Haardt, 165. According to Hans Jonas, "Hymn of the Pearl" is a misleading title given this text by translators. Part of the apocryphal Acts of the Apostle Thomas, its actual title is "Song of the Apostle Judas Thomas in the Land of the Indians." Jonas writes that "In view of the didactic intention and narrative form of the poem, 'hymn' is perhaps not exactly appropriate." Jonas, *Gnostic Religion*, 112. Jonas devotes an entire chapter to this quite beautiful text, more a fable than a hymn.

12. Edgar Allan Poe, "Eureka, an Essay on the Material and Spiritual Universe," *The Works of Edgar Allan Poe* (New York, 1876), II, 118.

that the history of the mind can be resumed in these terms: it is absurd by what it seeks, great by what it finds.

. . . . .

As for the idea of a beginning,—I mean of an absolute beginning—it is necessarily a myth. Every beginning is a coincidence; we would have to conceive it as I don't know what sort of contact between all and nothing. Trying to think of it one finds that all beginning is a consequence—every beginning completes something.

Totality, origin, light, truth—they are antithetical to us and to the language in which we try to explain ourselves. How can we know them, except as what exceeds and yet invests us?

We are besieged by what is remembered, what is possible, what is imaginable, what is calculable, all the possible combinations of our mind, at every degree of probability, at every state of precision. How can we form a concept of what is opposed to nothing? If it resembled something, it would not be the whole. If it resembles nothing . . . And if this totality has the same power as our mind, our mind has no hold on it. All the objections which are raised against an active infinity, all the difficulties one finds when wishing to order a multiplicity declare themselves. No proposition is capable of this subject so disorderedly rich that all attributes apply to it. Just as the universe escapes intuition, so it is transcendent to logic.

And as for its origin—IN THE BEGINNING WAS FABLE. It will be there always.[13]

13. "Comme la tragédie fait à l'histoire et à la psychologie, le genre cosmogonique touche aux religions, avec lesquelles il se confond par endroits, et à la science dont il se distingue necessairement par l'absence de vérifications. Il comprend des livres sacrés, des poèmes admirables, des récits excessivement bizarres, chargés de beautés et de ridicules, des recherches physico-mathématiques d'une profondeur qui est digne quelquefois d'un objet moins insignifiant que l'univers. Mais c'est la gloire de l'homme que de pouvoir se dépenser dans le vide; et ce n'est pas seulement sa gloire. Les recherches insensées sont parentes des découvertes imprévues. Le rôle de l'inexistant existe; la fonction de l'imaginaire est réelle; et la logique pure nous enseigne que *le faux implique le vrai.* Il semble donc que l'histoire de l'esprit se puisse résumer en ces termes: *il est absurde par ce qu'il cherche, il est grand par ce qu'il trouve.* . . . Quant à l'idée d'un commencement,—j'entends d'un commencement absolu,—elle est necessairement un mythe. Tout commencement est coïncidence; il nous faudrait concevoir ici je ne sais quel contact entre le tout et le rien. En essayant d'y penser on trouve que tout commencement est conséquence,—tout commencement *achève* quelque chose. . . . Ce qui est souvenir, ce qui est possible, ce qui est imaginable, ce qui est calculable, toutes les combinaisons de notre esprit, à tous les degrés de la probabilité, à tous les états de la précision nous assiègent. Comment acquérir le concept de ce qui ne s'oppose à rien, qui ne rejette rien, qui ne ressemble à rien? S'il ressemblait à quelque chose, il ne serait pas tout. S'il ne ressemble à rien. . . . Et si cette totalité a même puissance que notre esprit, notre esprit n'a aucune prise sur elle. Toutes les objections qui s'élèvent contre l'infini en

As Plotinus said, critically paraphrasing the gnostics, the soul must remain in error, "in failure," in the web of words and desire, so long, the gnostics themselves go on, as it is encumbered by the "demons" of "form," flesh and language.[14] But if the mendacity of words and flesh can be recognized as a speculum in which the fall of man is repeated along with his first being, and the negative image, as it were, of his divine, androgynous shape, fabulous origin, is mirrored by the broken pieces of its shatterment, then objects of "desire," whether books, words, or persons, can be as the robe of the *Pearl*, beautiful, intimations of inconceivableness, a mythically absolute anteriority, unity which is nameless, for which *gnosis* is a cipher.

The connection between knowing and desiring is implied by all of these gnostic fables of origin: man's desire of himself is coincident with his curiosity about the cosmos; God's creation of man represents a wish both to know himself and to take pleasure in himself. This is not by any means an idea confined to gnosticism. There is of course the well-known and quite orthodox biblical euphemism, "to know," meaning no less than "to have slept with." Contemporary psychoanalytic theory also offers a ligament to connect desire and knowledge, the Freudian concept of introjection: "Process revealed by analytical investigation: in phantasy, the subject transposes objects and their inherent qualities from the 'outside' to the inside of himself. Introjection is close in meaning to incorporation, which indeed provides it with its bodily model, but it does not necessarily imply any reference to the body's real boundaries (introjection into the ego, into the ego ideal, etc.). It is closely akin to identification." As Freud himself put it: "Expressed in the language of the oldest—the oral—instinctual impulses, the judgement is: 'I should like to

---

acte, toutes les difficultés que l'on trouve quand on veut ordonner une multiplicité se déclarent. Aucune proposition n'est capable de ce *sujet* d'une richesse si désordonnée que tous les *attributs* lui conviennent. Comme l'univers échappe à l'intuition tout de même il est transcendant à la logique. . . . Et quant à son origine,—AU COMMENCEMENT ETAIT LA FABLE. Elle y sera toujours." Paul Valéry, *Oeuvres*, ed. Jean Hytier, intro. Agathe Rouart-Valéry (Paris, 1957), 862–64, 866–67. My translation.

14. "The Polemic of Plotinus and his School against Gnosis," in *Gnosis*, ed. Haardt, 177. "The Paraphrase of Shem" speaks of "the demon of human form," and "The Teaching of Silvanus" asserts that "everything which is manifest is a copy of that which is hidden." *Nag Hammadi Library*, ed. Robinson, 321, 353.

take this into myself and to keep that out.'"[15] Identification, the self's confusion of itself with others, together with the closely associated desire to incorporate the other/self, are the psychoanalytic version of the Narcissus myth, the gnostic fall. These processes are, moreover, entirely normal and integral to our daily behavior, to the most banal thoughts and acts.

II.   Proust and Gnosis

What is striking about Proust is precisely the way in which he uses desire and literary aspiration as figures for each other. Love and the wish to write are the two experiences whose vicissitudes Proust's narrator chronicles relentlessly, to the point of his, and sometimes the reader's, exhaustion. But in all his work Proust is concerned with desire as a sense of something missing, something lost. He describes the progress of love, the pursuit of the beloved, as a sort of asymptotically progressive loss. The more the lover seeks to possess and define the object of his desire, the greater is his anxiety, his sense that he is failing to possess or to define, to "know"—for to Proust, the "possession" of someone loved is inseparable from an exhaustive knowledge of their past and present. The Proustian lover experiences desire as physically and emotionally debilitating, a "disease," a "drunkenness."

This failure to possess is epistemological as well as personal, one aspect of the bankruptcy of "objective" knowledge which preoccupied scholars and philosophers of Proust's day. The inadequacy of positivistic, scientific language and modes of analysis to deal with the realities of the differential, virtual self, in isolation and in a context of other virtual selves, suspended in perpetual flux, was perceived by such men as William James and Henri Bergson as a failure of communication, a failure of language.[16] Werner Heisenberg found that the mere act of perception alters reality, even under the most controlled circumstances, so that there can be no truly objective scrutiny of the real, no epistemologically valid "objective

15. Jean Laplanche and J.-B. Pontalis, *The Language of Psychoanalysis*, trans. Donald Nicholson-Smith (New York, 1973), 229–30.

16. James said that there was "no greater distance in nature than that between any two individuals." See William James, *The Principles of Psychology* (New York, 1923), I, 226; Henri Bergson, "Essai sur les données immédiates de la conscience," *Oeuvres*, ed. André Robinet (Paris, 1963), 85–92.

reality," and no sound basis for an exchange of facts, for "communication." The "deep self," to use Bergson's terminology, the self which perceives in isolation, cannot emerge through its linguistic carapace, for language is the mode of the "social self," the superficial and chimerical outer self.

So, from the vantage point of intellectual history, it should not surprise us that the two questions which obsess Proust's narrator are: What is love and how does one love? and What is literature and how does one do it? Lover, reader, writer, are all involved in the effort to decipher, to translate—in the pursuit, articulation, "possession" of something which eludes them, which by its nature is always slipping away.

In Freudian psychoanalytic theory, mourning and melancholia are responses of the psyche to a failure, real or perceived, to know: a miscarriage of introjection, the loss of a desired object, whether a person or some abstract entity, regardless of whether these were ever in any real sense "possessed" or even extant, accessible. As the movement of introjection describes the process of acquiring "knowledge," so the work of mourning corresponds to the perception—or, more accurately, the antithetical, un-perception, a psychic movement characterized by anxiety and uncenteredness—of the gnosis.[17]

To desire in the Proustian fashion is at the same time to mourn; Proust fuses the two psychic movements. What emerges from his treatment of desire is a severely antiphenomenological view of "knowledge" and of art, arrived at by nothing more or less than the pursuit of phenomenology to its logical and sensual ends.[18] The "knowledge" arrived at closely resembles the gnosis—that which cannot be known, but only perceived as something lost, missing, misplaced in the dark depths of self.

III.   A Word About Organization and Method

I propose to approach *A la recherche du temps perdu* from the point at which the discovery and elaboration of this antithetical knowledge is

17. Sigmund Freud, "Mourning and Melancholia," *General Psychological Theory*, ed. Philip Rieff (New York, 1963), 164–79.
18. Dr. Wilder Penfield has conducted experiments in which recollection, aided by artificial stimulation of the brain, has become virtually indistinguishable from present "reality." See Roger Shattuck, *Proust's Binoculars* (New York, 1963), 148–49.

most intense, the first half, roughly, of its fifth volume, *La Prisonnière*. Nowhere are the vagaries of desire more rigorously, relentlessly plotted; nowhere is Proust more proustian.

As Maurice Bardèche has shown, the original plan of Proust's work included everything, in remarkable detail, except the character of Albertine and the two volumes, *La Prisonnière* and *La Fugitive*.[19] That the *Recherche* reflects the careful execution of a plan of which the author was always firmly in control has been asserted in response to the hostile charge that the work is no more than the outcome of a monumental case of logorrhea. Though well-intended, this defense misrepresents Proust and indulges the mistaken and rather sentimentally positivistic interpretation of the work as a tale of the "triumph of art." Albertine and the parts in which she figures (by her absence as much as by her presence) are unforeseen extensions of Proust's initial project. The execution of his plan led him beyond it, to a radicalization of his own discourse which he himself could not have foreseen. Albertine is the narrative figure of that step beyond.

> Proust himself deludes himself when he speaks of the composition of his book, since he *discovered*, in the course of his work, vast, unforeseen zones of the intellectual domain which he wanted to explore; a step which is natural, but which excludes the affirmation that he knew perfectly where he was going, by what routes, and by what ports of call. In explaining Proust's work, one must not then forget this reality and this phantasmagoria of its composition. For they both exist: and this perhaps is what explains so many contradictory judgments or inconclusive attempts to give a rational explanation to what is explicable only historically.[20]

I would amend the end of the last sentence to read: "what is *not explicable*." The "plan" foreordained its own transgression; the incredible rigor and rationality with which Proust set out to map the vagaries of human

19. Maurice Bardèche, *Marcel Proust Romancier* (Paris, 1971), I, 224; II, 207–68.

20. "Proust lui-même s'illusionne lorsqu'il parle de la composition de son livre, puisqu'il a *découvert*, au cours de son travail de vastes zones imprévues du domaine intellectuel qu'il voulait explorer: démarche qui est naturelle, mais qui exclut l'affirmation qu'il savait parfaitement où il allait, par quels chemins, et par quelles escales. En expliquant l'oeuvre de Proust, on ne devra donc pas oublier cette réalité et cette fantasmagorie de sa composition. Car elles existent l'une et l'autre: et c'est peut-être ce qui explique tant de jugements contradictoires ou de tentatives peu concluantes pour donner une explication rationnelle de ce qui n'est explicable qu'historiquement." *Ibid.*, 301–302 [translation mine].

reality, intelligence, and desire led him inexorably towards the point at which reality and phantasmagoria, the rational and the irrational, are not clearly distinct. It is that point to which his entire narrative strains, and if critics have for the most part held back from special scrutiny of it, this may be for the very reason that Proust could not have foreseen its necessity. It is for the very same reason that this study departs from, and focuses on, that extremity.

But to illuminate this "negative space," intimated by Proust, one needs more than one kind of "light." The goal must be to explore as much of it as possible, and yet it has no specific topography which could be exhaustively, conclusively mapped. The choice of Proust, Flannery O'Connor, and François Villon is to some extent dictated by personal predilection. But it is also governed by the considered intention of illuminating this negative space fully yet economically, respecting its negativity. One has no practical choice but to proceed under the assumption that a well-chosen text, examined with rigor and eclecticism, can tell us a great deal about other texts by the same author, provided we have read them, and provided we make the necessary connections; and that, if artfully juxtaposed with texts by other authors, a limited, manageable corpus of material will finally allow us to stand back from our own reading, our own "text," and discern certain observations which might have application and relevance beyond the particular texts considered.

As for specific texts, a close reading of "The Enduring Chill" with references to O'Connor's other stories and two novels will elaborate the gleanings from Proust. "Chill" is one of her later works; it reached its final form after she had read Proust, and can be read as a strikingly parodic retelling of the "happy" tale which many readers seem determined to read in Proust's work—that is, Marcel's discovery of art as a vocation and his transmogrification as *artiste*—whether or not she had Proust consciously in mind.

For Villon, I have chosen *Le Lais* as point of entry to the other works. It is long enough, and short enough, to provide real access to the entire work, and economy of form, both of which are required for close reading. As in the cases of the other two authors, the choice of text does not imply an effort to impose any closure of interpretation but rather the opposite. Villon's opus confounds attempts to totalize it as surely as *Le Lais* refuses to be read without reference to Villon's other works.

All three writers are complemented by the discourses of Freud, Jung, Bergson, James, and others more recent such as James Hillman, but my aim has deliberately been to avoid a systematic subjection of the texts to a prescribed theoretical framework. Rather, by being read closely, the texts remain their own "theory," and finally overwhelm all of the various theoretical perspectives from which they are approached. Which is not in any sense to invalidate Freud, Jung, or any of the other theorists invoked; quite the opposite. A text must be approached from some angle, seen through some speculum. But the critical apparatus used to gain access to the text ought finally to be subject to the "theoretical" implications of the text itself, not the other way around. If this is procedural heresy, so be it.

On the one hand, Proust, O'Connor, and Villon appear here together because they are so unalike, in time, language, and genre. On the other hand, I chose them in particular because, as I was positively articulating this "negative" space to myself, I found that their works cast shadows which intersected at just the place I felt I wanted to go. Proust deals with this antithetical knowledge through a rhetoric of psychic violence, the violence of desire; O'Connor uses the metaphor of physical violence to describe it; finally Villon approaches it through the language of sexuality, in which the tropes of mind and body are intertwined. Villon is thus the apex of the "triangle."

But these writers really describe more a circle than a triangle, like Proust's novel, ending where it starts, forgoing conclusion—or swallowing it, "for the revolution ends where it begins." The symmetry observed here is a chiasmus. It begins by an application of the Freudian model of mourning to the texts, and ends by turning the texts on the model. The study takes place in the tension between these two kinds of text, the better to follow, observe, and enact that tension, which is nothing more or less than literature itself.

This is why I prefer to call my method here catholic rather than eclectic. Or at least to say that the eclecticism makes a point: that all methodologies, all modes of reading (and thinking), feed into, nourish, and also contaminate one another. Literary works are subject to the same contamination that flouts chronology and authorial intention. This study, in embracing and enacting such "contamination," looks for methodological precedent to Proust himself when, for instance, he wrote of "the

Dostoyevskian side of Madame de Sévigny."[21] "Purity" of text or of method is an illusion whose failure, like that of closure, I had no real choice but to enact, following Proust's dictum that "Dreams are not realizable, we know this; we wouldn't have any, perhaps, if it weren't for desire, and it is useful to have some so as to see them fail, and so that their failure may instruct."[22] Purity and closure are aspects of what Proust called the "mendacious flimsiness" of the narrative order. To observe its failure, we need to submit to "method," to the "narrative order" of critical reading, in as many of its avatars as can serve, while remaining within the bounds of rigor and the economy of these pages.

21. Proust, *A la recherche du temps perdu*, ed. Pierre Clarac and André Ferré (Paris, 1954), III, 378. Hereinafter cited by volume number I, II, or III [translation mine].
22. III, 183 [translation mine]. See note 34, Chapter 1.

PART I

The Landscape of the Self *(Pages 9–30)*

I. *The Landscape*

The narrator of *La Prisonnière* begins by telling us that he is not going to follow the usual mimetic conventions of storytelling. He awakes facing a wall, seeing nothing. But he describes the scene outdoors: "I already knew what the weather was like."[1] He is scarcely awake, but knows that the day is "glacial and pure."[2] This day depends, then, not on the sun, the clouds, and the elements in general, but on Marcel himself. His eyes are closed, and this "glacial and pure" day is taking shape in his head. It may resemble in some details the day as people are seeing it in the street outside, but only insofar as human beings share common notions and memories of what a day at this time of year in this particular street consists of. There are as many kinds of day in the street as there are people in the street, and Marcel's experience of the day is just as vivid, without his opening his eyes, as the perceptions of the people outside. Perception and experience are creative acts which draw on memory and imagination. In itself the present is a nullity. It depends on memory and expectation to become "real." The emanations from which Marcel fashions the day "slid through my sleep."[3] The implication is that waking perception and sleeping dream differ only in degree, that both are species of phantasm.

Right away Marcel has assumed a communication among the senses, even a correspondence, which makes it possible for him to describe and even to "be" in the streets without seeing them, without getting out of

---

1. "je savais déjà le temps qu'il faisait." III, 9. All translations from the French, including Proust's, are my own except where otherwise noted.
2. "glacial et pur." III, 9.
3. "glissée au travers de mon sommeil." III, 9.

bed. Proust had read Baudelaire and through him and other symbolists felt the influence of Swedenborg. Swedenborg believed that heaven existed in microcosm in every human mind, and that what was most innate in man was as near to divinity as one could come on earth.[4] The divine had to be pursued within the self. According to Baudelaire, the difference between nature as it exists (assuming it has any existence apart from perception, as a thing-in-itself) and the landscape of poetry, is the difference between disorder and order, control and confusion, anarchic prolixity. In *Rêve Parisien* he says that poetry ought to "canalize," contain the fluid infinity of reality, as symbolized by the sea. When Marcel says, before he has opened his eyes, that there is a "glacial and pure" morning outside, his "day" is the landscape of a poem, already contained, transmuted into clear shape and color, into *words*, already frozen. But Marcel doesn't recognize it as such. He lives and perceives after Baudelaire's example, rejecting the appearance of things as they are in favor of an imagined version of them. He takes for granted that perception and experience are creative acts, but he doesn't see that this transformation which he works on the "day," the present, is one step removed from art. Marcel's progress towards a conscious understanding of that metamorphosis of the world is the subject of this book, particularly the first half of it. He doesn't approach the issue as one of art so much as one of a pathology, motivated by curiosity about love and jealousy, what they are and how they work.

To de-cipher is literally to translate from an arcane medium into an accessible one, to undo a coded message, expose a "meaning." The word, and the idea of the writer as decipherer, assume the existence of a key by which "deciphering" may be performed, and that meaning has already been concealed in the thing to be deciphered. Meaning is not created but revealed. The "creative" act is not in fact creative but revelatory. The poet and the writer and the artist do not create, but transmutate, change things so that their "meanings" become explicit. Marcel doesn't yet see himself as a decipherer (*déchiffreur*) in the way that the narrator of Baudelaire's *Correspondances* is one. Yet he is already doing what a decipherer does,

4. Emanuel Swedenborg, *Angelic Wisdom Concerning the Divine Love and the Divine Wisdom* (New York, 1885), 81, 83, *passim*.

exposing "meaning" through disfiguration; he "sees" in the street (which he does not see, that willful blindness making his transforming "vision" possible), in the songs of the criers, in the milkmaids and bakerwomen, a mystery which is not apparent to the rest of the world.

Marcel feels drawn towards something, which at first he thinks is Albertine. Albertine incites him to reflect on art, assumes the role of siren—drawing Marcel to seduction and destruction—Prunikos, the lasciviously sexual woman and "transmundane mother" of gnostic mythology, and anima—in Jungian psychology, the female aspect of a male psyche, interlocutor between the conscious and the unconscious (the animus, male element of a female psyche, is its counterpart).[5] She is the fifth woman with whom Marcel has been infatuated over some period of time, having been preceded by his mother, Odette de Crécy, Gilberte Swann, and the Duchesse de Guermantes. Albertine is the last love before Marcel discovers his greatest love, which will be his work, his novel. Marcel is finding, as Donne put it, his own way of listening to the song of the sirens, in his search for women he can love, which also turns out to be the search for the vocation of writing, or, as Proust would say, Art.

Proust tells us in this first paragraph much the same thing as William James: the greatest distances in nature are those between any two individuals. "Neither contemporaneity, nor proximity in space, nor similarity of quality and content are able to fuse thoughts together which are sundered by the barrier of belonging to different personal minds. The breaches between such thoughts are the most absolute in nature."[6] The symbolists in poetry felt this and tried in their work to respond to it. Proust, in his work, attempts a more complicated and definitive answer. Bergson had codified the problem this way. The real self is the one which is expressed only within, i.e. the "deep self"—and to say that it is only expressed "within" is to say that it isn't expressed, signified, at all—it is that for which no signifier can stand. The social self, the self which the world sees, which makes conversation, explains itself, and is generally a phenomenon of signifiers, is not authentic but a mask, an inanimate exten-

---

5. Carl Jung (ed.), *Man and His Symbols* (New York, 1964), 186–98. Jonas, *The Gnostic Religion, passim.*
6. James, *The Principles of Psychology*, I, 233–34.

sion constructed *by* the real, inner self, in order that it may move and act in a world to which it is alien.[7] It is in this belief in a will, a creative "source" which cannot be represented but is concealed within the significative system and has brought the latter into being *as a tool*, that Bergson and Marcel appear to disagree with Jacques Derrida and others for whom language, if it can be called a "tool" at all, is a tool without a hand to move it, which moves on its own. For Marcel, however, the question whether communication among "deep selves" is possible is inextricably bound up with the question of what a "deep self" is. Marcel, no less than Bergson, is constantly grappling with this issue. At this juncture Marcel is situated in a landscape which really comprises himself only, which is of his own creation. A way out, an exit, would be one way of describing the thing he is looking for; another would be a means of completing, finishing, making whole that landscape of the self. "Love," says Marcel, "in painful anxiety as in nervous desire, is the exigency of a whole."[8] Marcel's relations with Albertine, with the other women of the novel, with all the characters, might accurately be described by Derrida as "differential," a system of mutually and inextricably involved "signifiers." On the plane of mimetic action, however, it is not true that Marcel accepts this differential reality passively. In abandoning the world for art, and bringing the cycle of the novel to a close, he abandons that "reality," turning to a vocation by which he hopes to become himself the source and "sense" which has seemed not to be there, but which in fact he has always been.

He recalls Bergson and Swedenborg in announcing the book's plan. "A little interior character" wakes him. There are several of these "little characters"; first a philosopher "in search of" the unity latent everywhere, of correspondences which may make that unity apparent. He is the orchestrator of the senses, he makes a coherent picture from disparate events and sensations, and he incarnates Swedenborg's doctrine of correspondences. His is the organizing instinct. He is concerned with *deciphering* the smells, sounds, images, everything which penetrates the outer perimeters of the self. The other "character" who is actively engaged in

---

7. Bergson, "Essai sur les Données Immédiates de la Conscience," *Oeuvres*, 85–92.
8. "L'amour, dans l'anxiété douloureuse comme dans le désir nerveux, est l'exigence d'un tout." III, 106.

helping Marcel get his bearings is called the "barometer." He only re-
sponds and reacts to what is going on outside, to the deciphered picture
given him by the philosopher. This barometer approximates the role of
Bergson's social self. The list is not exhaustive, says Marcel, but these are
the only particulars he gives about his "little characters." What is important is that he calls them "characters." They are no more or less than what
the other characters in the book are: hypostatizations of one imagination. In the case of the little characters, the imagination is Marcel the
narrator's; in the case of the "big" characters, Marcel the narrator and all
the others, the imagination belongs to Marcel Proust.[9]

They emblemize, the philosopher and the barometer, past and present.
The social self, which exists to deal with and in the present, corresponds
to the present. The rule of its existence is mutability. It is in a state of
perpetual adaptation and reaction. What the social self has been and done
become the concern of the philosopher, who, while assimilating the present, attempts to collate all the new information with all the old. His store
of information is the past, memory, and his business is to supervise the
transition of each instant from present to past.

The stage on which all this "occurs" is the apartment of Marcel's family
in the Hôtel Guermantes. Marcel has been living in the house of the
Guermantes, psychically as well as physically, since the beginning of *Le
Côté de Guermantes*, when his family moved there. In that volume, Marcel mentions that there is a new furnace in the apartment—a *calorifère*.
The newness of it is significant—the installation of the furnace is contem-
poraneous with Marcel's own installation in the place. But there are other,
more common words which might have been used for *furnace*, and the
word itself obtrudes in the passage as the reflective surface in which the
significance of the apartment and what goes on in it are "ciphered," but
whose significance—as a merely "mimetic" detail or something more—a
flame which heats and burns—is problematized by Marcel's uncertainty
as to his own nature as "narration" and "narrator." This word-furnace is
also a question, a suspicion of itself.

This *calorifère à eau* (water and fire, a functional paradox, "fluid flame")
is remarkable not for its heat, its supposed reason for being there, but

9. III, 9, 12.

rather for the "disagreeable noise" ("*bruit désagréable*") it makes. By association this noise (from time to time resembling a "hiccup") becomes imbued with Marcel's memories of Doncières and comes to "signify," by virtue of an arbitrary and "prolonged conjuncture" ("*rencontre prolongée*"), memories of an entirely different place. Like an alchemical retort, it *substitutes* one substance, substantiality, for another, aiming to arrive, via "filth," at the undisplaceable and incorruptible, the material antithesis of matter, metaphorical "gold." A *calorifère* comprises not only the source of heat, but the system of pipes used to distribute the heat.[10] What sort of "pipes" would these disagreeable noises be, what sort of "heat" are they distributing, containing, occulting? What is this "heat" which fuels *memory*, the sense of lost time and simply *loss*? The furnace is a noise; the "heat" it gives off is memory (the sense of loss); and the source of that heat is precisely the loss, what has been lost, the alchemical "gold" (unmediated being, perception, nondescriptive language) that the furnace's purely functional presence, as a "realistic" detail, intended for nothing more than to "provide mimetic heat" (belied by the importance Marcel gives it as a noisemaker), misplaces, displaces, contradicts. *The calorifère displaces, "burns up," its own signification.* Its "noise" substitutes one time and place for another, noise for heat, one mode of perception for another, and finally, with Marcel's collaboration, *recollected* (lost) perception for present perception, past for present, morning for afternoon. So that it undermines its own reality, its own "mimetic" nature—*as does the nar-*

10. "Depuis le matin on avait allumé le nouveau calorifère à eau. Son bruit désagréable, qui poussait de temps à autre une sorte de hoquet, n'avait aucun rapport avec mes souvenirs de Doncières. Mais sa rencontre prolongée avec eux en moi cet après-midi, allait lui faire contracter avec eux une affinité telle que, chaque fois que (un peu déshabitué de lui) j'entendrais de nouveau le chauffage central, il me les rappellerait." II, 347. A *calorifère* is defined as "Appareil de chauffage distribuant dans une maison, au moyen de tuyaux, la chaleur que fournit un foyer." *Petit Robert* (Paris, 1976), 217. Suggestively, the dictionary goes on to define *calorification* as "Production de chaleur dans un organisme vivant. *La calorification maintient le corps à une temperature constante.*" Life, the "steady" tension of Freudian Eros, is virtually defined as "calorification." Could Proust be giving us a definition of literary "life" here? The *Robert* gives as meaning of *foyer* (the source from which the *calorifère's* pipes branch out): focal point or *virtual* focal point: "point où *convergerait* les rayons réfléchis prolongés" (emphasis mine)—which invites comparison with Proust's "*rencontre prolongée*" of the *calorifère's* noise with Marcel's memory; and *wound*: "Siège principal d'une maladie; lésion." Perhaps most suggestively of all: "*Lieu où se propage une maladie*" (emphasis mine), 741. For a discussion of the retort in alchemical literature, see C. J. Jung, *Psychology and Alchemy* (Princeton, 1968), 236–38.

rative itself. It functions as a source of heat only if "heat" is understood as memory supplanting cognition, past substituting itself for present, the progressive, "transsubstantiative," "transtemporal" combustion of loss implicit in writing. The latter also corrodes, or seems to corrode, distinctions, exigencies of time and space. It is destructive of reality, of the present, both of writer and of reader, substituting for them a fictional world of the past or of some projected future, and of absence.

Proust, as a writer, intends to destroy still more. In his writing, he means very deliberately to annihilate his reader's last shred of mimetic "faith" in the present, in "reality," time and space, to throw off all the ballast impeding a view of the "gold." He meant his work as a purgatorial furnace, a revelatory machine which would wreak some ontological havoc as it revealed.

So Marcel is living in the atmosphere of this furnace, though as yet he doesn't know whether it is simply an everyday heater or something more. He is, however, progressively more aware of its heat. All the scenes and passages which I mean to discuss here are stages in Marcel's "burning clean." In the last scene of this reading, a sun does not set but simply collapses, burned out from within. It is never seen to set, but simply and suddenly is replaced by a new and altogether different orb as Marcel embraces the absence which defines him.

Albertine is a locus of the heat. In her many of Marcel's fond illusions, obstacles to gnosis, are combusted. Marcel is fond of saying that love and jealousy are an agony which must be cultivated. What he means is that they are in a sense the fuel of the flame, and it needs to get very hot indeed before it can accomplish its purpose. Marcel is the prisoner himself, prisoner in the furnace, that is until it has burned up all of him that it can. That prison might also be described as a "field of differential relationships," or as his latent vocation for writing, or as his love for Albertine. These are all ways of saying the same thing.

II. The "Big" Characters

In this first scene, Marcel's solitude is first physically broken by Françoise. But Albertine is unquestionably present, in Marcel's mind, from the first page. Here is further proof, if we needed it, that this is not a mimetic story of people "imitated" from reality: Marcel says that when Bloch used to visit him, he (Bloch) would hear voices, but "never found anyone in my room." And further, which is even more striking, he says that Bloch was quite wrong to think that Albertine was keeping him from going out. How can he have been wrong?—in his assumption of Albertine's presence, even of her positive existence. Bloch never saw her, so she did not really "exist" for him, in Proustian ontology. It was Marcel's mother who told Bloch that Albertine was living with Marcel at the time. But his mother was at Combray. Could she have known, any more than Bloch, if Albertine or anyone was there with Marcel? Not with certainty. She would have to take it on Marcel's word, or Françoise's, or someone's. Practically all of the action, if it can be called that, takes place in Marcel's bedroom. Marcel is the locus of the action and, most of the time, the only eyewitness to it.[11]

The only person who has seen Albertine with Marcel many times is Françoise. Who is Françoise? First she acts as a message bearer between them, speaking for them both. She assumes, for Marcel, the role of a secondary, a surrogate anima. Or perhaps it would be proper to call her the primary one: Albertine cannot enter Marcel's bedchamber without Françoise's permission. Marcel says that Françoise is "imbued with tradition." She contains for him all the history of peasant France as he imagined and idealized it from the *bas-reliefs* of the church of Saint-André-des-Champs. This elaborate system of notions subsumed under the heading of "the peasant past of France" he calls "the Code of Françoise."[12] Everything here recalls the opening sequence of *Du Côté de chez Swann*; the sleeping man in contact with the deepest strata of his psyche, and so according to Swedenborg and the gnostics, with unmediated good. The narrator holds "the string of hours, the chain of years," around his bed. Waking, he doesn't know where he is, has the feeling of ascending the scale of animal and historical orders, from reptile through primitive mammals and men, towards his own present. In a second, his "philosopher" has to inventory centuries of human evolution as well as all the stages of his own life, in order to "locate" him.[13] So it's the past which situates him, which is to say, in his code of characters, it's Françoise.

11. "ne trouvait jamais personne dans ma chambre." III, 9.
12. "le Code de Françoise." III, 16.
13. I, 5–6.

Lighting a fire, Françoise creates a "magic circle" capable of conjuring Marcel's past and resuscitating his memories of Combray and Doncières, so that "I was as happy as if I had been about to go walking on the Méséglise way or meet Saint-Loup and his friends when they were doing service in the country."[14] She is not the circle itself but she evokes it by something like a spell, worked with some twigs, which touches Marcel very deeply. The circle circumscribes his life, the universe in microcosm, both Swann (Méséglise) and Guermantes (Saint-Loup). Inside it, many former "presents" exist in a contemporaneity which excludes only that which is not yet past, only "now." Even if Marcel never again sees these places which are bound up with his past, the memories, which he calls "pictures" (*tableaux*), "make him over" (*refaire* is the word he uses) back into the child, adolescent, young man, he was. Françoise, with her magic circle, makes the bedchamber into a web of the past in which Marcel is "plunged again, invaded, by the joy of hopes long abandoned."[15]

If Françoise is, in Marcel's allegorical reading of his situation, the guardian of the past who brings Marcel into contact with the present, then the role of the present must be played by Albertine. She personifies in some ways the exterior, social self which adapts to the moment, reacts. This makes her very closely related to the "little barometric character." Perhaps she sometimes is indistinguishable from him. Marcel says that Albertine's tongue is his "daily bread"—an almost cannibalistic trope, until we consider the twist: if this is his daily bread, Marcel must be (spiritually) malnourished indeed, for he never swallows this "bread." The metaphor recalls the famous madeleine cake. One is always being forced to consume the present, having it forced into one's mouth—so to speak. But the present never lets us choke it down, digest, consume, possess it. It remains always the present, a literal intrusion in our bodies, noses, mouths, ears, pores, eyes, and minds. But this "tongue" in our mouths arouses us to a procreative tumescence—it makes us "secrete" the past. Albertine is in a state of perpetual metamorphosis. She is never a single image but a progression of "successive images" which are never fixed, a "germination, a multiplication of herself, a fleshy efflorescence of

---

14. "cercle magique"; "j'étais aussi joyeux que si j'avais été sur le point de partir en promenade du côté de Méséglise ou de retrouver Saint-Loup et ses amis faisant du service en campagne." III, 26.

15. "replongé, envahi, par l'allégresse d'espoirs abandonnés depuis longtemps." III, 26.

somber hue which had added to a nature previously quite null, now difficult to sound out."[16] She is that which cannot be assimilated, everything which Marcel feels in the depths of himself that he is not: woman, the boundless azure ocean—all that Marcel desires, and lacks. She is too vast and indistinct for him to "canalize" her. She never gets her bearings from the past. Marcel has secreted many memories around her shape, but these are his. She always belongs completely to the moment. Her body and her tongue are a sort of sacrament which takes its blessing from being loved and desired, but which cannot be consumed. Its blessing cannot redound to the sanctification of the lover and "blesser," because he has made of the tongue in his mouth something which it is only in his mind and memory, in the mental potion he has secreted around it, and finally confused with it.

So the loved object seems to be divine when the divinity has remained in the lover from the start. But what the loved person really is, is of no importance whatever. All that matters—that can matter—to the lover is what he thinks she is. Whatever Albertine is, Marcel says quite explicitly that she is not "human," but some kind of "domestic animal" who doesn't disturb him "as a person would have."[17]

Marcel receives a letter from his mother. His mother disapproves of his relations with Albertine. Love for the mother is the prototype for all others involving women, according to Freud. His mother's disapproval causes Marcel to feel ambivalent about Albertine. The jealousy of the mother gives rise to a conflict between past and present loves. To love in the present, the old love must be sublimated, if not repressed outright. But love for his mother seems, particularly for Marcel, to be the cornerstone of the possibility of love. The solution then is a non sequitur. Love must be got rid of before it can proceed. This is a plausible trope only on paper—there are no "real" non sequiturs. This in part is why Marcel needs to write books. The past must be got rid of, "killed" and buried, if it is to proceed as writing.

Before he turns to that most radical of solutions, however, Marcel must exhaust his faith in the present, in the prosaic sort of love which his mother, by her "abdication of will" in spending the night in Marcel's

16. III, 69. See note 12, Chapter 2 herein.
17. "bête domestique"; "comme l'eût fait une personne." III, 15.

room, allows him to believe in for a time—the length of time represented by the duration of the book. We all undergo a comparable suspension of disbelief during the time we read it. The book is a working through, a withdrawal of libido by infinitesimal degrees, both from women (the archetypal one, the mother, first and last) and from the past. This makes it very much like the Freudian "work of mourning."[18] It is finally for Albertine to put an end to that faith, to radicalize the sense of loss, lack, the "work" of mourning. It is through his bitter experience with her that Marcel begins to perceive that he has loved individuals and a past which, as palpable entities, were always beyond his reach, but which, as phantasmagorical images, have all along been his. His progression of loves is the process by which Marcel discovers the vocation of writing, but of course from our vantage point, and Proust's, it *is* the writing. Perhaps it will be useful to think of two sorts of "working through" in this respect: primary, the sort that applies to Marcel, and secondary, the sort which is synonymous with writing and art. This secondary process both prolongs the work of mourning and projects it outward in a form which may be "cathected" and worked through by readers. It substitutes for and postpones, perhaps indefinitely, the final step following the normal work of mourning, which is to cathect a new object, fall in love again, with a new and *accessible* object. For Marcel, and for Proust as well, we may assume, there is no such thing as an attainable, palpable object. For them, the end of desire is not possession of the object but desire itself, *which is synonymous with the process of mourning*, a profound sense of lack. Thus, the only exit from the primary process of mourning (desire) is the secondary one.

Marcel lives as a writer already. Albertine is not "real" for him; he has told us this in no uncertain terms. He calls her a "domestic animal." Perhaps more correctly, she is for him only a character, an invention of his imagination, a pasted together conglomeration of fragmentary memories and desires. As a woman, she represents what Marcel biologically is not. Woman is distinguished from man in the first place by what she is physically *without*; woman embodies otherness as absence and lack. As all of these things, she is inassimilable. She cannot be possessed so the

18. Freud, "Mourning and Melancholia," *General Psychological Theory*, 164–79.

lack she represents must be supplemented, and its absence (which is its nature) must be mourned, and finally embraced. This is what the writing does—or will do.

Finally, what sort of being is Marcel? Céleste Albaret, when Albertine was not in the chamber at Balbec, said that he was "a divinity of the sky deposited on a bed," a "dove," not "like those who voyage on our vile earth." He doesn't go to bed, she tells him, and never gets up from it. He is fixed, enclosed, imprisoned. "You never went to bed. No one ever saw a person in bed like that. You came and posed yourself there. Your pajamas, right now, perfectly white, with your movements of the neck, make you look like a dove."[19] Deposited—*déposé*—suggesting a fall of some kind. He is a divine bird of some sort then, like the Duchesse de Guermantes. Here is the premise of Swedenborg and the gnostics: there is a divine spark buried in the human form, a small parcel of light fallen into this darkness—or rather swallowed, in one version of the myth, by the archons, the gods of time and space and this "vile world." Attaining the gnosis involves a discovery and then a regurgitation, a forcing outward of this light. But the gnosis, and light, in a world of darkness, are negative entities. They have no positive existence *here*. They can only be discovered, perceived, as something missing, absent. A paradox is involved in this discovery: to discover the gnosis is to mourn it, and to mourn it is to attain it.

III. The Experience of Desire

In this moment, Marcel perceives his own desires only dimly. He doesn't really know what Albertine is or how to characterize her. Her eyes are very important in the incomplete and amorphous image that he develops little by little through the book. The changes which Albertine undergoes are above all ocular. "Her long blue eyes—more elongated—had not kept the same form; they were the same color, but seemed to have passed into a liquid state." Marcel sees in these eyes the sea at Balbec where he first saw Albertine—the infinite, gorgeous, and terrible azure of Baudelaire and Mallarmé: "when she closed her eyes, it was as with drapes one cuts

19. "Vous n'êtes jamais couché. A-t-on jamais vu personne couché ainsi? Vous êtes venu vous poser là. Votre pyjama, en ce moment, tout blanc, avec vos mouvements de cou, vous donne l'air d'une colombe." III, 17–18.

off a view of the sea."[20] Her eyelids are the canals of this ocean. Bergson, writing in a completely irrelevant context, offers what may serve as a tangential explanation of this use of the eye as metonymy. "The necessity of the whole, perceived through the contingency of the parts, is what we call moral obligation in general; the parts are, besides, only contingent in the *eyes* of society."[21] The actual object of desire is always perceived metonymically in Proust, never directly. As each woman is known only through the contingency of various fragments of her person or past, so each woman is only a metonymy of the greater object, woman, which is a metonymy for something still larger, which I call the gnosis for lack of any better name, and which does not have positive properties and cannot be described.

The present, embodied as Albertine awake, eyes open, and the mind which assimilates (Marcel) never stop changing and burgeoning. The latter always has a new increment to add to his past, in his constant effort to situate himself with respect to the present. This is Marcel's perpetual frenzy: the desire for stasis and permanence. This desire cannot be requited, just as it is impossible to obtain an answer to a question when one must do the answering as well as the asking. "The person asking the question and the person who could offer the memory were, alas, but one and the same person, myself, who had doubled momentarily, but without adding anything to myself. I had asked in vain, it was I who answered, and I learned nothing more."[22]

There are no objectivities in this ontology, only subjectivities. There is a constant dialectical process between subjects, but without what Hegel calls manifestation, without the result of a phenomenal objectivity. This is a differential reality, then. The problem, which can never be solved, in such a context, is how to situate oneself. If everything is relative to the

20. "Ses longs yeux bleus—plus allongés—n'avaient pas gardé la même forme; ils avaient bien la même couleur, mais semblaient être passés à l'état liquide"; ". . . quand elle les fermait, c'était comme quand avec des rideaux on empêche de voir la mer." III, 18.

21. "La necessité du tout, sentie à travers la contingence des parties, est ce que nous appelons l'obligation morale en général; les parties ne sont d'ailleurs contingentes qu'aux yeux de la société." Bergson, "L'Obligation Morale," *Oeuvres*, 1022 [emphasis mine].

22. "La personne qui se posait la question et la personne qui pouvait offrir le souvenir n'étaient, hélas, qu'une seule et même personne, moi, qui se dédoublait momentanément, mais sans rien s'ajouter. J'avais beau questionner, c'était moi qui répondais, je n'apprenais rien de plus." III, 85.

past, there remains the instability of the past itself—the "interior self," the storehouse of memory, is as awesome an abyss as present or future. James and Bergson had recognized a third variable in Pascal's equation, the nothingness within man. This nothingness is the territory which Proust seeks to map—not positively, as having a definite shape, but negatively, as what is not and cannot be represented. Proust's work is often, even usually, misconceived as simply introspective. It is not introspective at all. There is no more stability, objectiveness, within his characters than without. In a differential field, nothing can be what it is; the integrity of any entity is an illusion which is made possible by its involvement with what it is not, its noncoincidence with itself: "the truth," Marcel says in this first passage, "changes so much for us that others have trouble getting their bearings by it."[23] Albertine and Marcel are, each for the other, an unfathomably infinite chasm.[24] The important thing to recognize here is that neither Proust nor Marcel is championing the cult of the self. They could not possibly be farther from doing so. Proust contemplates, and often ridicules, the solipsism in which his characters indulge with a relentlessly grim irony.

Something which Proust designates as "chance" (*le hasard*) is a large part of instability, the failure to "situate oneself," and it figures in the "disease" of love. Love, Marcel insists over and over, is nothing if not arbitrary, accidental, fortuitous—everything he says he is in the coach of Doctor Percepied, when he fails to pierce through to the mystery of the belfries of Martinville and Vieuxvicq. He could just as easily have fallen in love with Andrée as with Albertine. Love fixes itself by some accident which occasions suffering, a sense of loss, lack, the failure to possess. To love is to suffer from this sense of something missing. "Love is perhaps no more than the propagation of those stirrings which, following an emotion, move the soul."[25] His love "fixes" on Albertine when she tells him that she knows Mademoiselle Vinteuil. This revelation arouses his

---

23. "la vérité change tellement pour nous que les autres ont peine à s'y reconnaître." III, 19.

24. III, 28–30.

25. "L'amour n'est peut-être que la propagation de ces remous qui, à la suite d'une émotion, émeuvent l'âme." III, 20.

jealousy and so revives a love on the verge of collapse. But he describes love almost in terms of a household plant, something "propagated": a pain to be sought and cultivated because it is only as a sense of something missing, something lost, that the gnosis may be experienced and known at all.

The object of desire—the *apparent* object—is of no importance. "Reality is only an allurement to an unknown towards which we cannot go very far."[26] What one loves, and perceives as the object of desire, is a fictional construct, made of one's own memories and inadequacies. Jealousy, and its concomitant dread, "can assume as many forms as the amorphous illness [lesbianism here] which is its object."[27] Marcel calls desire "the bringing together of the famished"[28]—everyone always famished for what he or she lacks, seeing in someone else an "allurement" (*amorce*, which also can mean "beginning") towards that dark mystery. Male and female, self and other, the opposed and yet complementary forces of the universe are not distinct from each other, but differentially involved with the other(s), in a state of mutual contamination which admits of no stability, no certainty, no possession, and no truth—no positive truth. According to the gnostic, what they seek is union with the God of whom they are part, whom they recognize obscurely in the objects of their desire. This attraction of one desirer for another is described in *Sodome et Gomorrhe* by the small drama of the bee and the flower, against the metaphorically similar background of Charlus' and Jupien's encounter. The part that receives—the feminine part, whether it belongs to male or female party—is related to the flower by analogy. All the flowers in the novel—and there are many—have to do with this metaphor. The object of desire is not only passive, but might as well be seen as inert, inanimate, utterly beyond perceiving the desirer, responding to its "penetrator's" violence or even feeling it. Charlus and Jupien, as often happens, are each other's objects, so that each is both flower *and* bee.

In similar fashion, Marcel describes the sexual trysts in which he imag-

---

26. "La réalité n'est qu'une amorce à un inconnu sur la voie duquel nous ne pouvons aller bien loin." III, 24.

27. "elle peut revêtir autant de formes que le mal incertain qui est son objet." III, 22.

28. "le rapprochement des affamés." III, 22.

ines Albertine taking part as *dualistic*, like any figure, "sign": the "congenital evil" and the "ephemeral cause."[29] The difference between the two is the difference between love and loves, between a disease and its specific symptoms and incidences. This calls to mind the theory of Claudel and Mauriac that all loves constitute a single love, a single pattern which is endlessly repeated.[30] The same, or a very similar notion, is implicit in much of Freud's work. Marcel says that the desire for women is, literally, a desire to go out into the street: the desire, metaphorically phrased, of the self to go out beyond its own boundaries and make direct contact with the present, the unassimilable otherness of the moment (Albertine, woman). But in fact he knows that the desire can never be requited, because that woman, that moment, that street, are phantasms of his own making. "If I had not accompanied Albertine on her long round, my mind only wandered the more for it and, for having refused to taste that morning with my senses, I enjoyed in imagination all such mornings, past or possible . . . for the sharp air turned the necessary pages of itself, and I found everything indicated before me, so that I could follow it from my bed, the gospel of the day."[31] It is as if—*as if*—Albertine were his eyes, his senses, and felt for him. As if she were an appendage, an extension of himself. *His* Albertine, the Albertine of Marcel's desire, is just that, an appendage of himself. "My thought," he says, "followed her on her walk, described a distant, bluish horizon, engendered around the center which was myself a mobile zone of uncertainty and vagueness."[32]

29. "mal congénital"; "cause éphémère." III, 22.

30. Paul Claudel, *Partage de Midi* (Paris, 1949); François Mauriac, *Génétrix* (Paris, 1925); Wallace Fowlie, "The Art of François Mauriac," *A Mauriac Reader* (New York, 1968); Henri Peyre, *French Novelists of Today* (New York, 1955), 118–19.

31. "Si je n'étais pas allé accompagner Albertine dans sa longue course, mon esprit n'en vagabonderait que davantage et, pour avoir refusé de goûter avec mes sens cette matinée-là, je jouissais en imagination de toutes les matinées pareilles, passées ou possibles . . . car l'air vif tournait de lui-même les pages qu'il fallait, et je trouvais tout indiqué devant moi, pour que je puisse le suivre de mon lit, l'évangile du jour." III, 26.

32. "Ma pensée la suivait dans sa promenade, décrivait un horizon lointain, bleuâtre, engendrait autour du centre que j'étais une zone mobile d'incertitude et de vague." III, 28. There is a strong case to be made that these passages are based entirely on the sketches which appeared in *Contre Sainte-Beuve*. Compare, for instance, these passages from "L'article dans 'Le Figaro'" and "Conversation avec Maman": "Je fermai les yeux en attendant le jour. Je pensai à cet article que j'avais envoyé il y a longtemps déjà au *Figaro*. J'avais même corrigé les épreuves. Tous les matins, en ouvrant le journal, j'espérais le trouver. Depuis plusieurs jours, j'avais cessé d'espérer et je me demandais si on les refusait tous ainsi. Bientôt j'entends tout le monde se lever." *Contre Sainte-Beuve* (Paris, 1954), 105. "Et tandis

This is the rarified atmosphere (an air "unknown on this earth"[33]) of a self on the verge of the knowledge that it is both the center and outer limit of itself; on the verge of making that knowledge into a written art. This knowledge is not the gnosis but it certainly is prerequisite to reaching the gnosis—whatever the latter may be. For Marcel, Albertine is the eye of his self, his sensual link with the outside, which makes it possible for him to make that world over, re-create it, incorporating all of his past and—so Proust, and Jung as well, believed—that of his ancestors. There is no distinguishing the "real" town from Marcel's version of it, just as there is no distinguishing the "real" Albertine from Marcel's version of her. For Proust and for Marcel, there is no material reality apart from our perceptions of it. To make such a statement is not solipsistic, but rather gnostic. Marcel is perfectly straightforward in giving the intellectual and spiritual creed of the work of which he is part: "Dreams are not realizable, we know this; we wouldn't have any, perhaps, if it weren't for

---

que Maman parlait, je voyais le soleil non pas directement, mais dans l'or sombre qu'il plaquait sur la girouette en fer de la maison d'en face. Et comme le monde n'est qu'un innombrable cadran solaire, je n'avais pas besoin d'en voir davantage pour savoir qu'en ce moment, sur la place, le magasin qui avait baissé sa toile à cause de la chaleur allait fermer pour l'heure de la grand-messe, et que le patron qui était allé passer son veston du dimanche y déballait aux acheteurs les derniers mouchoirs . . . que sur le marché les marchands étaient en train de montrer les oeufs et les volailles. . . . Mais maintenant ce n'était pas cela que l'éclat du soleil de dix heures du matin, plaqué non plus sur les ardoises de l'église, mais sur l'ange d'or du campanile de Saint-Marc, quand on ouvrait sur la petite calle ma fenêtre du Palazzo . . . à Venise. Et de mon lit je ne voyais qu'une chose, le soleil, non pas directement, mais en plaques de flammes sur l'ange d'or du campanile de Saint-Marc, me permettant aussitôt de savoir qu'elle était exactement l'heure et la lumière dans tout Venise et m'apportant sur ses ailes éblouissantes une promesse de beauté et de joie plus grande qu'il n'en apporta jamais aux coeurs chrétiens, quant il vint annoncer 'la gloire de Dieu dans le ciel et la paix sur la terre aux hommes de bonne volonté.'
    "Les premiers jours cet éclat d'or sur l'ange me rappelait l'éclat plus pâle, mais marquant la même heure sur les ardoises de l'église du village, et tout en m'habillant, ce que l'ange semblait me promettre de son geste d'or, que je ne pouvais fixer tant il éblouissait, c'était de descendre vite au beau temps devant notre porte, de gagner la place du marché pleine de cris et de soleil, de voir l'ombre noir qu'y portaient les devantures fermées ou encore ouvertes, et le grand store du magasin, et de rentrer à la maison fraîche de mon oncle." *Ibid.*, 135–37. The sun here is like a giant *calorifère*. Perception occurs as a series of substitutions, made possible by memory and association, the sequence of which can begin anywhere and end anywhere—or nowhere. "Maman" here seems to be the prototype for both Albertine and Françoise. The latter two characters double or split the mother figure, just as the act of writing doubles the writer: "A chaque phrase, dès le premier mot se dessine d'avance l'idée que je voulais exprimer; mais ma phrase me l'apporte plus nombreuse, plus detaillée, enrichie, car auteur, je suis cependant lecteur." *Ibid.*, 108.
    33. "inconnu sur cette terre." III, 30.

desire, and it is useful to have some so as to see them fail, and so that their failure may instruct."[34]

> The universe is true for all of us and dissimilar for each of us. If we weren't, for the order of the story, obliged to confine ourselves to frivolous reasons, how many more serious ones would permit us to show the mendacious flimsiness of the beginning of this volume where, from my bed, I heard the world awaken, now to one sort of weather, now to another! Yes, I have been forced to cut the thing down and to be a liar, but there isn't one universe, there are millions, almost as many as there are human eyes and intelligences, that wake up every morning.[35]

His desire to tell a story, and the "order" of that story, its narrative exigencies, the gesture toward sense and closure which the genre demands, prevent Marcel from acceding to the absence of any "truth," any unmediated essence, so that he is forced to approach unmediated being (the gnosis) through the mediation of language. "Otherwise," he seems to say, "if I did not have to try to tell a story, I could expose the thing itself; I would not be obliged to lie." Here Marcel is closest to revealing the true significance of Bergson's and his own concept of a deep self: we know of it only through the mediation of the "social self," only as what is never realized, what we perceive within ourselves as lost, missing, misplaced: unmediated being, the light shrouded in darkness, the gnosis. It is only Marcel's amazing twofold innocence that makes the "story" possible: on the one hand, he wants to tell a story, while on the other hand, believing that to tell a story he must forgo a direct approach to the deep self, he seems to affirm that a direct approach might be possible under some hypothetical circumstance. He wants to tell a story, and at the same time he believes in the transcendent, "inner," nonreferential self which narration—*language*—can only approach as an absence, only intimate negatively, by telling "lies," by "failing."

34. "Les rêves ne sont pas réalisables, nous le savons; nous n'en formerions peut-être pas sans le désir, et il est utile d'en former pour les voir échouer et que leur échec instruise." III, 183.
35. "L'univers est vrai pour nous tous et dissemblable pour chacun. Si nous n'étions pas, pour l'ordre du récit, obligé de nous borner à des raisons frivoles, combien de plus sérieuses nous permettrait de montrer la minceur menteuse du début de ce volume où, de mon lit, j'entends le monde s'éveiller, tantôt par un temps, tantôt par un autre! Oui, j'ai été forcé d'amincir la chose et d'être mensonger, mais ce n'est pas un univers, c'est des millions, presque autant qu'il existe de prunelles et d'intelligences humaines, qui s'éveillent tous les matins." III, 191.

CHAPTER 2

Albertine and Art—The Mind and Desire *(Pages 64–76)*

I. Creative and Destructive Desire

The first woman in all of *À la recherche du temps perdu* appears in the first pages of *Du Côté de chez Swann*. Her "body" is Marcel's thigh, pressing against its pair. She is 1) Marcel himself, and 2) phantasm—but one which corresponds to a physical reality, namely the sensation of two legs rubbing together.

This woman is ephemeral, a dream. The dream of the present moment in which, as Bergson says, we learn, assimilate, nothing:[1] "In themselves, what were Albertine and Andrée? To find out, you would have to immobilize yourself, to live no longer in that perpetual waiting on yourself in which you are always passing further on; you would have to stop loving yourself in order that you become fixed, in order that you no longer know of your own interminable and ever disconcerting arrival."[2] This, of course, is addressed to Albertine and Andrée. But they are fictive creations, part of the same fictive "world" as Marcel the narrator. He must be speaking here not only of the love of women, but of the love of self, addressing himself, in fact. To attain absolute liberty, to utterly defeat fear, one must conquer the greatest of specific fears, which is that of death. Dostoievski had, albeit contemptuously, inscribed this belief in such characters as Kirilov and Stavrogin in *The Devils*, and Dostoievski, of the Russian writers, was Proust's favorite.[3] Proust says in the passage

---

1. Bergson, "La Mémoire et l'Esprit," *Oeuvres*, 281–84, 291.
2. "en elles-mêmes, qu'étaient Albertine et Andrée? Pour le savoir, il faudrait vous immobiliser, ne plus vivre dans cette attente perpétuelle de vous où vous passez toujours outre; il faudrait ne plus vous aimer pour vous fixer, ne plus connaître votre interminable et toujours déconcertante arrivée." III, 64.
3. Céleste Albaret, *Monsieur Proust* (Paris, 1973), 157.

above that one must "immobilize oneself" in the sense of suppressing all of oneself which comprises the social self, all of oneself which is not oneself, which comes from "without" and which cannot be subordinated to the will, which is subject to chance and the present. As Mallarmé says in the first verse of *Le Tombeau d'Edgar Poe*, "Tel qu'en lui-même enfin l'éternité le change" ("So finally eternity turns him into himself"). He must exterminate his "love" of the present and the world, society, in favor of a solitary "immobilization" in which he may cease his *attente*, literally his "waiting": stop the ever incomplete effort to become, to pass from one moment to the next. James expressed the effort this way:

> Whilst we think, our brain changes, and . . . like the aurora borealis, its whole internal equilibrium shifts with every pulse of change.

> Our state of mind is never precisely the same. Every thought we have of a given fact is, strictly speaking, unique, and only bears a resemblance of kind with our other thoughts of the same fact. . . . Often we are ourselves struck at the strange differences in our successive views of the same thing. . . . the women once so divine, the stars, the woods, and the waters, how now so dull and common (the young girls that brought an aura of infinity, at present hardly distinguishable existences).

> Experience is remoulding us every moment, and our mental reaction on any given thing is really a resultant of our experience of the whole world up to that date.[4]

Only death can arrest this succession of "presents."

Proust, in the writing of *A la recherche du temps perdu*, was quite literally committing slow suicide. He suffered all his life from a physical infirmity which confined him to bed a good portion of every day. In 1914, he stopped eating anything at all save some milk and, very occasionally, a fried fish; even before that year he had not been accustomed to eating more than one or two croissants daily. No one knows how much he slept during the last years of his life, when he was working on the *Recherche*, but the evidence implies that it was very little. His brother Robert has made this mournful and slightly maudlin summation: "Marcel could have

---

4. James, *The Principles of Psychology*, 233–34, 226.

lived longer if he had been willing to live as everyone else lives. But he wanted it, he wanted it for his work; we have only to bow our heads."[5]

But why did he want it, for his work or himself? There is every indication that Proust believed with Bergson that, in the social world, self-possession is impossible. In the social persona, one is in perpetual *attente* for oneself. He seems also to have prefigured Jung in believing that one projects the past—the female aspect of the self (anima)—onto the form of a specific woman and becomes infatuated with her. To say that one loves is the same as to say one loves oneself. So one cannot kill love. To kill it would amount to a kind of suicide. Rather, one waits for possession of the loved object to be realized. Meanwhile, the women themselves never stop becoming:

> Oh successive rays in the whirlwind in which we palpitate to see you reappear even as we scarcely recognize you, in the vertiginous speed of the light. This speed, we would ignore it perhaps and everything would seem immobile to us, if a sexual attraction did not make us run towards you, ever dissimilar drops of gold which always surpass hope. Each time, a young girl resembles what she was the previous time so little (dashing to bits as soon as we perceive her the memory which we had kept and the desire which we intended) that the stability of nature with which we endow her is only fictive and for the convenience of language.[6]

Marcel adds that "very often a love is no more than the association of the image of a young girl (who without that association would have quickly become intolerable to us) with the heartbeats inseparable from an interminable and vain waiting, and from having been stood up by the young lady. All that is only true for young and imaginative people confronted with unstable young girls."[7]

5. "Mon frère aurait pu vivre plus longtemps s'il avait accepté de vivre la vie de tout le monde. Mais il l'a voulu, il l'a voulu pour son oeuvre, nous n'avons qu'à nous incliner." Albaret, *Monsieur Proust*, 70.

6. "ô rayons successifs dans le tourbillon où nous palpitons de vous voir reparaître en ne vous reconnaissant qu'à peine, dans la vitesse vertigineuse de la lumière. Cette vitesse, nous l'ignorerions peut-être et tout nous semblerait immobile, si un attrait sexuel ne nous faisait courir vers vous, gouttes d'or toujours dissemblables et qui dépassent toujours notre attente. A chaque fois, une jeune fille ressemble si peu à ce qu'elle était la fois précédente (mettant en pièces dès que nous l'apercevons le souvenir que nous avions gardé et le désir que nous nous proposions) que la stabilité de nature que nous lui prêtons n'est que fictive et pour la commodité du langage." III, 64.

7. "bien souvent un amour n'est que l'association d'une image de jeune fille (qui sans cela nous eût été vite insupportable) avec les battements de coeur inséparables d'une attente

The writer needs to dispossess himself of this ignorance which is fictive. He must learn to be disdainful of physical attractions, even if he does not or cannot forsake them altogether. It is an important premise of Proust's theory of art that the love of individuals must be sacrificed before the creative energies can be released. Art destroys reality, and it destroys the present, present-ness. The artistic milieu, and the artistic temperament, refuse time and space. So they must leave no "fiction," no "fictive lack of knowledge" intact, however attractive it may be and however much it may partake of the reasonable and the palpably "real." Knowledge, the writerly gnosis, must be pursued and is worthy of being pursued even though it may appear awful and ugly. The genealogy of this notion is easily traceable to Lautréamont and Baudelaire, and even further back, to Sade. Proust, of course, does not seek expressly to shock. He is not a surrealist, but rather a skeptic, and not simply a skeptic but that very rare creature, a *mystical* skeptic. He is as dubious about the validity of reason as a concept, a practice, and a criterion for sorting "real" from "unreal," as about anything else.

Albertine particularly, in this passage, is never more than possible. Every moment contains untold myriads of latent futures. None of them is ever more than possible and latent because we remain captives of the moment, of the possible. One fails to attain freedom because one fears losing the present—the present which, Proust keeps telling us, has no value. All knowledge, the writerly gnosis, remains latent for Marcel at this point in the cycle.

II. Albertine, Balbec, and the Ocean: Woman and Azure

Marcel makes an analogy between Albertine and "the purple light which fell at the feet of my curtains at Balbec."[8] Behind both girl and curtains, he says, "shone like mother-of-pearl the bluish undulations of the sea."[9] Albertine's attraction for Marcel is the same as that of the "insolent and florid retinue which unwound the length of the beach,"[10] but concen-

---

interminable, vaine, et d'un 'lapin' que la demoiselle nous a posé. Tout cela n'est vrai que pour les jeunes gens imaginatifs devant les jeunes filles changeantes." III, 66.
  8. "la lumière pourprée qui tombait aux pieds de mes rideaux à Balbec." III, 67.
  9. "se nacraient les ondulations bleuâtres de la mer." III, 67.
  10. "cortège insolent et fleuri qui se déroulait le long de la plage." III, 67.

trated, personified. The trope recalls the flowers of Swann's way and of the Vivonne on the Guermantes way: love and art, which all the parts of the *Recherche* represent a monumental effort to reconcile. Albertine contains both, both "ways." In her are the "anxiety" (*émoi*) of Méséglise and the "unquiet vanity, the wandering desires of the life of oceanside resorts"[11]—the world of aristocracy, the "periwinkle blue" eyes of the Duchesse de Guermantes.

Now, since he has known her, Albertine has undergone so many subtle metamorphoses in Marcel's mind (and doubtless in hers as well), through the course of so many "presents," that he can scarcely recognize her. This chaos is, he says, "due, moreover, to the superimposition not only of the successive images which Albertine had been for me, but also of great qualities of intelligence and of heart, defects of character, both the ones and the others unsuspected by me, which Albertine in a germination, a multiplication of herself, a fleshy efflorescence of somber hue, had added to a nature previously quite null, now difficult to sound out."[12]

The loved person is a hollow receptacle. What disconcerts and disorients the lover is that of himself with which he has filled and embellished this urn of living flesh. The receptacle, however, breathes and moves and has its own life. The horror of this displacement outwards, which is love, is the discovery that one does not and cannot possess oneself. However much lovers may enjoy themselves trying, they can never succeed in rubbing, fondling, pummeling, or devouring each other's bodies into one integral and immutable whole. The succession of moments, possibilities, becomes overwhelming. If the ocean is behind the eyes of Albertine, the water of the ocean oozes from those eyes—eyes which at once suggest and conceal that terrifyingly pristine azure, contain it and set it loose. The sight of what there is beyond them unsettles, reveals the body as mirage, "receptacle." It menaces one's belief in the fiction of reality, one's faith in the present and in desire, the love of individuals.

The only moments of bliss which Marcel experiences with Albertine

11. "la vanité inquiète, les désirs errants de la vie des bains de mer." III, 67–68.

12. "dû, d'ailleurs, à la superposition non seulement des images successives qu'Albertine avait été pour moi, mais encore des grandes qualités d'intelligence et de coeur, des défauts de caractère, les uns et les autres insoupçonnés de moi, qu'Albertine en une germination, une multiplication d'elle-même, une efflorescence charnue aux sombres couleurs, avait ajoutés à une nature jadis à peu près nulle, maintenant difficile à approfondir." III, 69.

are the times when she is asleep. Her eyes are mercifully sealed then, and her body seems to enclose the azure in those eyes—the superimposed images of past identities. She appears simply to be, rather than to be becoming. When Albertine is asleep, metaphor controls reality, language is purified and verse tames nature. The would-be artist (who thinks wrongly to have attained possession of what he desires at such moments) tastes an unreal and "fictive" satisfaction. Asleep, says Marcel, "I saw her as a long stem in bloom which had been laid out there. . . . In this way, her sleep realized, in a certain degree, the possibility of love: alone, I could think of her, but I missed her, I didn't possess her; present, I spoke to her, but was too absent from myself to be able to think. When she was sleeping, I had no longer any need to speak, I knew that she no longer looked back at me, I didn't have to live on the surface of myself."[13] Marcel says that when Albertine is there with him, he is "absent from myself." This is because he has projected himself onto and into Albertine. He is as alone as ever, but he has the pleasure of seeming not to be alone. There is nothing to clash with, contest his own will and imagination, nothing to remind him that his self does have boundaries. He has the satisfaction of appearing to encompass everything in his sight (and his desire). He has the sense of belonging to himself, of self-possession. The anima becomes an obstacle between the self and the unconscious; it must be pursued, but to arrive at the past, one must reach beyond, through it—or seem to.

III. Woman and Art

This hidden azure (ocean, blue of eyes) is emblematic of the past, hoarded as it is in the unconscious. Albertine asleep, as the anima of Marcel's psyche, threatens tantalizingly to reveal this fecund emptiness. The present suppressed, the past underneath seems to rise to the surface and hover, just out of view. Albertine is like a book, containing an exhaustive superimposition of presents and characters but which, closed, becomes an in-

13. "je lui trouvais l'air d'une longue tige en fleur qu'on aurait disposée là. . . . Par là, son sommeil réalisait, dans une certaine mesure, la possibilité de l'amour: seul, je pouvais penser à elle, mais elle me manquait, je ne la possédais pas; présente, je lui parlais, mais étais trop absent de moi-même pour pouvoir penser. Quand elle dormait, je n'avais plus à parler, je savais que je n'étais plus regardé par elle, je n'avais plus besoin de vivre à la surface de moi-même." III, 69.

animate, finite, and easily portable object. "Each time she moved her head, she created a new woman, often unsuspected by me. I seemed to possess not one but innumerable girls."[14] Seeing Albertine asleep is a metonymic vision of art realized, of his work whole and finished before him, and also of his own death, himself become an inanimate object and so liberated from the successive tethers of the moment. Death means freedom from chance, the present, the social self, unrequitable desire; embracing death means that one no longer fears to lose the present, that one has "fallen out of love" with the present. Only then can the self be unencumbered—eyes closed, perfidious present contained: "Her brows, arched as I had never seen them, surrounded the globes of her eyes like the soft nest of a halcyon. Races, atavisms, vices rested on her face."[15] So Albertine assumes the immobility and (relative) immutability of a painting. "Her hair, which had fallen the length of her pink face, was laid beside her on the bed, and sometimes an isolated and straight lock gave the same effect of perspective as the thin, pale, lunar trees which one sees standing up stiffly in the background of Elstir's Raphaelesque paintings."[16]

This scene is a dream, Albertine is a dream, and art, as far as Proust is concerned, is the transcription of a dream—the dream of attaining, possessing the beautiful. From the first scene of *Du Côté de chez Swann*, Proust underlines the idea that art is something not of this world. One is nearest it in sleep, dreaming. Only then does the unconscious become accessible. The artist seeks to realize that freedom (that *apparent* freedom) consciously, with his eyes open. Art then represents an effort to bring into this world that which is fundamentally unlike it, and to make a shared experience of something which by its nature can only be felt in solitude. Love is the same effort, but does not know that it is. The artist

14. "Chaque fois qu'elle déplaçait sa tête, elle créait une femme nouvelle, souvent insoupçonnée de moi. Il me semblait posséder non pas une mais d'innombrables jeunes filles." III, 72.

15. "Ses sourcils arqués comme je ne les avais jamais vus entouraient les globes de ses paupières comme un doux nid d'alcyon. Des races, des atavismes, des vices reposaient sur son visage." III, 72.

16. "Sa chevelure descendue le long de son visage rose était posée à côté d'elle sur le lit, et parfois une mèche isolée et droite donnait le même effet de perspective que ces arbres lunaires grêles et pâles qu'on aperçoit tout droits au fond des tableaux raphaëlesques d'Elstir." III, 71.

dreams of catching beauty in his work; the lover dreams of possessing the object of his desire: "it was an entire physiological existence before me, mine; as long as I had remained in times past stretched out on the beach, in the moonlight, I would have stayed there watching her and listening to her. Sometimes one would have said that the sea was getting rough, that the storm was making itself felt all the way into the bay, and I lay against her to hear the roaring of her breath."[17] The sea is enclosed, the azure contained, the anima, the muse, the mediating archons definitively defeated.

IV. The Word

This dream ends with one of the two times in all of the *Recherche* that Marcel is called by his *nom de baptême*, literally his "baptismal name": "My Marcel," "my dear Marcel."[18] Throughout gnostic literature, the askesis of knowledge is preceded by such a calling of the seeker by his "divine" name, a "baptism" by speech from the "higher" world. Theologic terminologies arise because of the ancient identity, in most cultures, and certainly our Western one, of scripture and text, exegesis and reading, "scripturality" and textuality. The word for Christian divinity is *Word—Logos*. In gnostic theology this implies a radical and irreducible paradox which it does not for Christianity, one not subject to resolution, an epistemological oxymoron: mediated unmediatedness. It is too easy to dismiss references to theosophy of any kind as anachronistic and maudlin fanaticism, and to do so would be to miss the point and to overlook a powerful current in Proust's text. The idea of sacredness, of a soul, is bound up in our culture with the concepts of perception, of being, of mind, through the mediation of scripture, text, the act of exegesis, reading. Marcel calls Albertine his *oeuvre*.[19] She is for him a text, a figure for

17. "c'était toute une existence physiologique qui était devant moi, à moi; aussi longtemps que je restais jadis couché sur la plage, au clair de lune, je serais resté là à la regarder et à l'écouter. Quelquefois on eût dit que la mer devenait grosse, que la tempête se faisait sentir jusque dans la baie, et je me mettais contre elle à écouter le grondement de son souffle qui ronflait." III, 73.

18. "Mon Marcel"; "Mon chéri Marcel." III, 75.

19. Marcel is able to experience "ardent sentiments" for Albertine only insofar as he is able to assimilate her to the creation and perception of art. At such moments she takes on for him "l'apparence d'une oeuvre d'Elstir ou de Bergotte," and he sees her in the "*recul*,"

the text, with which he is engaged in a violent exegetical struggle. "Marcel" is the name not only of the narrator-character, but of the author himself: "She would say: 'My' or 'My dear,' followed, the one or the other, by my Christian name, which, *giving to the narrator the same first name as to the author of this book, would have made*: 'My Marcel,' 'My dear Marcel.'"[20] The writer has with a peculiar but appropriate ironic phrasing given his name to his narrator (his work—*oeuvre*), through the mediation of the narrator's "work" (Albertine). The author's text, somewhat equivocally, names him; in it, by it, he names himself—or rather, is named in and by his absence, his text, from which he is absent. Thus reading and writing are *parabasis*—the author's "voice," "name," within his own work, which only underlines his absence from it, is a discrepancy of the text with itself which renders the work absolutely ironic. Schlegel called irony "permanent parabasis."[21] Proust seems to be calling desire, writing, and reading, the production of the text, permanent parabasis. No rhetoric is so violent as this one. Where is the writer? In the text? Then there is no writer, but only a text. Who is this Marcel? Character or author? Lover or beloved? Writer or written, reader or "read"? It seems we must acknowledge that he is only a character within the text. Where does this leave the lover Marcel, "author" of Albertine? Where does it leave Proust and his reader, we ourselves? Where indeed, but *lost*.

---

the "back step," the "distancing," the "regression" of art and imagination, as a condition of their backward movement and inseparable from it. III, 56. "Mais ma chambre ne contenait-elle pas une oeuvre d'art plus précieuse que toutes celles-là? C'était Albertine elle-même." III, 382. Of course, as is so often the case with Proust, this statement is brazenly contradicted on the very next page. "Mais non; Albertine n'était nullement pour moi une oeuvre d'art." III, 383. She is and she isn't, depending on when Marcel happens to ask himself the question, on whether jealousy is fueling his disfiguring imagination or not. The same is true of a book or a painting. It may be "art" at one moment and simply an object the next.

20. "elle disait: 'Mon' ou 'Mon chéri,' suivis l'un ou l'autre de mon nom de baptême, ce qui, en donnant au narrateur le même prénom qu'à l'auteur de ce livre, eût fait: 'Mon Marcel,' 'Mon chéri Marcel'" [emphasis mine]. III, 75.

21. "Die Ironie ist eine permanente Parekbase," Friedrich Schlegel, "Philosophische Fragmente," Erste Epoche II [1796–1798], "Philosophische Lehrjahre 1796–1806, nebst philosophischen Manuskripten aus den Jahren 1796–1828," *Kritische Friedrich-Schlegel-Ausgabe*, ed. Ernst Behler (Paderborn, 1963), XVIII, 85. The origin of the word *parabasis*, meaning an intrusion of the author's voice within the text, is in Old Greek Comedy: "During an intermission in the action the chorus, alone in the orchestra and out of character, came forward without their masks to face the audience and delivered, in song or recitative, views which the author felt strongly on various matters." *Princeton Encyclopedia of Poetry and Poetics* (Princeton, 1974), 597–98.

V. Bloom's Map of Misreading and the Rhetoric of Gnosis

Irony, and particularly irony as parabasis, is Proust's "trope of power," as Harold Bloom might say. Irony, according to Bloom, is a trope "of contraction or limitation," which "withdraws meaning through a dialectical interplay of presence and absence."[22] At this point in my analysis, Proust can be plotted on Bloom's "map of misreading" quite readily. This irony of parabasis is the first movement away from the "precursor-text" (I might be more inclined to call this the hypothetically ideal and irremediably lost object of desire, but if we are to use Bloom's map we may as well use his terms); for Proust this would be a composite of, say, Ruskin, Stendhal, Balzac, Flaubert, and the Duc de Saint-Simon. The irony introduces a dialectic of presence and absence. Following on the "absence" is synecdoche, the refiguration of the "absent" Albertine into a synecdoche of femininity, of all that Marcel might desire. This synecdoche, as the next, the middle, stage, becomes metonymy, that is, Albertine as a figure for Balbec, the "life of oceanside resorts," the "bluish undulations" of the boundless ocean, the present. At this point, the image of Albertine appears by turns empty and full, null and nauseously rich, as according to Bloom's paradigm it ought. For metonymy is substituted hyperbole, and Albertine becomes Françoise, present becomes past—grotesque but endowed with magical powers, a sorceress, a goddess of the past. This moves us into images of inside and outside characteristic, in Bloom's paradigm, of metaphor (it is only *within* Françoise's magic circle, *within* his room that Marcel can feel the past; Albertine is *outside* of the circle, but her absence within, presence somewhere *out there* in the realm of absence makes it possible for Marcel to imagine the day, create the present, turn it into the past). This would correspond to Marcel's vision of Albertine as a plant, in which she seems to be enclosed, entirely *within*, contained, sparing him the necessity of "living on the surface of himself."

This attempt at limitation always fails, however, and gives way to the trope of metalepsis, transumption, "a taking across to the poem's farther shore." Bloom cites Quintillian: "It is the nature of *metalepsis* to form a kind of intermediate step between the term transferred and the thing to which it is transferred, having no meaning in itself, but merely providing

22. Harold Bloom, *A Map of Misreading* (New York, 1975), 95.

a transition."[23] This, of course, is the ultimate figure which Albertine represents, being for Marcel no more than an *amorce*, a beginning over, a movement towards other women, "tropes." All of the women in the novel follow the same progression for Marcel, ending finally with Mademoiselle de Saint-Loup, at whose appearance the novel's ending turns into its beginning: Marcel decides to write what he has narrated, or as Bloom might put it, the text casts its belatedness into an earliness, "precedes" its precursors. Bloom sees in a text's final movement a recuperation, a "healing" of loss, a "completion" of the work of mourning. For Bloom metalepsis is the apotheosis of trope, "a figure of a figure," "a representation against time."[24] Of course, we must remember that in Bloom's theory the order in which these substitutions occur in the text is not important.

Proust, however, seems to undercut this model in a most ironic fashion. Is not the metaleptic figure of Albertine also a parabasis? Her "mask" is removed and she steps forward with the other women in the novel, like a chorus, to impel Marcel, in the name of the "author," in the name of his own sense of himself as a lover and an author, toward new desires, finally toward art. Doesn't the very same parabasis of irony govern all the tropes which Albertine at various times represents? As the object of desire, the absent, unassimilable eye of the present, isn't Albertine always the author's (silent) voice, naming Marcel, impelling him toward his end and re-commencement? Isn't Marcel himself in fact nothing but parabasis? His is the author's name. His is also the author's voice. How are we to know when Marcel is wearing his mask of a character and when he is not? It is this parabasic irony that governs Proust's text, not metalepsis, not any "trope of representation which strengthens language and the self"—the latter is nothing more or less than the "mendaciously flimsy" "*ordre du récit*," the dream which instructs by failing—but an irony of parabasis which is always misplacing, losing language and losing the self, losing the self in language. *Irony* is the rhetoric of desire, loss, and gnosis, the rhetoric of gnostic textuality.

23. *Ibid.*, 102; see also 84. For a revealing discussion of metaphor in Proust, see Paul de Man, "Reading (Proust)," in *Allegories of Reading* (New Haven, 1979), 57–78.
24. *Ibid.*, 103.

CHAPTER 3

Jealousy as a State of Mind *(Pages 99–119)*

I. Speaking Without Seeing: The Failure of Communication

Albertine is awake now, no longer "a long stem in bloom," and Marcel glibly announces the theme of this passage as "the impossibility where love collides with itself."[1] The dream of desire requited, art and love accomplished, is broken and the lover is faced with the unyielding reality of the flesh as an obstacle. The lover confronts the body he desires not as a barrier but as a goal; the artist, or the potential artist, sees it as a wall and hurls himself against it quite deliberately, though perhaps desperately and without a very clear understanding of what he is doing or why he does it. Proust takes such a banal harbinger of the plastic age as the telephone as a metaphor for any social encounter—the child of technological science, servant of the social self and of language at its most superficially social. Speaking on the telephone, one never sees what one hears and speaks to:

> I knew that I alone could say "Albertine" in that particular way to Andrée. And yet, for Albertine, for Andrée, and for myself, I felt that I was nothing. And I understood the impossibility where love collides with itself. We imagine that it has as its object a being whom we can see lying down before our eyes, enclosed in a body. Alas! It is the extension of this being to all the points in space and time which that being has occupied and will occupy. If we do not possess its contact with such-and-such a place, with such-and-such an hour, we do not possess it.[2]

1. "l'impossibilité où se heurte l'amour." III, 100.
2. "Je savais que moi seul pouvais dire de cette façon-là 'Albertine' à Andrée. Et, pourtant, pour Albertine, pour Andrée, et pour moi-même, je sentais que je n'étais rien. Et je comprenais l'impossibilité où se heurte l'amour. Nous nous imaginons qu'il a pour objet un être qui peut être couché devant nous, enfermé dans un corps. Hélas! Il est l'extension de cet être à tous les points de l'espace et du temps que cet être a occupés et occupera. Si

Marcel is more pessimistic about desire here than he has generally been before. "We waste precious time on an absurd course and we pass by the truth without suspecting it."[3] The love of individuals, and telephone conversations, are a waste of time.

It's interesting to note that in 1914, at about the time he was beginning the crushing regimen of work and solitude which he pursued until his death, Proust had his telephone removed. His housekeeper, Céleste Albaret, says that "in reality, it was that he didn't want to be bothered any more except when he chose to be. He made himself the master of his outings, his visitors, master of all his relations."[4] He was apparently weary of what he saw as the fatuousness of the social world, and wanted to make room for a world which would comprise himself and his will and imagination only. "His sole concern became the tranquillity of writing. For that, he needed solitude."[5]

The world and the self, the social self and the deep self, the self and its anima conflict. The tension and attraction between Marcel and Albertine resume the dynamic of these relationships. Marcel knows he is wasting his time but goes on wasting it because he is *jealous*. Jealousy is not to be subdued by mere force of will. "It is curious that a first love, if it clears the way for future loves by the fragility it leaves in our hearts, does not at least give us, as the very identity of symptoms and suffering, the means of curing them."[6] This is a disease which admits of no cure. Marcel has already made a list of its symptoms: "How many persons, towns, paths, does jealousy thus make us avid to know! It is a thirst for knowing thanks to which, on points isolated one from the others, we end up by having in succession all possible notions save the ones we would like to

---

nous ne possédons pas son contact avec tel lieu, avec telle heure, nous ne le possédons pas." III, 100.

3. "nous perdons un temps précieux sur une piste absurde et nous passons sans le soupçonner à côté du vrai." III, 100.

4. "En réalité, c'est qu'il ne voulait plus être dérangé que quand il le désirait. Il s'est rendu maître de ses sorties, de ses visiteurs, maître de toutes ses relations." Albaret, *Monsieur Proust*, 64.

5. "Son seul souci est devenu la tranquillité d'écrire. Pour cela, il avait besoin de solitude." *Ibid.*, 64.

6. "Il est curieux qu'un premier amour, si, par la fragilité qu'il laisse à notre coeur, il fraye la voie aux amours suivantes, ne nous donne pas du moins, par l'identité même des symptômes et des souffrances, le moyen de les guérir." III, 97.

have."[7] Marcel is convulsed by a violent fit of jealousy upon learning that Albertine plans a visit to the Verdurin household. He fears, for no good reason, that she intends to make contact there with some "refugee from Gomorrha." He experiences that peculiar pain which, instead of turning one away from desire as Pavlov's researches suggest it ought, only hones the obsession. Marcel is not a dog, and love and art nourish themselves on anguish.

II.   Fog and the Aviator

Two images seem particularly significant here. Albertine warns Marcel about the bad weather when he proposes accompanying her to the Verdurins. "There's an atrocious fog," she says. "I wouldn't want you to get sick from it."[8] What is more likely to make him sick is Albertine herself, who is as obscure and oppressive as any fog. This fog is like Albertine, and also like the moment, the present, all the many shapes of the ephemeral wall against which desire compels the lover to hurl himself suicidally. The social self (Albertine) warns its insular comrade: Beware. This world to which you would make yourself known is perfidious. You risk too much. It is not worth the trouble.

The other image, which comes a little later in the passage, is, like the telephone, a device of the modern age. An aviator flies away in his airplane, by means of mechanical wings. Marcel looks at the sky into which the flying machine and its master disappear, and sees his walks at Balbec "which I gloried in seeing last all of an afternoon and which I would contemplate afterwards, standing out like beautiful beds of flowers against the rest of Albertine's life as against an empty sky before which one dreams peacefully, without thought."[9] This is the azure past—the ocular periwin-

---

7. "Combien de personnes, de villes, de chemins, la jalousie nous rend ainsi avide de connaître. Elle est une soif de savoir grâce à laquelle, sur les points isolés les uns des autres, nous finissons par avoir successivement toutes les notions possibles, sauf celles que nous voudrions." III, 86.

8. "il y a un brouillard atroce . . . je ne voudrais pas que cela vous fasse mal." III, 104.

9. "que je m'enorgueillissais de voir durer tout un après-midi et que je contemplais ensuite, se détachant en beaux massifs de fleurs sur le reste de la vie d'Albertine comme sur un ciel vide devant lequel on rêve doucement, sans pensée." III, 106. The choice of an airplane here is surely not accidental. A great deal has been made of Proust's chauffeur, Alfred Agostinelli, as one of the prototypes for Albertine in the *Recherche* (see George Painter, *Proust: The Later Years* [Boston, 1965], 96, 115; Justin O'Brien, "Albertine the

kle hue of the Guermantes, the color of the Guermantes way and the way of art. The plane reminds him of "a boat sought by a tourist who wishes to go make a tour (*randonnée*) on the ocean."[10] The plane is inert. One must drag it, like a boat, "on the sand."[11] Finally it rises from the ground, but cannot evade the force of the earth's attraction, cannot avoid the bonds of necessity, natural necessity, which tie it to the earth. Thus the flights of love endure—precariously, and for a short time only. The "fiction" (of flight) must sooner or later suffer displacement by an unwieldy and leaden reality, take back "its materiality, its greatness, its volume, when, the duration of the excursion approaching its end, the moment would have come to return to port."[12]

The most interesting word here is *randonnée*, "circuit," "tour," what the tourist wants to do with his hired boat. The word contains two pho-

---

Ambiguous," *PMLA*, December 1950; Harry Levin, "Proust, Gide, and the Sexes," *PMLA*, June 1950). There is a passage in *Pastiches et mélanges* in which Agostinelli is depicted as the agent of the very sort of "doubling," alchemical substitution, which the Venetian statue of an angel had suscitated in *Contre Sainte-Beuve* and which Proust described in the latter volume as identical with literary experience, writing and reading (see note 32, Chapter 1 herein): "C'était mon mécanicien, l'ingénieux Agostinelli qui, envoyant aux vieilles sculptures le salut du présent dont la lumière ne servait plus qu'à mieux lire les leçons du passé, dirigeait successivement sur toutes les parties du porche, à mesure que je voulais les voir, les feux du phare de son automobile.* Et quand je revins vers la voiture je vis un groupe d'enfants que la curiosité avait amenés là et qui, penchant sur le phare leurs têtes dont les boucles palpitaient dans *cette lumière surnaturelle*, recomposaient ici, comme projetée de la cathédrale dans un rayon, la figuration angélique d'une Nativité" [emphasis mine]. The asterisk marks the insertion of this note: "Je ne prévoyais guère quand j'écrivis ces lignes que sept ou huit ans plus tard ce jeune homme me demanderait à dactylographier un livre de moi, apprendrait l'aviation sous le nom de Marcel Swann dans lequel il avait amicalement associé mon *nom de baptême* [see pages 44–45 herein] et le nom d'un de mes personnages et trouverait la mort à vingt-six ans, dans un accident d'aéroplane, au large d'Antibes." *Contre Sainte-Beuve*, ed. Pierre Clarac and Yves Sandre (Paris, 1971), 66 (emphasis mine). Objects of desire, whether "Maman," through the recollected mediation of a statuary angel, as in "Conversation avec Maman" (see note 32, Chapter 1 herein), or Agostinelli here, and whether "intentionally" or not, manipulate *light*—sunlight or headlights—in such a way as to set in motion the figuration and defiguration, substitution and doubling, of "literary" perception, so that the title becomes "supernatural," "angelic," "divine." One real such object was for Proust intimately and *fatally* connected with airplanes. Moreover, in *Albertine Disparue*, an outright link is made between Venetian angels (painted by Giotto) and aviators, between the imaginary supernatural, art, and aviation, mechanical flight (III, 648; see Painter, *Later Years*, 272).

10. "une barque demandée par un touriste qui veut aller faire une randonnée en mer." III, 105.

11. "sur le sable." III, 105.

12. "sa matérialité, sa grandeur, son volume, quand, la durée de la promenade approchant de sa fin, le moment serait venu de rentrer au port." III, 106.

nemic elements: the verb *donner* and the prefix *ra-*, which means "again," indicates a restoration of a previous state. A matter of going to sea, then, to give something back? There is also the anagrammatic sense of *ren(dre) (un) donné—r(endre) un donné—*to render in the sense of turning over, or simply turning, altering, reproducing, representing in a different medium, translating, deciphering, breaking (rending) the "given" (the "given" circumstances of writing and experience: language and desire). This interpretative violence would be the gift itself, the gift rendered in the rending (giving) of the given (gift), irreducible paradox emblemizing the *circuit*, movement outwards, of the desiring and writing self into self-displacement, introjection and projection, the reflexivity of its narration and its desire. The prefix *ra-* points to the always belated and repetitive nature of this reflexive displacement (work of mourning), and to its inability to requite, complete, objectify itself, short of death. Marcel must finally discover that this "given gift" is the gnosis itself, the gold absent from Proust's literary furnace (*calorifère*), missing but unnervingly present by its absence. The word *mer* (*mère*), an imagistic and phonemic emblem of maternal femininity, situates, specifies the direction of the circuit: to rend(er) the mother (the first love object), the generative female matrix into a different medium from the flesh (into writing), by this act of violence and regeneration to become one's own generative matrix at the same time as one penetrates it, both consummating original desire and transcending, undoing it. *Faire une r(endre) un donné(e) en/un mer/mère.*

III.   *Sadomasochism in Love and Art*

I have just acknowledged a subspecies of masochism—jealousy—as the animating force of this "grace," the phenomenon which motivates its pursuit. It is the hallucinogenic which causes men to "see" periwinkle blue skies (and eyes) in a magical, even a divine, light. But sadism is involved as well. Marcel, following Baudelaire, announces that he, too, is both knife and wound (see the latter's *L'Héautontimorouménos*). Scolding Albertine, he finds himself in the role his parents used to occupy before him. Albertine has assumed his former part. He recognizes himself in the childishness of her face. He has doubled "like those plants which double themselves as they grow," so that "before the sensitive child whom I uniquely had been, there was now a man opposed, full of good sense, of severity for the sickly sensibilities of others, a man resembling what my parents had been for me."[13] Loving Albertine, he is in love with himself. Abusing Albertine, he abuses himself. Seeking to possess Albertine, without any hope of success, he seeks to possess himself, and of course fails. The idea seems to be that love consists of these alternating currents of attraction, the positive (sadism) and the negative, a sense of repugnance (masochism); it is a force comprising opposite forces, sky and earth, heaven and hell. Pain inflicted redounds to the inflictor. So it is that Marcel says "the coupling of contrary elements is the law of life, the principle of fecundation, and, as we will see, the cause of much misfortune."[14] His is quite a zoroastrian view of things. Suffering and fecundation, creation, are inseparable. "Here," he ominously announces, "I call love a mutual torture."[15]

IV. *The Loss of Faith, the Dream, Grace, and the Artist as Holy Man*

Albertine is never able to comfort Marcel as his mother did. He feels with Albertine only anxiety, "the anguish of those nights when my mother scarcely told me goodnight, or did not even come up to my room."[16] He acknowledges that this anguish localizes itself in a love, in the present, for a time only, and then dissipates, to taint every experience and memory: "once again spread over all."[17] It seems safe to say that Marcel has lost what little faith he had in the present. He still had some when his mother came up every night to kiss him. But women, kisses, the moment no longer have any power to appease his advanced and advancing anxiety. He suffers particularly at this moment because he is living in a state of limbo. He has seen that love is nothing but a sort of hopelessly banal martyrdom, but he has not understood that desire and its concomitant

13. "en regard de l'enfant sensitif que j'avais uniquement été, lui faisait face maintenant un homme opposé, plein de bon sens, de sévérité pour la sensibilité maladive des autres, un homme ressemblant à ce que mes parents avaient été pour moi." III, 107.
14. "l'accouplement des éléments contraires est la loi de la vie, le principe de la fécondation et, comme on verra, la cause de bien des malheurs." III, 108.
15. "J'appelle ici l'amour une torture réciproque." III, 109.
16. "l'angoisse [de ces soirs] où ma mère me disait à peine bonsoir, ou même ne montait pas dans ma chambre." III, 111.
17. "de nouveau étendue à toutes." III, 111.

anguish may be leading him to something more important than Albertine. He is beyond mere melancholy, but he has not begun to spin the web of mourning which will be his work. "I no longer knew how to say: I am sad."[18]

He has lost the *logos*, the puerile innocence which allowed him to find some solace in the present. Young children live exclusively within the confines of the present moment; the future does not exist for them. It is pointless to promise a child that he will have such-and-such a thing in six months or a year—you might as well tell him he will never have it. The present is his reality, and as far as the child is concerned, what is not now, is not. His mother embodied this present for Marcel the child; now Albertine personifies many of its attributes. So he says of her that "she continued . . . like a watch which does not stop, like a climbing plant, a convolvulus which continues to spread its branches, whatever support is given it."[19]

When she is asleep, he is able to see her as a receptacle through which his own will might express itself; so he dreams of restoring an equilibrium between himself and the present, of closing the gap between himself and Albertine, all "objects of desire." Otto Rank believed that this was the dream and deepest desire of every artist.[20] This vision of Alber-

18. "je ne savais plus dire: je suis triste." III, 112.

19. "elle continuait . . . comme une montre qui ne s'arrête pas, comme une plante grimpante, un volubilis qui continue de pousser ses branches quelque appui qu'on lui donne." III, 113.

20. "My feeling is insistent that artistic creativity, and indeed the human creative impulse generally, originate solely in the constructive harmonizing of this fundamental dualism of all life." Otto Rank, *The Myth of the Birth of the Hero, and Other Writings*, ed. Philip Freund (New York, 1959), xi. Proust's work contradicts this statement most tellingly: it is by a *destructive dissonance* that the creative impulse undoes the metaphysic of dualism. With this revision of terms, Rank's theory of creativity is perhaps closer to Proust's, and to my concept of the gnostic art, than any other in psychotheory, prior to James Hillman. Compare, for instance, these statements (appropriately revised) from Rank to my "Freudian" reading of Proust at the end of Chapter 5 and to the conclusion of this study: "From the side of art and that of science, the way seems prepared for the decisive crisis, in the midst of which we stand—but also for its solution, which I foresee in a new structure of personality. This will be able to use in a [de-]constructive form the psychological insight that is so destructive when it exists as introspection, and the individual impulse to creation will turn positively [negatively] toward the [de-]formation of its own personality. . . . This is the goal that has hitherto been vainly sought by the so-called neurotic; in earlier ages [historical moments when more orthodox, rather than gnostic, arts could flourish] he was occasionally able to achieve creatively, thanks to some collective art-ideology, but today all collective means fail and the artist is thrown back onto an individual psychotherapy. [I

tine, however, assumes possession of her, which is never realized: "as if she had been an instrument on which I had played and on which I executed modulations of tone, drawing from one and the other of its strings, different notes."[21]

This is what he will do in the making of his books, in the transformation of Albertine into a character. In the dream, the female body becomes a receptacle for the masculine will. He fills it with his breath. Marcel calls the breathing of Albertine asleep "the pure song of Angels. And in that breathing, however, I suddenly said to myself that perhaps many names brought back by memory must have figured."[22]

In the dream, the sequence of ancestral pasts accumulated in the memory becomes nearly accessible to the conscious senses. The body of the anima becomes "translucid" and permits a glimpse of "the world just underneath." "So that her sleep appeared to me as a marvelous and magical world in which there occasionally arose, from the depths of the scarcely translucid element, the confession of a secret which no one will understand."[23] What he hears is the divine and eternal "feminine principle," as Goethe called it, which drives men "to reach beyond themselves."[24] "I

---

would argue that this is not only happening today, but has happened at various historical moments, for instance that of Villon's lifetime.] But this can only be successful if it sees its individual problem as one conditioned both by time and by culture, whereas the modern [gnostic] artist is driven by the unattainability of his ideology into that neurosis out of which the neurotic vainly seeks a creative escape—vainly, because the social ideologies are lacking that could fulfill and justify his personal conflict. Both will be achieved in a new [de-]formation of personality, which can, however, be neither a therapy of neuroses nor a new psychological art-ideology, but must be a [de-]constructive process of acceptance and development [dispersal] of one's individual personality as a new type of humanity, and in order to create the new it will have to give up [lose] much that has been received from tradition and become dear to it." *Ibid.*, 210. "And the creative type who can renounce this protection [dispersal] by art and can devote his whole [de-]creative force to life and the [de-]formation of life will be the first representative of the new human type [the gnostic type], and in return for this renunciation will enjoy, in personality-creation [-dispersal] and expression, a greater happiness [freedom]." *Ibid.*, 244.

21. "comme si elle eût été un instrument dont j'eusse joué et à qui je faisais exécuter des modulations en tirant de l'une, puis de l'autre de ses cordes, des notes différentes." III, 113.

22. "le pur chant des Anges. Et dans ce souffle pourtant, je me disais tout à coup que peut-être bien des noms humains apportés par la mémoire devaient se jouer." III, 114.

23. "translucide"; "ce monde sous-jacent"; "Alors son sommeil m'apparaissait comme un monde merveilleux et magique où par instants s'élève, du fond de l'élément à peine translucide, l'aveu d'un secret qu'on ne comprendra pas." III, 114.

24. Goethe, *Faust*, trans. Walter Kaufman (Garden City, 1961), 503: "The Eternal Feminine Lures to Perfection."

remembered still other voices, voices of women particularly . . . ; I re-
called one by one the voices of each of the girls I had known at Balbec,
then that of Gilberte, then that of my grandmother, then that of Madame
de Guermantes . . . I saw rising towards God by the tens, hundreds,
thousands, the harmonious and multisonorous salutation of all the
Voices."[25] This is the "Word" which announces the "creation," and the
"divinity," which comes bearing "grace"—in French, *salut—salut-ation*.

In his dialogue, his desire, his "intertextuality" with Albertine, Marcel
the character "reads" his name, names himself. In the impersonal and
constant, directionless drone of Albertine's breath there are "multisonorous" voices, bearing greeting, "grace." But can this be "grace" in the
sense in which it is understood by so many goodhearted descendants of
Françoise, of peasant Catholicism, Wednesday night bingo-players, novena-
sayers? Or is it, more likely, Flannery O'Connor's sort of "grace"—a "*coup
de grâce*"—a blow to terminate an agony? Or, more ironically, perhaps,
dispensation, exemption, a temporary clemency, suspension of a death
sentence? As we shall see in discussing O'Connor's work, there is in her
application of the term much the same ironic indeterminacy. What we
can say is that this self-naming, in which any reader is engaged as he
projects his voice into a "text," some Albertine, making it speak to him
as if it were another's voice, name him, situate him, suspends us in a
violent indeterminacy. The "work" threatens at once to save us, to tell us
what we want so furiously to know, and so to finish us, cut off our striving and our indeterminacy, our groping after ourselves, our lust for closure, finish us by some unforeseeable violence (*coup de grâce*)—and yet
what it does is more unsettling than any blow: to suspend us in the
arbitrariness, the inscrutability, of a sound, a name, a sign, a text, reducing us to something else which we must "read." So we ourselves become
signs, and self-displacing signs, furnaces making "disagreeable noises."
The gnostic divinity, if it is "within us," is not the *logos*, but its antithesis,
neither presence nor the name of presence but absence, antithesis, the
inconceivable other. It is towards this that Albertine, as a text, is leading

25. "je me rappelai d'autres voix encore, des voix de femmes surtout . . . ; je me rappelai
une à une la voix de chacune des jeunes filles que j'avais connues à Balbec, puis de Gilberte,
puis de ma grand-mère, puis de Madame de Guermantes . . . je voyais s'élever vers Dieu
par dizaines, par centaines, par milliers, l'harmonieuse et multisonore salutation de toutes
les Voix." III, 101–102.

Marcel, the still frustrated lover/reader—frustrated, because he has not learned to love loss.

This dream, appearing for the second time in this one novel, is Proust's *Paradiso*, Albertine being his Beatrice. ("Beatrice looked up [toward God] and I looked at her."[26]) Albertine awake, the present, represents the inferno of jealousy. Sleep, which resuscitates the past, is as near to paradise as mortal man may come. Life and the metamorphosis of *paradiso* into palpable form (which, to the creative temperament, might be almost interchangeable) amount to a purgatory. But Proust's work calls the careful segregation of these three states into question. At various times, Albertine is a figure for all three. Or rather they are figures for her. If it is the *inferno* of jealousy which drives Marcel towards the ephemeral *paradiso* of possession and the *purgatorio* of writing, it is the same Albertine who is an emblem for them all. What this suggests is that the entire economy of recuperation, totalization, possession, toward which this progression of *inferno*, *purgatorio*, and *paradiso*, is directed, might be entirely fallacious. The real paradise might lie beyond wishing to possess, nostalgia for possession, in the violence of loss, in the alchemical power of words (and desire) to disfigure and re(dis)figure, to transmutate things and persons by naming, renaming them, losing them in the texts of their and our being.

What distinguishes Marcel from everyone else is that he hears these "divine voices" practically everywhere. Often one has the feeling that Proust has cast his narrator in a mystery play without the latter's knowledge. "How I would have wished to grasp the meaning of it all,"[27] says Marcel. The action, in the Aristotelian sense,[28] of the mystery play centers on, even in, the body of Albertine. The female criers in the street are the chorus, all singing the same "confession of a secret which no one will understand."[29]

The language of the criers seems strange to Marcel. He hasn't yet mastered the art of deciphering, the art of the *déchiffreur*, as Mallarmé called

---

26. "Beatrice in suso et io in lei guardava." Dante, *Tutte le Opere de Dante Alighieri* (3rd ed.; Oxford, 1904), *Paradiso*, canto two, line 22, p. 105.
27. "Comme j'aurais voulu en saisir le sens." III, 114.
28. See Francis Fergusson, *The Idea of a Theater* (Princeton, 1949), 229–34.
29. "aveu d'un secret qu'on ne comprendra pas." III, 114.

it. "It has always been difficult for me to understand why these very clear words were gasped in such an inappropriate, mysterious tone, like the secret which makes everyone sad in the old palace where Mélisande has failed to bring any joy, and profound like a thought of the old man Arkel who seeks to utter in very simple words all of wisdom and destiny."[30] It seems almost that this refrain is a secularized mass, a travestied gregorian chant, so disguised as not to be recognizable even to those who sing it. Marcel and his century have lost the key to such mysteries. Bergson said that they had lost the instinctive faculty.[31] It comes to nearly the same thing. Positivism has deprived men of the sense that the material world is not the only one, and that they have lives and worth beyond their bodies, their stomachs and brains. It is consistent with some popular versions of existentialism that Proust should have conceived the artist as the one who, by the effort of will which is his work, restores the will of humanity. Modern man is like a child, giving all his faith to the moment, looking to it to answer his desires. That means that he is in a fallen state, a state of *ignorance*, of not knowing, in which the truth, gnosis, spirit, both within him and outside of him, in others, is hidden. It is for art, rather than scripture, to reveal it, or at least to give some sense that it exists. It is to that task of restitution and revelation that Marcel finally, at the close of the cycle, decides to devote himself, and through it, to deliver himself from the swaddling ignorance of the present and the flesh by embracing it, not as a nullity of not knowing but rather as the knowing of an absence. In fact, what Proust is about is not so much restoring the will of humanity as reaching beyond it, and beyond nostalgia for it. It may be that in that "revelation" of losing there is something beyond loss, a kind of liberation.

Marcel senses the mystery of the commercial refrains chanted out in the street but cannot precisely define it. The mystery, for a gnostic anyway, is simply that every man is a god (or a piece of one) and does not know it, is deprived by "evil" forces of the knowledge of his own divinity. We are reminded that Marcel has not realized his vocation just as we

---

30. "Il m'a toujours été difficile de comprendre pourquoi ces mots fort clairs étaient soupirés sur un ton si peu approprié, mystérieux, comme le secret qui fait que tout le monde a l'air triste dans le vieux palais où Mélisande n'a pas réussi à apporter la joie, et profond comme une pensée du vieillard Arkel qui cherche à proférer dans des mots très simples toute la sagesse et la destinée." III, 117.

31. Bergson, "L'Evolution créatrice," *Oeuvres*, 635–44.

were in the first scene of the book. Françoise brings in *Le Figaro*: "my article still had not appeared."[32]

Marcel explains the failure to decipher the mystery. It is like "the secret which makes everyone sad in the old palace where Mélisande has failed to bring any joy."[33] The mystery is "the impossibility where love collides with itself," just beyond the jealousy animating specific desire. Marcel is beginning to suspect that the women with whom he has been in love have only been the conduits of something much larger and that the failure to discover this larger force may be the source of the frustration he always feels in the presence of Albertine. Evoking the myth of Mélisande, he implies that the love of individuals is by nature tragic. It is too "factitious," too "heavy," like the airplane which takes off only to land again. Jealousy, if it fuels the flight, is also a considerable ballast.

The sounds of the courtyard remind him of the same thing that the airplane did: "The iron 'curtains' of the baker, the milkseller, which had been lowered last night over all the possibilities of feminine happiness, rose now like the canvas of a ship which is setting sail and about to follow, over a transparent sea, a vision of young female assistants."[34] But the noise of desires past, present, and possible is not all he hears. "This noise of iron curtains being raised would perhaps have been my sole pleasure in a different part of the town." But this is Marcel's part of town, the private and unique part of someone who is going eventually to write books, though he does not yet know it. He knows, nevertheless, that his experience of the world is not like everyone else's. He says that "if I lacked the instinct of the artist, it is quite possible that I would be content with feminine happiness. But I hear other sounds, other mysteries in this quarter": "a hundred others made my joy."[35] He is learning to celebrate the violent indeterminacy, the suspension, of this constant and reflexive naming, with no will or identity behind it, which is nothing more or less than perception, be it in reading or desire.

32. "mon article n'avait toujours pas passé." III, 119.
33. "le secret qui fait que tout le monde a l'air triste dans le vieux palais où Mélisande n'a pas réussi à apporter la joie." III, 117.
34. "Les 'rideaux' de fer du boulanger, du crémier, lesquels s'taient hier soir abaissés sur toutes les possibilités de bonheur féminin se levaient maintenant, comme les légères poulies d'un navire qui appareille et va filer, traversant la mer transparente, sur un rêve de jeunes employées." III, 116.
35. "Ce bruit du rideau de fer qu'on lève eût peut-être été mon seul plaisir dans un quartier différent." III, 116. "cent autres faisaient ma joie." III, 116.

CHAPTER 4

The Perfidious Present and
the Perfidious Female (Pages 131–50)

I. Libido Sciendi: The Desire to Know—the Failure of
Knowledge in the Present

Marcel is wracked by a new fit of jealousy. The divertissements in which
Albertine may have indulged on her trip to Versailles have just occurred
to him. The chauffeur who accompanied her assures him, deceitfully, of
Albertine's innocence. But this does nothing to quell his suspicions. Gilberte's *femme de chambre* comes to tell him that during the time he was
seeing Gilberte almost daily, Gilberte was also seeing someone else. This
causes Marcel a good deal of mental anguish despite the time elapsed
since his infatuation with Gilberte. Jealousy is not bound to the passage
of time, to the present, or to the truth. "Facts" have nothing to do with
its potency.

Jealousy is peculiarly ironical. It depends no more on truth than on
what one may believe one knows. One lives, without thinking too much
about it, by a faith in the present and in "knowledge." This faith is often
betrayed, but as there is no simple alternative, seldom obliterated entirely. Jealousy is governed by nothing but chance. Will has no power
over it, neither does the mind. Jealousy is part of the outside, of the
signifier, if you will, and there can be no *direct* approach to the signified,
the "inside," via the "outside."

Jealousy is a phenomenon of doubt, of what one does not know but
may feel or suspect. "Jealousy struggles in the void, uncertain as we are
in those dreams in which we suffer for not finding in his empty house a
person we have known well in life but who may be someone else here
and have only borrowed the traits of another character, uncertain as we
are to an even greater extent after waking when we seek to identify this

or that detail of our dream."[1] It is always a dream, one in which identity scarcely exists. Here, it is a dream of absence, of an empty house, the failure of a search. The house is surely Marcel's psyche, or better, his "world," and Proust's novel. The person for whom he searches is in some sense Albertine, and also himself, as well as the gnosis—the latter again an arbitrary term for something at once intensely familiar and unknown, lost. The house Marcel occupies is a house of jealousy. He does not suffer now because of the chauffeur's dishonesty. What concerns him is a humiliation long past. Jealousy, and that part of the self which is afflicted by it, have their own sense of time which rarely corresponds to that of the clock (we will shortly see that it is Françoise who obeys this "untime"). It is the same faculty which animates memory, which depends on the "barometric character," that is, on the present, on the chance of the moment, to resuscitate the past.

The locus of this passage and much of the novel's treatment of love is the postcard—a fine example of the tendency of dream and of the writer's unconscious to invest an inconsequential object with great psychic significance (displacement). The connection is the one which Proust always makes between place and person, love and the desire, for instance, to see Venice. "The curiosity of love, like that which the names of places excite in us: always disappointed, it is reborn and remains ever insatiable."[2] "The postcards from Versailles . . . gave me a slightly disagreeable impression every time my eyes fell onto them while arranging some papers."[3] He is afraid that Albertine might have bought the cards without ever going to the places they "signify," that she may have sent them only to throw him off the scent of her vices.

Postcards are nothing but two-dimensional images of a place. Why buy them? If not to send, then to keep as souvenirs of a trip. The image and the place are not the same thing, surely. But it is part of our faith in

1. "La jalousie se débat dans le vide, incertaine comme nous le sommes dans ces rêves où nous souffrons de ne pas trouver dans sa maison vide une personne que nous avons bien connue dans la vie mais qui peut-être en est ici une autre et a seulement emprunté les traits d'un autre personnage, incertaine comme nous le sommes plus encore après le reveil quand nous cherchons à identifier tel ou tel détail de notre rêve." III, 147.

2. "La curiosité amoureuse, comme celle qu'excitent en nous les noms de pays: toujours déçue, elle renaît et reste toujours insatiable." III, 143.

3. "les cartes postales de Versailles . . . me donnaient une impression un peu désagréable chaque fois qu'en rangeant des papiers mes yeux tombaient sur elles." III, 135.

the present, the faith that few acknowledge but most (excepting suicides and some lunatics) share, that we believe in this identity. Buying the card, the tourist believes it—that he is taking home a bit of the place he has visited. Even more fetishistic examples are common. Many a notable place has been stripped of woodwork, plaster, even stone, by sightseers who wished to carry a little of it home with them. That their act of homage and remembrance is also an act of destruction seems not to occur to them—or in any case, does not deter them. Always the desire to possess is apparent in the most trivial of human acts.

What Marcel says about postcards might just as well be applied to the women in his life.

> For two years intelligent men, artists, found Sienna, Venice, Granada, a bore, and said of the most inferior omnibus, of every wagon: "There is something beautiful." Then this taste passed like the others. I'm not even sure that we're not coming back to "the sacrilege which is to destroy the noble things of the past." In any case, a first-class car ceased to be considered *a priori* more beautiful than Saint Mark's in Venice. One would say rather: "It is in the former that life is, the return to the past is a factitious thing," but without drawing any clear conclusion.[4]

This is one of Baudelaire's most famous dicta: beauty is factitious, and every age invents its own. But Proust suggests that real beauty consists of something more. The difference between image and place is similar by analogy to the difference between signifier and signified, with the proviso that the latter exists. It is notable and surprising that Proust should have assumed that most people believe only in "signifiers," lend no credence to and don't even think about any "signified"; the ironic "nobility" of Marcel comes from his recognition of this discrepancy within the sign, his self-consciousness of the sign's duality which sets him apart from everyone else, and his persisting nostalgia for the naïve assumption of unity reflected in popular concepts of beauty—the assumption of identity

---

4. "Pendant deux ans les hommes intelligents, les artistes trouvèrent Sienne, Venise, Grenade, une scie, et disaient du moindre omnibus, de tous les wagons: 'Voilà qui est beau.' Puis ce goût passa comme les autres. Je ne sais même pas si on n'en revint pas au 'sacrilège qu'il y a de détruire les nobles choses du passé.' En tout cas, un wagon de première classe cessa d'être considéré a priori comme plus beau que Saint-Marc de Venise. On disait pourtant: 'C'est là qu'est la vie, le retour en arrière est une chose factice,' mais sans tirer de conclusion nette." III, 136.

between signifier and signified, of the totalization of the sign. Marcel is looking for something which everyone else appears to him to have found, when in fact what sets him apart is to be the only one aware of the loss, of the discrepancy within the sign, of its non-coincidence with itself. Marcel thinks that the emperor must be wearing clothes if everyone else sees them, and cannot understand why those clothes should be invisible to him. This Chaplinesque ingenuousness is a source of much comedy in the novel. Marcel cannot yet see that love and art are nothing but undressing, dressing, and dismembering the "emperor," the naked and null corpse of the real, and that he is already engaged in that process, turning Albertine into a musical instrument, his "work," a text. This difference between beautiful "things" and the idea of "beauty" is the difference between the person one loves and love itself, the difference between present and past, even that between the social self and the deep self. The love object, be it male or female, is for Proust a kind of trope, a mirage, an imagistic signifier. Jungian psychology suggests that what one is looking for exists only within the self. "Deep selves" cannot communicate with one another in the social world of social selves. "We are," says Marcel, "sculptors. We wish to obtain from a woman a statue completely different from the one which she presents to us."[5]

Again Marcel makes a rhetorical connection between lover and artist, and between the object of desire and the raw material of art. To desire is to make, to create, or rather to project a shape in the imagination outside of the self, to create or re-create an aspect of the self from the body and features of someone or something—else.

II.   The Choir of Female Voices

Inebriated by the music of the courtyard, Marcel decides to send for one of the criers. He suspects, in their noise and the glimpses he catches of them, some occluded mystery.

> In a butcher shop, where to the left was an aureole of sunlight and to the right an entire beef carcass hung up, a butcher boy, very tall and very thin, with blond hair, his neck rising from a sky-blue collar, with vertiginous speed and religious intensity put on one side the exquisite fillets of beef, on the other the

5. "Nous sommes des sculpteurs. Nous voulons obtenir d'une femme une statue entièrement différente de celle qu'elle nous a présentée." III, 142.

worst cuts of the rump, placed them on a dazzling balance surmounted by a cross, and from which hung beautiful chains and—though he did nothing afterwards but arrange some kidneys, steaks, ribs in the window—gave in reality much more the impression of a beautiful angel who, on the day of final Judgment, will prepare for God, according to quality, the separation of the Good and the Bad and the weighing of souls.[6]

Marcel doesn't just see a butcher, he sees a painting of Giotto. He always has the feeling that there is more before him than what is literally visible or audible, there in his "part of the town." The same thing which he dimly sensed behind the belfries of Martinville and Vieuxvicq, and past the trees at Hudimesnil, he senses now in the streets of Paris, in the milkmaids. Their mystery and their allure are derived from their nature as "fugitive beings" (*êtres de fuite*); they are sufficiently unknown and amorphous for Marcel that he may create them, invest them with whatever significance he wishes to. He knows nothing of their lives, so he is free to imagine them. Like latent statues, they so lack form and detail that he can chisel them in the image of his desire. But their allure depends on their remaining shapeless. "The nostalgic view which I had of these little girls, could I believe it very exact? Wouldn't she have been different if I had been able to keep her immobile next to me for several instants, one of those whom, from the height of my window, I saw only in a store or in flight?"[7]

He asks Françoise to send for one of them "for an errand which I needed to have done."[8] It isn't to send her on an errand and it isn't to see a single, certain woman that Marcel so instructs Françoise. The woman he is looking for is the one absent from every street, the hypothetical apotheosis of woman, like the flower which Mallarmé alludes to in *Crise*

6. "Dans une boucherie, où à gauche était une auréole de soleil, et à droite un boeuf entier pendu, un garçon boucher, très grand et très mince, aux cheveux blonds, son cou sortant d'un col bleu ciel, mettait une rapidité vertigineuse et une religieuse conscience à mettre d'un côté les filets de boeuf exquis, de l'autre de la culotte de dernière ordre, les plaçait dans d'éblouissantes balances surmontées d'une croix, d'où retombait de belles chaînettes, et—bien qu'il ne fît ensuite que disposer pour l'étalage, des rognons, des tournedos, des entrecôtes—donnait en réalité beaucoup plutôt l'impression d'un bel ange qui, au jour du Jugement dernier, prépara pour Dieu, selon leur qualité, la séparation des Bons et des Méchants et la pesée des âmes." III, 138.

7. "La vue nostalgique que j'avais de ces petites filles, pouvais-je la croire bien exacte? N'eût-elle pas été autre si j'avais pu garder immobile quelques instants auprès de moi une de celles que, de la hauteur de ma fenêtre, je ne voyais que dans la boutique ou en fuite?" III, 138.

8. "pour une course que j'avais à faire faire." III, 139.

de Vers: "I say: flower! and . . . musically there rises . . . that one which is absent from every bouquet."[9] In Marcel's quarter, love and art consist of the creation of something which has no material being, no phenomenal reality, of giving form to some aspect of the lover's or the artist's self, perhaps to something only latent in his or her personality, only apparent as something missing, absent. Sending for this milkmaid, Marcel understands perfectly well what he is about.

> I was like Elstir who, obliged to remain closed up in his studio on certain days in spring when to know that the woods were full of violets gave him the sudden urge to see some, would send his concierge's wife to buy him a bouquet of them: so it was not the table on which he had placed the little vegetal model, but all the carpet of underbrush where he had seen at other times, by the millions, their serpentine stems, bending beneath their blue beaks, that Elstir believed he had before him, like an imaginary zone enclosed in his studio by the limpid odor of the evocative flower.[10]

The actual, deep self, Bergson says, is always latent, always "enclosed." The only outlet it may have, Proust seems to suggest, is in the work of art. Even there it remains sharply constrained. It awaits a reader or a viewer to make something of its "evocative odor." Note the repeated rhetorical connection between women and flowers. The flowers which Elstir sends for are blue, of a slightly more intense shade than azure. Elstir does not aspire to possess the latter. He simply needs a small goad from the present to aid him in the making of his own bank of flowers. It is enough for him to know that the flowers are there where they ought to be, and *used* to be, and to supply his "barometric character" with a little of their look and smell, to set his "philosopher" to reconstructing the memory of the flowers, idealizing and organizing it as it never was in fact, in the present, before it was a memory.

The milkmaid arrives, and in arriving loses all her mysterious allure,

9. "Je dis: une fleur! et . . . musicalement se lève . . . l'absente de tous bouquets." Mallarmé, "Crise de Vers," *Oeuvres complètes*, ed. Henri Mondor and G. Jean-Aubry (Paris, 1945), 368.

10. "J'étais pareil en cela à Elstir qui, obligé de rester enfermé dans son atelier, certains jours de printemps où savoir que les bois étaient pleins de violettes lui donnait une fringale d'en regarder, envoyait sa concierge lui en acheter un bouquet: alors ce n'est pas la table sur laquelle il avait posé le petit modèle végétal, mais tout le tapis des sous-bois où il avait vu autrefois, par milliers, les tiges serpentines, fléchissant sous leur bec bleu, qu'Elstir croyait avoir sous les yeux, comme une zone imaginaire qu'enclavait dans son atelier la limpide odeur de la fleur évocatrice." III, 139.

her phantasmagorical irreality. The matter of her body is too substantial, too fixed, for Marcel to mistake it for the feminine principle. He can add nothing to her as she is—unless he were to become well enough acquainted with her to suspect her of telling lies, concealing vices. Another problem is that he does not know how to respond to her as a sign. He is still acquainted only with the present moment. As a writer, he knows the power of absence only instinctively. Reality, if one lets it, will immobilize the will. "She took on a crest-fallen look for not having more (instead of ten, twenty, as I remembered one after another without being able to fix my memory) than one nose, rounder than I had thought, and which gave an impression of stupidity and had in any case lost the power to multiply itself. This flight, captured, inert, obliterated, incapable of adding anything to her poor plainness, no longer had my imagination to collaborate with it. Fallen into the immobile real, I tried to rebound."[11] This *crémière* is absent presence personified, and to experience it and her, to feel it deeply, requires imagination. This is the force which is driving Marcel towards writing, the anguish of feeling that one's desires are frustrated, misled, deceived. This sense of despair and obstruction animates the faculty of recollection, sets the "philosopher" to organizing, fitting bits of memory together in an idealized and distorted fashion. In this way jealousy acts to *créer mon hier* ("create my yesterday"), which, abbreviated, of course, becomes *crémière*.

Marcel is "fallen into the immobile real." But he begins to recognize the absence which the milkmaid evokes. "I raised my eyes onto the curly, golden locks, and I felt that their swirling was bearing me away, my heart beating, into the light and gusts of a hurricane of beauty."[12] Jealousy is reinforced by this sense of lack which it helps to bring about. It is a phenomenon of the present, in which, according to Bergson, we do not live our real lives, do not learn anything. The present can only evoke. It

11. "Elle prenait un air tout penaud de n'avoir plus (au lieu des dix, des vingt, que je me rappelais tour à tour sans pouvoir fixer mon souvenir) qu'un seul nez, plus rond que je ne l'avais cru, qui donnait une idée de bêtise et avait en tout cas perdu le pouvoir de se multiplier. Ce vol capturé, inerte, anéanti, incapable de rien ajouter à sa pauvre évidence, n'avait plus mon imagination pour collaborer avec lui. Tombé dans le réel immobile, je tachai de rebondir." III, 143.

12. "Je levai les yeux sur les mèches flavescentes et frisées, et je sentis que leur tourbillon m'emportait, le coeur battant, dans la lumière et les rafales d'un ouragan de beauté." III, 144.

is real and exists only by virtue of what it makes us recall. The impossibility of possessing the object of desire, her or his inexorable absence, and his or her connection with every man or woman, place and thing which one has wished or wishes to possess, constitutes the essence of jealousy, which for Marcel, and for Proust, is the essence of desire.

III.   *The Revival of Jealousy*

Marcel discovers that the actress Léa, whom he suspects of Gomorrhean tendencies, and who knows Albertine, will appear at the Trocadéro, precisely where he has sent Albertine to foreclose the possibility that she might attempt to gratify her vices at the Verdurin household. At this realization his jealousy resurges violently, despite the chauffeur's reassuring lies. He remembers seeing Léa at Balbec with two girls whom Albertine, "without appearing to see them, had watched in the mirror one afternoon in the Casino."[13] He remembers Albertine's false denials that she knew Léa. These memories make Albertine again an unknown being, without shape, and which summons forth the "sculptor" in Marcel, whose marble refuses to lie still under the chisel. Marcel has already suggested that love is a disease to be cultivated. He repeats that sentiment here, and explains himself somewhat. "Chagrin penetrates us and forces us, by curiosity, to penetrate."[14] Desire is both active and passive, the desire to penetrate indivisible from the desire to be penetrated. The desire of the self is a desire for itself. Why then should desire, love, be cultivated? Because it makes one desire more. Active desire reinforces passive desire and vice versa. They are like diastolic and systolic movements of the self, which fuel its work of mourning, the process of imaginative digestion by which the self creates and expands its "world" or its "quarter."

Finally Marcel resumes this entire passage in a sentence already cited: "Jealousy struggles in the void." Lover and artist inhabit a landscape of dream, absence, void. It has no real existence but is a patchwork of lacunae. The lover "struggles in the void" to fix, give some shape of his own to what he loves, so bring it into himself—psychically devour it. He

13. "sans avoir l'air de les voir, avait, un après-midi, au Casino, regardées dans la glace." III, 144.

14. "Le chagrin pénètre en nous et nous force par la curiosité douloureuse à pénétrer." III, 146.

tries to immobilize the sequential movement, flow of presents "in which we are always passing beyond," where what he desires is always fleeing, becoming. The artist is about the same business, but consciously. His work is fixed, in a factitious sense, but in another, it is as "fugitive" as any individual or time. It is constantly transmuted in the minds of those who read or look at it. Both artist and lover "waste their time on an absurd route." If heroic in any sense, they are either comic or tragic at the same time. Probably they are both: ludicrous and yet somehow persistently noble in their pathos.

Jealousy narrowly escapes being utterly futile, unless art, and desire, are themselves utterly futile. We see it here as the force driving Marcel to become the consummately self-conscious lover—a writer of books. He cannot have the desire to penetrate and be penetrated, to destroy and be destroyed, the desire to make and to be made, without the goading spur of jealousy.

CHAPTER 5

The Sinking of Desire and the Sun *(Pages 153–75)*

I. Françoise and the Past

Carl Jung has described his dreams of descending lower and lower in a house whose furniture becomes progressively more ancient the lower one descends, ending finally in a cave, the floor strewn with bones and primitive drawings scratched on the walls.[1] In this passage of *La Prisonnière*, Françoise emerges as the anima, leading Marcel towards "the most remote epochs of the past."

The scene coalesces around Françoise and her language. She speaks a patois with her daughter which Marcel cannot understand. But, as he has deciphered the aristocratic dialect of the Duchesse, Marcel begins to penetrate this language too. Marcel, as Stephen Dedalus does also, sees languages as obstacles to be overcome.[2] The language itself takes the role of anima, interlocutor, between writer and reader, and because the work is made of words, between the author and himself, the conscious and the unconscious. Along with dream, writing is the only medium in which both express themselves, in which the two elements of the self confront each other directly, or come as near it as ever: "Keys become useless when the one we would keep from entering can use a pass-key or a burglar's jimmy. The patois becoming a defense without value, she began to speak with her daughter a French which quickly became that of the most remote epochs."[3]

1. Carl Jung, *Memories, Dreams, Reflections* (New York, 1965), 158–59.
2. James Joyce, *A Portrait of the Artist as a Young Man* (New York, 1964), 203.
3. "Les clefs deviennent inutiles quand celui qu'on veut empêcher d'entrer peut se servir d'un passe-partout ou d'une pince-monseigneur. Le patois devenant une défense sans valeur, elle se mit à parler avec sa fille un français qui devient bien vite celui des plus basses époques." III, 155.

The word *key* recalls Mallarmé's phrase: "O golden clasps of old missals," and evokes the entire symbolist ideology of secrecy and esoterism.[4] The poem, as Freud astutely remarked, is a defense of sorts. But it is a defense which invites its own undoing, beckons us to decipher it, unclasp its binding and pass into the writer or some simulacrum of him which he and we in collusion have created. It is like a wall with a door in it, erected so that the door might be opened. Without the wall there could be no point of entry. Language acts as both barrier and revelation, a point of entry, albeit arbitrary, a point at which more than one mind may *appear* to converge. Proust knows this and Marcel begins to know it.

Françoise is jealous of the attention which Marcel lavishes on Albertine. "Albertine renewed, after so many years, the same torture of envy of which Eulalie had been the cause when she had worked for my aunt."[5] Françoise, I have already noted, embodies for Marcel the past of peasant France, the past which he has seen in, or which he has been provoked to imagine by, the *bas-reliefs* of Saint-André-des-Champs. Her jealousy of Marcel's time allegorizes the attraction of the past, which draws Marcel into himself, as the desire for solitude which he feels almost always. When he is alone, and even more when he is alone with Albertine and she is asleep, he can "create her day," create Albertine as he would have her be, play her like a reed pipe. This preference of Marcel was shared by Proust, an aspect of what he called his neurosis—a preference for solitude and the past.[6]

Marcel is more conscious in this passage of Françoise and the past she embodies than he has been before. She absolutely lacks the sense of proper time, "clock" time. Marcel finds it impossible to situate himself according to her sense of temporality. Françoise is disdainful of duration as it is understood by most people. "When Françoise, having thus looked at her watch, if it were two o'clock, would say: it is one o'clock, or it is three o'clock; I have never been able to understand if this phenomenon which was occurring was situated in Françoise's vision, or her thinking, or her

4. "O fermoirs d'or de vieux missels." Mallarmé, "Hérésies Artistiques, L'Art pour Tous," *Oeuvres complètes*, 257.

5. "Albertine renouvelait, après tant d'années, le même supplice d'envie que lui avait causé jadis Eulalie auprès de ma tante." III, 154.

6. Albaret, *Monsieur Proust, passim*.

language; what is certain is that this phenomenon always took place. Humanity is very old. Heredity, crossbreeding have given an insurmountable force to bad habits, faulty reflexes."[7] Some modern sociologists and psychologists would think it altogether quaint that Proust should have insisted on the hereditary nature of not only physical traits but behavioral ones as well—although science at present seems to be rediscovering this line of thought. Proust would probably have agreed with Luther Burbank that "heredity is nothing but inherited environment." The past, experience, becomes a physiological, neurological burden which is passed on to one's descendants. Marcel sends this past, his private idealization of it, off in search of the present, of Albertine, at the Trocadéro. He recalls again the first scene of *Du Côté de chez Swann*, in which the narrator, awakening, must situate himself in the present by way of the past. It is also in that passage that his leg becomes an imaginary woman. So he depends on the past (phantasm) to situate him in the present, the present in which phantasm is represented as a female body.

Françoise, having found Albertine, has someone telephone Marcel. She does not speak to him herself. There are two interlocutors, the operator and the woman to whom Françoise is speaking, at the other end. So communication—and experience (of the present)—take place via intermediaries. The intermediaries, for Marcel, are always women, always the sexual "other" of himself. These two, from whom he learns that Albertine is on her way back, are seconded by, and analogous to, Françoise and Albertine, the real interlocutors, intermediaries. Jealousy and imagination, as we have seen, cannot operate without an overlapping of past and present, certainty and chance. The ultimate intermediary, or "receptacle" of the will (Albertine fits this description only when asleep), will for Marcel be language. Marcel and Proust both accept this halter. Communication, and in a larger sense, experience, do not occur otherwise. Dream and written work represent a reconciliation of the two aspects of the self, or at the least a juxtaposition of them.

7. "Quand Françoise, ayant ainsi regardé sa montre, s'il était deux heures disait: il est une heure, ou il est trois heures, je n'ai jamais pu comprendre si le phénomène qui avait lieu alors avait pour siège la vue de Françoise, ou sa pensée, ou son langage; ce qui est certain, c'est que ce phénomène avait toujours lieu. L'humanité est très vieille. L'hérédité, les croisements ont donné une force insurmontable à de mauvaises habitudes, à des réflexes vicieux." III, 156.

This milieu which we do not see, but through the translucid and changing intermediary of which we were seeing, I her actions, she the importance of her own life; that is the beliefs which we do not perceive but which are no more assimilable to a pure void than is the air which surrounds us; composing around us a variable atmosphere, sometimes excellent, often unbreatheable, they are worthy of being noted and recorded with as much care as the temperature, the barometric pressure, the season, for our days have their physical and moral originality.[8]

What is this medium coloring the lovers' perceptions of one another and themselves but an interface between them, and more, between those aspects of themselves which they have projected onto each other, and introjected into themselves?

The distance between individuals (and within them) which James saw as unbreachable truly haunts Marcel. He says in this passage that, under the hand of the artist, such voids are no longer simply void. In such gaps the artist erects an intermediary, a surrogate, which is his work, not to span the gap, but to *radicalize* it. This is one of the most positive passages in Proust's entire corpus of work. He affirms what James and Bergson believed, that the "true" self (which, it must be admitted, they defined variously and ambiguously) is imprisoned in an adamantine emptiness, and that language cannot penetrate that prison. Perhaps it cannot translate the essence of the deep self, and perhaps it cannot establish a directly communicative link between persons, but by amplifying the emptiness it may create the *image*, the figure, of such a linkage. And it may be that that is all that is necessary for the linkage to effectively exist. As imagination and memory make the place familiar and unthreatening, so the work of art may make the failure of communication, James's unbreachable distances, tolerable.

This passage recalls the two visits to Balbec. The first, during which Marcel was so unaccustomed to the new surroundings that he could not sleep; the other when, returning to Balbec, he finds himself enveloped

---

8. "ce milieu que nous ne voyons pas, mais par l'intermédiaire translucide et changeant duquel nous voyions, moi ses actions, elle l'importance de sa propre vie, c'est-à-dire ces croyances que nous ne percevons pas, mais qui ne sont pas plus assimilables à un pur vide que n'est l'air qui nous entoure; composant autour de nous une atmosphère variable, parfois excellente, souvent irrespirable, elles meriteraient d'être relevées et notées avec autant de soin que la température, la pression barométrique, la saison, car nos jours ont leur originalité physique et morale." III, 148–49.

not by an unfamiliar emptiness but by an atmosphere of his own creation, which his imagination has had time to assimilate, work its psychic
rhetoric of projection and introjection on. The place is so much a part of
him that it forces him, for the first time, to acknowledge the reality of
his grandmother's death. Life, and more than ever the life of a serious
writer, is a matter of filling in the gaps with images from one's own mind
and memory.

Art is not the only means of effecting such a "filling-in," and certainly
writing is not. Proust reverses an ancient tenet of rational thought: to be
real, a thing must objectively, phenomenally exist without reference to
anything else. He implies that the contrary is true, that nothing is real
until a person has "made it over" in his own mind. Not only is there a
psychic reality but there is no reality but the psychic one. The self assimilates as it expands. The chair which the eyes see exists only for the pair
of eyes and the mind which see it. It is, in Mallarmé's sense, an "absent"
chair. Life consists in fabricating the appearance of presence from the
raw material of absence. Art represents an effort both to communicate
and to appear to solidify and so negate that absence. James was right as
far as he went, Proust seems to say; reality, as he understood the word,
is void. But the human intellect is not limited to physical reality. In fact,
it only knows of physical reality by way of the mediation of psychic
reality. Everyone, in his or her psychic life, spends his or her time deny-
ing the integrity of so-called physical reality, making it over in his or her
own image. The artists and the writers make this everyday practice of
creating what does not exist into an *apparently* (that appearance in this
system *is* reality) communicative process.

It should surprise no one that Marcel is able to say, receiving a letter
from Albertine, a written communication, that "I was more the master
than I had thought."[9] This passage began with an example of his mastery
as decipherer. Remember that he calls Albertine "a work" (*une oeuvre*).
His hope, as a budding writer, must be that the human will does not
only "struggle in the void," that there is more to living and desiring than
the pain of jealousy, and more to jealousy than the failure of possession.
But he also recalls the beginning of the passage by the sentence follow-

9. "J'étais plus maître que je n'avais cru." III, 157.

ing: "More the master, which is to say, more the slave."[10] He has just described Françoise as a reservoir of the past. The age of humanity is so great that we are prisoners of many traits—good, bad, and indifferent—which are ours at birth, for instance the venerable spirit which will not permit Françoise to live by the time of the rest of the world, which denies her this sense of a common reality. The writer is born into a trap, an emptiness, which he devotes his life to filling, completing. But the same is true of any human. When it is complete, he or she is complete, and death marks the arbitrary point of closure. What sets the writer and the artist aside is that they are not blindly engaged in this process. They seek actively to manipulate it. They seek a past they have inherited in a present which is strange to them—they strive to digest, assimilate, the world without so that it resembles the world within. What the artist does that others do not do is to make of this process itself a thing in the present which will be for others a thing to be assimilated, a thing which may stimulate, enrich, and embellish their own lives as creators.

II.   The Vulcanian Art

Waiting for Albertine (his "work"), Marcel plays the piano. It may be instructive to recall here that Norpois called Bergotte a "flute player" (*joueur de flûte*). The implication being that writing books is a frivolous and futile expenditure of time. Marcel specifically plays the Vinteuil sonata. He imagines not the "redness" of his past, the "red" way of Swann, poppies, Montjouvain, the house of jealousy, but "the walks on the Guermantes way—where I had myself wanted to be an artist."[11] The sonata exorcises jealousy; he no longer feels it. The sonata no longer calls to mind the red way of Montjouvain, but the periwinkle blue of the Duchesse de Guermantes' eyes: love purged of jealousy, of all expectation of possession, having become desire for its own sake. The music makes Marcel feel something which has no material reality. He recognizes in it Elstir and himself: the realization of art consists in an overlapping of phantasms, of imaginations engaged in "making over," "filling in" the emptiness of the real. The artist furnishes the medium in which this

10. "Plus maître, c'est-à-dire, plus esclave." III, 157.
11. "des promenades du côté de Guermantes—où j'avais moi-même désiré d'être un artiste." III, 158.

"overlapping" can occur. He projects himself outward in his work, and the listener (if the art is music), hearing, projects himself, his memory, into the sounds he hears. In this process they seem to recognize themselves in one medium, one sound, and so seem to be the same thing—they experience an intimation of the gnosis. Marcel experiences a communication beyond society and jealousy.

> The music, quite different in this way from the company of Albertine, helped me to descend within myself, to rediscover there: the variety which I had vainly sought in life, in travel, for which however this sonorous tide, whose sun-drenched waves died at my side, gave me a sense of nostalgia. Double diversity. As the spectrum exteriorizes for us the composition of light, the harmony of a Wagner, the color of an Elstir permit us to know that qualitative essence of another's feelings into which love for another being does not let us penetrate. Secondly, diversity in the breast of the work itself, by the sole means there is of being diverse: to unite diverse individualities.[12]

It is only a sound—a *spectre*, in both senses of the French word—which accomplishes what desire fails to do. The art of Elstir, like any art, consists in a reciprocal involvement, of intellect, imagination, memory, which are subsumed under the rubric of perception, and this mutual involvement gives life to absence, familiarity to strangeness. The artist constructs the receptacle, the meeting place. Both composer and listener project themselves and mingle their pasts, the pasts of their ancestors (if one goes along with Proust, Jung, and to some extent, Freud as well). A kind of communication, or the illusion of it, seems to occur which James and Bergson might have thought impossible.

Marcel thinks of Wagner as he plays. He recognizes some notes from *Tristan* in the sonata. He repeats the name of this opera three times on a single page, evoking what the name of Debussy's opera, the name of Mélisande, evoked: fatal love. The tragic art limits itself to a love founded on and fueled by jealousy, which is no more "true" or "transcendent"

---

12. "La musique, bien différente en cela de la société d'Albertine, m'aidait à descendre en moi-même, à y découvrir du nouveau: la variété que j'avais en vain cherché dans la vie, dans le voyage, dont pourtant la nostalgie m'était donnée par ce flot sonore qui faisait mourir à côté de moi ses vagues ensoleillées. Diversité double. Comme le spectre extériorise pour nous la composition de la lumière, l'harmonie d'un Wagner, la couleur d'un Elstir nous permettent de connaître cette essence qualitative des sensations d'un autre où l'amour pour un autre être ne nous fait pas pénétrer. Puis, diversité au sein de l'oeuvre même, par le seul moyen qu'il y a d'être effectivement divers: réunir diverses individualités." III, 159.

than Marcel's love for Albertine. He wondered as he sat down at the piano if he had lost something real by not pursuing a career in art. He seems here to answer no, that these artists have only transcribed and elaborated jealousy, which he knows too well. Their art is nothing more than what he has experienced in life, and does no more than imitate the failure of desire.

Their art is for Marcel something like Mallarmé's swan which cannot break the ice in which it is frozen. He thinks of the works of Michelet (*La Bible de l'Humanité*), Balzac (*La Comédie Humaine*) and Hugo (*La Légende des Siècles*) in which he recognizes this same lack of transcendence, of a "surreality." They are all examples of what he calls a vulcanian art, meaning that their unity is mimetic. These writers have failed to close the circles of their works. They have remained infatuated with the present, chance, and not gone beyond, not overcome the romantic allure of the eye to attain some intimation of the blue beyond. They have taken their own specific desires too literally. This makes them not artists but "fabricators," forgers.[13] They merely imitate, duplicate, what they see and live. Marcel concludes that "if art is only this, it is no more real than life, and I had no cause for regret. I went on playing *Tristan*."[14] Art has not yet cured him of jealousy, but only given some temporary relief to its symptoms, a momentary anesthetic. Perhaps this fleeting comfort has come from the possibility, suggested by the sonata and by Marcel's interaction with it, of a communication which would not involve the social self at all, or only tangentially—a possibility innate but still latent in art.

He returns to the airplane as a metaphor for factitious art, and says clearly that this is not the swan of Lohengrin, the bird free to fly, but one closer akin to Mallarmé's, bound even in its flight to earth. "The technical expertise of the worker only served to make them leave the ground more freely, birds not like the swan of Lohengrin but like that airplane I had seen at Balbec change its energy into elevation, float above the waves, and become lost in the sky. Perhaps, as the birds which fly the highest, which fly the fastest, have stronger wings, these actual, material apparati were necessary to explore the infinite, these hundred-and-twenty-

13. "fabricateur," III, 161.
14. "Si l'art n'est que cela, il n'est pas plus réel que la vie, et je n'avais pas de regrets à avoir. Je continuais à jouer *Tristan*." III, 162.

horsepower motors, marked Mystery." The sentence continues, and here is the key: "where, however, no matter how high one floats, one is a little hindered from tasting the silence of space by the powerful roar of the motor."[15]

III.   Albertine's Ring and the Solar Myth

When Albertine has returned, Marcel notices that she is wearing a ring which he hasn't seen before. "A ring on which spread the wide and liquid expanse of a clear sheet of ruby." A red stone bought, she explains, with the savings made possible by cohabiting with Marcel. He will say a little later: "To tell the truth, I had come with Albertine to that moment (provided that things go on the same, that things go on happening normally) past which a woman is no longer of any use to us except as a transition to another woman."[16] But things do not go on the same. Albertine is the last in the sequence of loves which give way to the great love, which is art. Love dies a sort of ritual death, that is to say, the *loves* die, to re-emerge as the creative impetus to write. This ruby is a sign of the death of Albertine, of the end of Marcel's love for her, and, more close at hand, of the death of Bergotte (another "forger" of vulcanian art, a "flute player"—he only "plays" life, he doesn't transfigure it). Marcel can barely make out, in the stone, a man's head, "grimacing." A death's head, Bergotte's head, Marcel's own perhaps; his eyes are too weak to make out the image. This ring represents the economic investment, displacement of his own value, his own libido and self, onto Albertine. It is red, the color of suns which are about to set, and an emblem of the death of Albertine, of the end of Marcel's interest in her, of Bergotte's death, all of which will lead to Marcel's maturation as a writer. So that it's a sun which sets to rise.

15. "l'habileté technique de l'ouvrier ne servait qu'à leur faire plus librement quitter la terre, oiseaux pareils non au cygne de Lohengrin mais à cet aéroplane que j'avais vu à Balbec changer son énergie en élévation, planer au-dessus des flots, et se perdre dans le ciel. Peut-être, comme les oiseaux qui montent le plus haut, qui volent le plus vite, ont une aile plus puissante, fallait-il de ces appareils vraiment matériels pour explorer l'infini, de ces cent vingt chevaux marque Mystère"; "où pourtant, si haut qu'on plane, on est un peu empêché de goûter le silence des espaces par le puissant ronflement du moteur." III, 162.

16. "A vrai dire, j'en étais arrivé à ce moment où (si tout continue de même, si les choses se passent normalement) une femme ne sert plus pour nous que de transition avec une autre femme." III, 169.

The color calls to mind Bachelard's *Psychanalyse du Feu*. Fire purifies and liberates, but by destroying. Albertine, the flame, desire, will consume itself, be purged of the dross of jealousy.[17] The color recalls, within the cycle of novels, the poppies of Swann's way, Méséglise: jealousy, the anguish which finally produces art, and the debauchery that art has to "expiate" (it is after all the depraved *amie* of Mademoiselle Vinteuil who will "decipher" the great red septet of her father). Later there is the episode of the Duchesse's red slippers, in which the motifs of Swann's imminent death, Marcel's infatuation with the Duchesse and the world of the aristocracy, and the approaching demise of that infatuation, focus around the emblem of the slippers. There too, the death of a person coincides with the end of an era in Marcel's life.

It is important to note that Marcel has just reviewed these "red" motifs through the artist's cold eye, Swann's way from the perspective of the Guermantes. He has looked at desire without feeling jealousy, but doesn't yet see that there is more to desire and to art (potentially, at least) than tragedy. Here he simply rejects both love and art. An ending is realized but the new beginning isn't yet in view. The ring, however, is a sign of both, and so an enigma which Marcel cannot decipher. "'I cannot distinguish the cuttings around the ruby, one would almost say a man's head, grimacing. But my eyes aren't good enough.' '—Even if they were better it wouldn't do you any good [replies Albertine]. I can't make it out either.'"[18] The scene retains the demeanor of a mystery play, disguised beyond the ken of the players in it.

17. Hans Jonas suggestively juxtaposes the gnostic view of fire as a symbol and that of Heraclitus and the Stoics: "What to the Stoics is thus the bearer of cosmic Reason, to the Valentinians is with the same omnipresence in all creation the omnipresence of Ignorance. Where Heraclitus speaks of 'the everliving fire,' they speak of fire as 'death and corruption' in all elements. Yet even they would agree that as far as *cosmic* 'life' so-called and *demiurgical* 'reason' so-called are concerned these are properly symbolized in fire, as indeed in many gnostic systems the Demiurge is expressly called the god of the fire; but since that kind of 'life' and of 'reason' are in their true nature death and ignorance, the agreement in effect amounts to a subtle caricature of the Heraclitan-Stoic doctrine." *The Gnostic Religion*, 198. So we might say that Proust's novel is a "subtle caricature," an ironic subversion, of the traditionally mimetic, "happy" love story, and Albertine a grotesque parody of the heroines of such tales. See also note 10 of Chapter 1 herein, in which Proust's own version of the fire symbol, the *calorifère*, is discussed.

18. "je ne peux pas distinguer les ciselures autour du rubis, on dirait une tête d'homme grimaçante. Mais je n'ai pas une assez bonne vue—Vous l'auriez meilleure que cela ne vous avancerait pas beaucoup. Je ne distingue pas non plus." III, 165.

This is the eve of Marcel's discovery of his own "imprisonment" in art, writing. As if he felt that Albertine (and the desire and jealousy which she represents) were leading him towards asceticism and art, he seems to perceive, dimly, some drama of death and rebirth occurring around him. "As one does on the eve of a premature death, I added up the accounts of pleasures of which I was deprived by Albertine's putting an end to my liberty."[19] Albertine's presence keeps Marcel from being swallowed up in "the Wagnerian tempest." His work will not be limited to the merely tragic vision of Tristan. "If Albertine had not gone out with me, I could have heard at that moment, in the circus at the Champs-Elysées, the Wagnerian tempest make the strings in the orchestra groan, drawing to itself, like a light foam, the air of the reed-pipe I had just played, making it fly, forming it, deforming it, dividing it, dragging it along in a growing whirlwind."[20] Albertine, or rather Marcel's affection for her, has forced Marcel beyond her, and he sees that she could not have given herself any more than she has: "We have in effect possessed her, exhausted everything she consented to deliver of herself."[21] Now she is only a point of transition to "new lips."[22] But the new lips will not be human, they will belong to a goddess. "The presence of Albertine kept me from going to them, and perhaps in this way from ceasing to desire them. The man who wishes to keep alive within himself the desire to live and the belief in something more delicious than the ordinary, must walk, for the streets, the avenues, are full of Goddesses."[23] But they are all Melusines, "as fugitive, alas! as the years": "the Goddesses do not let themselves be approached."[24] Marcel has his own mythology. In this he is genuinely gnos-

19. "Comme on fait à la veille d'une mort prématurée, je dressais le compte des plaisirs dont me privait le point final qu'Albertine mettait à ma liberté." III, 168.

20. "si Albertine n'était pas sortie avec moi, je pourrais en ce moment, au cirque des Champs-Elysées, entendre la tempête wagnerienne faire gémir tous les cordages de l'orchestre, attirer à elle, comme une écume légère, l'air de chalumeau que j'avais joué tout à l'heure, le faire voler, le pétrir, le déformer, le diviser, l'entraîner dans un tourbillon grandissant." III, 168–69.

21. "Elle, en effet, nous avons possédé, épuisé tout ce qu'elle a consenti à nous livrer d'elle-même." III, 169.

22. "lèvres neuves," III, 169.

23. "La présence d'Albertine me privait d'aller à elles, et peut-être ainsi de cesser de les désirer. Celui qui veut entretenir en soi le désir de continuer à vivre et la croyance en quelque chose de plus délicieux que les choses habituelles, doit se promener, car les rues, les avenues, sont pleines de Déesses." III, 169.

24. "les Déesses ne se laissent pas approcher." III, 169.

tic, not expecting to find what he is looking for in the flesh, or in the love of the flesh, in the periwinkle blue eyes of any woman, even of a duchess. Marcel is certain now that eyes are as inassimilable as the present. "Aren't the eyes we see all penetrated by a look whose images, the memories, the waits, the disdains, we don't know and from which they cannot be separated?"[25]

But Marcel doesn't know where to look for whatever it is that is drawing him, if not in the eyes of women, in the streets, in the city, in the present. He does have a vague presentiment of another possibility. He makes a tropological connection between eyes and precious stones, saying that they are very different in their impact on the observer. "We don't look at the eyes of a girl whom we don't know as we would at a little slab of opal or agate. We know that the little ray which makes them iridescent or the grains of luster which make them sparkle are all we can see of a thought, a will, a memory in which resides the familial house we don't know, the dear friends whom we envy."[26] The stone, a hard, raw material which needs shaping and polishing, is a hackneyed metaphor for the unfinished artwork, or even for a youth at the outset of his education, before he knows what he wants to do with his life. This passage harks back to Albertine's ring. Jung has associated precious stone in his own dreams with the *lapis* of alchemy, the stone which is at once dead and alive.[27] The *lapis*, then, the concept of it, merely literalizes the contradiction which art seeks to effect by appearing to be "alive," the aporia which the text embodies.

In Swedenborg's philosophy, the seat of love and divine wisdom is the sun, the great fire which symbolizes the ultimate correspondence uniting spirit (wisdom) and senses (love). The two should, according to Swedenborg, nourish each other: "Wisdom or understanding, from the strength that love gives it, can rise up and receive such things as are of

25. "Les yeux qu'on voit ne sont-ils pas tout pénétrés par un regard dont on ne sait pas les images, les souvenirs, les attentes, les dédains qu'il porte et dont on ne peut pas les séparer?" III, 169.
26. "nous ne regardons pas les yeux d'une fille que nous ne connaissons pas comme nous ferions d'une petite plaque d'opale ou d'agate. Nous savons que le petit rayon qui les irise ou les grains de brillant qui les font étinceler sont tout ce que nous pouvons voir d'une pensée, d'une volonté, d'une mémoire où réside la maison familiale que nous ne connaissons pas, les amis chers que nous envions." III, 171.
27. Jung, *Memories, Dreams, Reflections*, 210–11.

the light of paradise, and perceive them."[28] This source of light and heat is the way to unmediated being, then, pure perception.

Finally, this passage and, I would even hazard to say, all the past to be sought and rediscovered later, in *Le Temps Retrouvé*, collapses in Marcel's strange vision of a *dying* sun. He describes it (the setting sun and the landscape which is its backdrop) as a great bed of flowers, a poppy (the redness of jealousy) disintegrating against a background of more flowers, reflected in a blue water (the limpid complexion of art, which, in Proust's world, reflects and refracts the violence of love): "Albertine admired, and by her presence kept me from admiring, the reflections of the red sails on the wintry blue water, a tile house huddled in the distance like a single poppy in the clear horizon of which Saint-Cloud, on the horizon, seemed the fragmentary petrifaction, crumbly and ribbed."[29] Then, abruptly, the intensity of day is no more. Marcel is in a nocturnal calm, and the red sun has been replaced by the moon which sheds a cold, white light—a perfectly sculpted sphere—another stone, perhaps, which is not a source of light itself but draws light from other sources and disperses it. "The daylight [was], still bright enough so that I thought I had time to do everything I wanted before dinner, when, only a few instants later, at the moment when our car was approaching the Arc de Triomphe, it was with a brusque movement of surprise and fright that I noticed, above Paris, the full and premature moon, like the face of a stopped clock which makes us think we are late."[30] There: time has stopped—or appeared to. Marcel is late in commencing his real work. But now he is within the solitary and tranquil zone in which his kind of art is made. He will never be anywhere else, from this moment. He is more than ever the prisoner. His is a prison of dream—of absence. It will be his work to furnish it commodiously, with the stuff of his memory and imagination.

28. Swedenborg, *Angelic Wisdom Concerning the Divine Love and the Divine Wisdom*, 199. See note 17 above.

29. "Albertine admira, et par sa présence m'empêcha d'admirer, les reflets de voiles rouges sur l'eau hivernale et bleue, une maison de tuiles blottie au loin comme un seul coquelicot dans l'horizon clair dont Saint-Cloud semblait, plus loin, la pétrification fragmentaire, friable et côtelée." III, 174.

30. "le plein jour, si clair encore que je croyais avoir le temps de faire tout ce que je voudrais avant le dîner, quand, quelques instants seulement après, au moment où notre voiture approchait de l'Arc de Triomphe, ce fut avec un brusque mouvement de surprise et d'effroi que j'aperçus, au-dessus de Paris, la lune pleine et prématurée, comme le cadran d'une horloge arrêtée qui nous fait croire qu'on s'est mis en retard." III, 175.

CONCLUSION

I.   A Jungian View

Jung says that every individual comprises a sexual duality. This has nothing to do with so-called bisexuality, or with an individual's sexual preferences or practices, latent or overt. This theory addresses a purely intrapsychic phenomenon, which may or may not carry over into interpersonal relations. The end of Marcel's search is completion, not only of the work but of that which projects the work, the self. This completion entails integrating the masculine and feminine principles, Swann and Odette, Saint-Loup and the Duchesse, Swann and Guermantes, Marcel and Albertine, in one entity. Once this reconciliation, integration, has been achieved, if it ever is, Marcel may have found a cure for the "material impossibility against which love throws itself," the biologically inexorable fact that three bodies result from the effort of two to become one. This is "the law of life" and "the cause of much unhappiness": "the coupling of opposite elements"—masculine and feminine.[31]

Jung explained infatuation as the lover's effort to complete himself by projecting onto a love object the features and images associated with his own inadequacies and lacks, the features which make up his anima (the female negation of his predominantly masculine psyche) and seeking to possess it, to make it part of himself. He is in love with something missing, or only negatively present, within himself, and the image which he "loves" is always cracked and jarred by the autonomous flesh and mind onto which it is projected, like the colored murals thrown on the walls of Marcel's room by a "magic lantern" in an earlier and celebrated passage of the *Recherche*.

Self-composition, however, is an oneiric process. Art, insofar as it partakes of dream, may be part of this process. To complete himself, an individual needs to attain a psychic androgyny. To begin his work, Marcel the writer needs to come to terms with the feminine aspect of his self. He needs to liberate his anima from the dominion of time, the present, carnality, the devouring force which is the memory of childhood, pre-

31. "la loi de la vie"; "la cause de bien des malheurs"; "l'accouplement des éléments contraires." III, 108.

sided over by the mother. All of these things, however, are for Marcel the promise and the hope of love, the reasons for his persisting faith in the present, in chance, in jealous desire, in love first for his mother and then for a sequence of other women. These infatuations, "failures of will," date from the "abdication of will" by Marcel's mother in the *drame de mon coucher* of *Du Côté de chez Swann*.

Marcel's story is that of the hero who must kill the monster (the mother, time, memory, the past) to liberate a new femininity: Theseus who, by killing the minotaur, frees Ariadne. Proust no less than Marcel is in the business of exorcising this past, his childhood and the oppressive affections of his mother, which would eclipse the feminine aspect of his own nature, and so prevent satisfactory love relations.[32] Recently Professor Theodore Johnson has advanced the thesis that Proust suffered from severe neuroses.[33] I wonder if Proust himself would not have concurred in part with Johnson, though he might have been amused and bewildered to find himself blamed for his mental "devils," for their mark on his work. To a great extent they *are* his work. Rilke, for instance, vowed never to undergo psychoanalysis because, while it might have taken away his devils, it might also have deprived him of his angels.[34] It is very easy to argue that no well-adjusted, "normal" person would set pen to paper or brush to canvas. Any work of art is the product of a special need. For Marcel, it proves necessary to destroy time, and desire, to arrive at the possibility of desire. It seems a foolish gesture to sacrifice the obvious parallels between Marcel's fictional life and Proust's actual life to a zeal for ideological purity—specifically, the useful but abused principle that the man is not the work. Marcel's Ariadne is Mademoiselle de Saint-Loup, the daughter of Robert de Saint-Loup and Gilberte Swann. Proust, apparently, found no man or woman capable of liberating him from the maternal hold of the past. Instead of accepting this absence, he set about to make up such a person, and the "person" is the corpus of his work.

32. Jung (ed.), *Man and His Symbols*, 111–18.

33. J. Theodore Johnson, "Against 'Saint' Proust," in *The Art of the Proustian Novel Reconsidered*, ed. L. D. Joiner (Rock Hill, S.C., 1979), 105–43.

34. Jean Strouse, "Perchance to Dream," *Newsweek*, September 3, 1979, p. 63—a review of *The Dream and the Underworld*, by James Hillman, and *The Innocence of Dreams*, by Charles Rycroft.

II.   *The Freudian View*

Jealousy is the motive force of Marcel's search. Jealousy is the awareness of lack, of the highly unstable status of every subject with respect to every other subject. All of us exist in the present, which is to say, in Heidegger's terms, that we exist only in a negative sense; the present defines itself in terms of memory and desire, expectation; it is the middle, the point at which past becomes future. If we could impose closure on all the subjects which by their interaction and involvement with us threaten to define us and by doing so deprive us of stable "meaning," we could become as words in some hypothetically unmediated language, return to the inorganic stasis which Freud believed the death instinct will sooner or later lead us all to. Thanatos, after all, is only a more radical Eros—the latter seeks temporary reductions of tension within the organism, while the former seeks to obliterate all tension once and for all. Jealousy, in Proust's novel, is the emotional counterpart of the desire for closure, which is a desire for meaning, and which may resemble Eros in the short run but which eventually comes to resemble Thanatos. Without some semblance of finitude, there can be no "sense," no shape to a text—or a life, for that matter. Beginning and ending, however arbitrary, however ephemeral, however illusory, are the two pillars on which the concept of sense, meaning, rests. On the level of literary analysis, and in a much larger sense as well, Thanatos might be described as the desire to make sense.

To speak of the death of God is to risk wallowing in truisms. But it is certainly true that the idea of God has been a source of "closure" and so of meaning, of order, to a great many people—and still is to many. The *logos* of religion has been a guarantor of stability at every level of human thought and interaction. If it abandons this foundation, literature must find a replacement, discover some way of carrying on without any *logos*, or simply cease to be, become silent. Belief in a God, and all the corollary beliefs that go with it, guarantee the stability of linear relations, that the Cartesian space is not absolute, that subjects, objects, and subjects can signify and can reach one another via language. It has guaranteed those relations partly by the notion of a divine substance subtending all things, and partly through the idea of an Apocalypse, a universal ending which will impose closure on everything, which by promising closure enforces these linear relationships.[35] The collapse of the belief cancels the second term in all these "semiotic equivalencies" which human thought and action have for so long assumed. There are no longer any positive values, only variables. If there is to be no Apocalypse, then literature must learn to invent endings on a smaller scale, and endings of a different nature altogether—endings which are not "linear," which do not look to a grander and ultimate end—or give up on endings altogether, and on form, and on meaning, and espouse chaos and nonsense as the basis of art.

If literature pursues the first of these options, it must learn to rehearse death and to discover a new transcendence in its own self-destruction as mimesis, in the alienation of the self from the world, and the analogue, a disintegration of the relation of language to physical and human reality, the world.

Without God, "suicide," the literary analogue of it, might appear to contemporary art as a tempting and simple option, but so far it has proved too much fascinated with itself to take the pills or open the veins. What it has frequently done instead is to reenact the failure to believe, to signify, or to give up on form altogether. Its unreachable ideal might be to isolate one or more subjects—a "Marcel" and his "Albertine"—and destroy them, punctuate their sentence with a very final period, out of desire for containment. "Love," Marcel tells us, "in painful anxiety, as in nervous desire, is the exigency of a whole."[36] Indeed. It is very closely akin to the sense of form which demands that books, events, films, places, and lives, have a beginning, a middle, and an end.

I have already said that Albertine is the latest in a series of female hypostatizations of the present. We have witnessed a Freudian conflict between the origins of desire and the aims of desire when Marcel received a letter from his mother expressing doubts about his relations with Albertine. As Harold Bloom likes to say, substitutions, sublimations, never satisfy the psyche of a strong poet. The poet's anxiety derives from a compulsion both to return to the original object of desire and to make that beginning over again in his own image, to recast his "belat-

---

35. See Frank Kermode, *The Sense of an Ending* (New York, 1968).
36. "L'amour, dans l'anxiété douloureuse comme dans le désir nerveux, est l'exigence d'un tout." III, 106.

edness" into a precedence. Now, without following through with an application of Bloom's theory of influence, the relevance to my reading of Proust, and to Marcel's relations with his mother, should be apparent. His mother is unhappy with his liaison with Albertine. Marcel knows this, and is ambiguous himself in his feelings for Albertine. The act of writing transforms original desire; it creates a new "feminine ego ideal" which is both exterior, exteriorized in the text, and internal, derived entirely from Marcel's self. It is in the imaginary being of Mademoiselle de Saint-Loup, at the end of the cycle, that what Freud somewhat archly calls an "ego-syntonic erotic cathexis" becomes possible for Marcel, and the conditions for "happy love" are fulfilled: "the primal condition in which object-libido and ego-libido cannot be distinguished." Happy love, however, is not for Marcel what it is for most people. Instead of falling in love with Mademoiselle de Saint-Loup, Marcel falls in love with pen and paper. Though the cure may be unusual—if it were not, Marcel would not be a writer—writing for Proust and finally for Marcel as well, seems to be the final stage of a self-analysis, a search for a "cure" as well as for the past—a homeopathic "uncure" which treats the disease by radicalizing it. "Where narcissistic gratification encounters actual hindrances, the sexual ideal may be used as a substitutive gratification. In such a case a person loves (in conformity with the narcissistic type of object-choice) someone whom he once was and no longer is, or else someone who possesses excellences which he never had at all. The parallel formula to that given above runs thus: whoever possesses an excellence which the ego lacks for the attainment of its ideal, becomes loved."[37] Marcel's mother, by acceding to him in the scene which Proust characterized as "an abdication of will" (*le drame de mon coucher*), placed an insurmountable obstacle in the way of narcissistic gratification. (The economy of Marcel's libido is permanently broken by the *dependence* for which this event is a narrative figure. The "event" and the dependence are not causally related, however, as a purely Freudian reading might see them, for the dependence conditions the event as much as the event conditions the dependence.) At the same time his mother gave him the false hope that he might find in women what he lacked. So she condemned him to a search,

37. Sigmund Freud, "On Narcissism," *A General Selection from the Works of Sigmund Freud*, ed. John Rickman (New York, 1957), 122.

a series of repetitions, substitutions, a search for an "ego-syntonic libido cathexis" which must be futile until Marcel's ego-libido equals his object-libido. One might well question, with Proust, whether this can ever be the case. So long as his object-choices are patterned after the first one—his mother—there can be no possibility of fulfilling the requirements of "happy love." Marcel must somehow transcend the origins of his desire as he returns to them. It is not enough to match, to repeat the primal paradigm of love, for it was itself unsatisfactory; he must "rewrite" that scenario, make it over, as Bloom might say, *precede* it.

Each woman in this novel might be read as a synecdoche. The whole to their part would be the perfect subject, the ego-ideal, that love object with whom an ego-syntonic love attachment would be possible. In Marcel's case, this individual is like Mallarmé's perfect flower, that one which is "absent from every bouquet." The same kind of ideal for contemporary, godless art might be the closure which is death, total destruction. Marcel's death, of course, is permanently postponed by the circular structure of Proust's narration.

Why not one of the simpler options—theocentric mimesis, silence, or an aesthetic of non-sense—instead of this endless circular self-generation, with only the implication of closure somewhere beyond the bounds of the text? Freudian psychoanalysis may furnish a partial—and speculative—solution. If we assume that Proust faced psychic circumstances in which no satisfactory relation to an object, to "real" objects in a "real" world was possible, we can infer other things about his psyche as well. This could occur when tension between the id (desire) and the superego (the imperatives of culture which tend to become more extreme and constrictive as the culture advances) becomes so great that the ego is forced to *try* to withdraw all libidinal energy into itself. For the ego to invest such libido in itself, however, would be very difficult so long as there are impediments to "narcissistic gratification," as there appear to have been in Marcel. So that the ego is impeded in both directions, and must seek a working through of those memories and psychic residues which stand in the way of gratification. Let's not forget that the superego is of like substance with the id because it is patterned after the id's first object-choices. The like substance is desire itself. But those first object-choices, in the Freudian paradigm, though perhaps not inevitably, turn out to be interdictions on desire. The superego, as ideal or original object, constrains desire, and in extreme cases might even strangle it. To close the inner distance from id to superego in such an extreme case would be to embrace Thanatos, death, to force desire into the arms of the antierotic superego. That union becomes idealized, and desired, but also feared and dreaded. To avoid all this ambivalence, the writing ego attempts to suppress the second term of all equivalencies such as signifier/signified, form/content, self/other, ego/superego. Life, and the text, become a mourning for the lost object/world, which, as it "works through" the memories which impede narcissistic gratification, "undoes" them or, in Freudian terminology, "binds" them, becomes a means of narcissistic gratification, the generation of an illusory love object, like Mademoiselle de Saint-Loup, which instead of absorbing libido, reflects it. Marcel does not fall in love with Mademoiselle de Saint-Loup, because she is himself; she is the negative image of all his memories and experiences.

To close the work of mourning, embrace real objects, fuse object-libido and ego-libido as Freud says should be normal in cases of personal loss,[38] is equated with death, self-destruction—to be feared and desired. The ego works through the obstacles to narcissistic gratification but still cannot embrace the superego, the prototype for all object-choices. The result in Proust's case would seem to be a perpetual mourning of the other/object, the superego, which enforces the self's distance from its objects and from its inner object, the superego, while it brings them nearer "asymptotically." Mourning becomes a way of appeasing erotic desire, extending the self, postponing ultimate gratification, death, at the same time that it is a preparation, not to return to mimesis, the literary analogue of object-relations, but to abandon the latter completely, for death. Closure, death, is a morphological necessity for the text, and yet we cannot locate an end point on a circle. Death has become a transcendence of the text itself; the second terms of all the equivalencies associated with the mimetic one have been displaced outside of the text, and cannot be found. We could postulate the very same psychic pathology for those alchemists who were fond of characterizing Mercurius, the embodiment

---

38. See Freud, "Mourning and Melancholia," *General Psychological Theory*. This chapter also owes much to Walter Benjamin's "The Storyteller," in *Illuminations* (New York, 1969), 83–110.

of the opus, "the sun-moon hermaphroditic *rebis*," as a serpent devouring itself.[39]

Finally, to return to a point I made earlier, how does this circularity of texts relate to the modern "loss of faith"? Freud would have us believe that the Judeo-Christian God is a collective father image, in some sense a collective superego. If this is the case, then for Proust embracing God is the same as embracing death. Insofar as religious feeling involves the belief in a common substance subtending all things, it must be symptomatic of an id and a superego which can find common ground in this world, in real objects. If tension between desire and superego is as extreme as it appears to have been in Proust, we cannot sustain belief in a traditional, Judeo-Christian God any more than we can write in the traditional, "mimetic" mode. Religious feeling, if expressed at all, emerges as the sense of something missing, something lost. That sense of lack becomes a way of knowing that which cannot be known—the gnosis.

Thus the point of Proust's narrative, as of Marcel's involvement with Albertine and all of the women in the novel—what emerges from the mutual figuration of desire and writing (or the desire *to* write) which Proust valorizes—is precisely the "flimsiness" and "mendaciousness" of desire and writing, their utter inability to requite themselves, their perpetually reenacted failure to transcend their *dependent* beginnings, to "reestablish" a psychic and literary economy which always exceeds and precedes them. They cannot transcend time and "live," express, the transcendence temporally (within "l'ordre du récit"), embrace death (the mother) and not die, go on living, pursuing Albertine, Gilberte Swann, Odette de Crécy, Oriane de Guermantes, and finally Mademoiselle de Saint-Loup, herself a human allegory of writing and memory, the multiplicitous duplicities of desire. Art cannot imitate, "signify," and be whole, its own object. Such an unmediated mimesis would be the literary analogue of "happy love relations" and suggests powerfully the "mendaciousness" of such "happiness." Marcel's story suggests the circular paradox implicit in both Jung's and Freud's models of the self. The desiring self cannot totalize itself or its object precisely because of the sexual and temporal multiplicity which Jung allegorizes as self and anima and which

39. Jung, *Psychology and Alchemy*, 251–53.

he says it must realize before it can totalize (or be totalized, totalize it-self). The ultimate object of Freudian desire (Eros) turns out to be its antithesis (Thanatos), undesire, interdiction, stasis, the return to some hypothetical state of being prior to desire, to "life," in which the self's (and the signifier's) economy would function infallibly. This novel knows that *it* is just such a paradox, as Marcel finally knows that he, in his pursuit and loss of Albertine, is too. Both the narrator and the narration of which he is an emblem know their impotence and rage against it in their mutual figuration by describing, reflecting, radicalizing it. The novel renders its "gift" by rending the given, doing violence to itself, violence to desire, violence to violence. Marcel finds no escape, no rescue from the world's flimsiness unless we define exacerbation as escape, loss as recuperation. The moon which Marcel does not see rising because it has been his "sun" all along, a reflective, scattering absence of light, and not Swedenborg's totalizing sun, not Freud's or Jung's hypothetically "well-adjusted" self, is what illumines all these pages. But the moon's cold, dead glow suggests a source, a sun invisible but present by its absence, projecting light. The light precedes and exceeds attempts to locate, "im-mobilize," it; it is the virtual and hypothetical focal point of memory's "prolonged conjuncture" with the noise of Marcel's furnace, of our pro-jected and introjected conjuncture with the silent combustion of loss, the "disagreeable noise" of Proust's novel-furnace. We cannot plot that point in space or time. Art only "cures" by making us sicker, not letting us pretend that we are not sick. Indeed, Proust's novel may differ from oth-ers ("happy," "well-adjusted" ones) only in its gnostic consciousness of its own failure, in that it knows—and says—that it cannot say what it wants to, can only say it by saying that it cannot say it. It seems most apt that Proust should have glossed his own novel before he wrote it when, in his introduction to Ruskin's *Le Sésame et le lys*, he wrote that "a truth which is obtained by letters of recommendation," "which lets itself be copied in notebooks," is not the truth which interests him. Even if, "pour l'ordre du récit," we must inevitably fall into the trap of such a "truth," we ought finally to remind ourselves that a book is properly no more than "the angel who flies away as soon as he has opened the gates of the celestial garden," that it is as true of Proust himself as of writers in general that "by a singular and moreover *providential* law of the *optic* of minds (law which means perhaps that we cannot receive truth from anyone, and that we have to create it ourselves), that which is the closure of their wisdom appears to us only as the beginning of ours, so that it is at the moment when they have told us everything they could tell us that they arouse in us the feeling that they haven't told us anything yet."[40] What

40. "une vérité qui s'obtient par lettres de recommandation"; "une vérité qui se laisse copier sur un carnet"; "l'ange qui s'envole aussitôt qu'il a ouvert les portes du jardin céleste"; "Mais par une loi singulière et d'ailleurs providentielle de l'optique des esprits (loi qui signifie peut-être que nous devons la créer nous-mêmes), ce qui est le terme de leur sagesse nous apparaît comme le commencement de la nôtre, de sorte que c'est au moment où ils nous ont dit tout ce qu'ils pouvaient nous dire qu'ils font naître en nous le sentiment qu'ils ne nous ont encore rien dit" [emphasis mine]. "Journées de lecture," *Pastiches et Mélanges* (Paris, 1919), 236, 237, 229. Most of this article was included in Proust's introduction to his translation of *Le Sésame et le lys* (Paris, 1906; reprint 1933).

This passage, and indeed much of the article, can be read as a preemptive revision of Harold Bloom's theory of influence (see *The Anxiety of Influence* [New York, 1973] and *A Map of Misreading* [New York, 1975]). Proust implies that books, "precursors," like love objects, do not inspire anxiety and repression so much as a sense of loss, gratuitous desire. The jealousy they arouse is reflexive nostalgia. The reading/desiring self knows no phenomenal, totalized other (including itself). The text is a *pre*text just as are all objects of desire and memory; they self-combust like Marcel's furnace. We attach value to them according to the most arbitrary associations, such as those which make the furnace's noise remind Marcel of Doncières. The reading and writing self confronts other texts (selves) not so much as influences, or rather not as willful, positively directed influences, but as labyrinthine and reflective optics. "Et c'est là, en effet, un des grands et merveilleux caractères des beaux livres (et qui nous fera comprendre le rôle à la fois essentiel et limité que la lecture peut jouer dans notre vie spirituelle) que pour l'auteur ils pourraient s'appeler 'Conclusions' et pour le lecteur 'Incitations.'" Like "reality," he implies that books are only "une amorce à un inconnu sur la voie duquel nous ne pouvons aller bien loin"; III, 24. Which books we read, which Albertine we happen to fall in love with, does not matter, for they are simply goads, spurs. "Nous sentons très bien que notre sagesse commence où celle de l'auteur finit, et nous voudrions qu'il nous donnât des réponses, quand *tout ce qu'il peut faire est de nous donner des désirs.* . . . D'ailleurs, si nous leur posons des questions auxquelles ils ne peuvent répondre, nous leur demandons aussi des réponses qui ne nous instruiraient pas. Car *c'est un effet de l'amour que les poètes éveillent en nous de nous faire attacher une importance littérale à des choses qui ne sont pour eux que significatives d'émotions personelles*" [emphasis mine]; *Pastiches et Mélanges*, 229. The "truth" of reading, in reading, is not in the book or the reader but in the desire, striving, displacement which occurs between them. The truth is not "une chose matérielle, déposée entre les feuillets des livres comme un miel tout préparé par les autres et que nous n'avons qu'à prendre la peine d'atteindre sur les rayons des bibliothèques et de déguster ensuite passivement dans un parfait repos de corps et d'esprit"; *ibid.*, 234. It is just such *rest* which books, reading, and desire itself, deny us by doubling us, turning desire on itself. Proust repudiates in advance his own legions of scholarly "idolaters," those "malsains de goût" who believe in "une vérité sourde aux appels de la réflexion et docile au jeu des influences . . . une vérité qui se laisse copier sur un carnet . . ."—those guilty of "respect fétichiste pour les livres"; *ibid.*, 236–37. Though, he admits, this is not

his novel adds is that this identity of beginning and ending, questioner and answerer, lover and beloved, reader and writer, applies not just to "them" and "us," but to us and our selves in our inevitably solitary strife and search for the "celestial garden" whose gates disappear even as the ephemeral "angel" opens them.

---

the most dangerous misconception of truth that there can be, and it is a trap into which the most astute and "unfetishistic" of readers and writers must perhaps inevitably fall "in this vile world of appearances," forgetting, "pour l'ordre du récit," that the book is "l'ange qui s'envole" and not "une idole immobile"; *ibid.*, 237.

PART II

CHAPTER 6

Proust, Flannery O'Connor, and the Aesthetic of Violence

> Until the sun slipped finally below the tree line, Mrs. Turpin remained there with her gaze bent to them as if she were absorbing some abysmal life-giving knowledge. At last she lifted her head. There was only a purple streak in the sky. . . . A visionary light settled in her eyes. She saw the streak as a vast swinging bridge extending upward from the earth through a field of living fire. Upon it a vast horde of souls were rumbling toward heaven. There were whole companies of white-trash, clean for the first time in their lives, and bands of black niggers in white robes, and battalions of freaks and lunatics shouting and clapping and leaping like frogs. . . . She could see by their shocked and altered faces that even their virtues were being burned away. . . . At length she got down and turned off the faucet and made her slow way on the darkening path to the house. In the woods around her the invisible cricket choruses had struck up, but what she heard were the voices of the souls climbing upward into the starry field and shouting hallelujah.
>
> —Flannery O'Connor, "Revelation"

I. O'Connor, Proust, Grace, and the Devil

If Proust is not, as I maintained at the outset of this study, a practitioner of the "mimetic" principle or principles—*i.e.*, does not concern himself much with simulating "objective" realities or observe unities of time, place, or even character—Flannery O'Connor could be taken as an exemplary case of the writer who observes those principles scrupulously. Her fictions are so palpably anchored in a particular time and place as to color her readers' perceptions of the place itself. If her stories and novels appear fantastic to some, it is probably because they are unfamiliar with the rural South of which she wrote.

Despite this technical difference between Proust and O'Connor, not to mention breaches of culture and language, I have always had the feeling that there existed a profound kinship between them. Close examination reveals this as more than their common attraction for me. O'Connor shares Proust's belief in a spirit occulted in the flesh, though it might be argued that she states her case for it less arcanely. Though she insisted that her vision of humanity was not "Manichean" (her catchword for all things gnostic, which as a devout Catholic she regarded as heretical), she is interested above all in the distances which humans are at pains to place between themselves and the spiritual in themselves, the sacred in and around them, and in the terrible violence with which the Holy finally and inevitably erupts into their willfully profane lives. "The theologian," she wrote, "is interested specifically in the modern novel because there he sees reflected the man of our time, the unbeliever, who is nevertheless grappling in a desperate and usually honest way with intense problems of spirit."[1] It is just this sort of ontological violence which overtakes Marcel. What Proust represents psychically, O'Connor represents physically, but Marcel's anxiety before Albertine and his lengthy analyses of it are closely related to the Misfit's homely theosophic peroration in "A Good Man Is Hard to Find," which culminates in murder, or the grandmother's discovery of Christian virtue in herself in the same story.

Of course, Proust does not share any of O'Connor's Catholic orthodoxy—or pretensions to it. Yet it is precisely in making those pretensions that she is closest to Proust, in the practice of her art and in spirit.

> I am always having it pointed out to me that life in Georgia is not at all the way I picture it, that escaped criminals do not roam the roads exterminating families, nor Bible salesmen prowl about looking for girls with wooden legs. . . . If the writer believes that our life is and will remain essentially mysterious, if he looks upon us as beings existing in a created order to whose laws we freely respond, then what he sees on the surface will be of interest to him only as he can go through it into an experience of mystery itself. His kind of fiction will always be pushing its own limits outward toward the limits of mystery, because for this kind of writer, the meaning of a story does not begin except at a depth where adequate motivation and adequate psychology and the various determinations have been exhausted. Such a writer will be interested in what we don't understand rather than in what we do. . . . The kind of writer I am describing will use the concrete in a more drastic way. His way will much more obviously be the way of distortion.[2]

It is the writer's work to exhaust the concrete, to so wear out and stretch the mimetic principle that the reader is forced to confront the inexplic-

---

1. Flannery O'Connor, *Mystery and Manners*, ed. Sally and Robert Fitzgerald (New York, 1961), 158.
2. *Ibid.*, 38, 41–42.

able which lies beyond, within, wherever one chooses to locate the place of *otherness*, of gnostic realities.

This artistic principle of distortion, aesthetic violence, has something in common with Maurice Blanchot's idea of communication. It entails a sense of disintegration, dissolution, epistemological conflagration. For Blanchot, of course, *la communication* is not an aesthetic principle and has nothing to do with the content of a work of fiction but describes that strange and distinctly gnostic (negative, antithetical) space which the act of reading conjures, delineates as a negative, unknowable, indescribable, unentity—it is language betraying its antithesis.

> The communication of the work is not in the fact of its becoming communicable, by reading, to a reader. The work is itself communication, an intimacy in the struggle between the limits of the work as it is accessible and the excess of the work as it tends toward impossibility, between the form in which it is seized and the boundlessness in which it refuses itself, between the decision which is the being of beginning and the indecision which is the being of beginning again. This *violence* lasts as long as the work is a work, ever implacable, but also the calm of a harmony, strife which is the movement of understanding, understanding which perishes as soon as it ceases to be the approach to that which cannot be understood.[3]

But O'Connor is not content to consider this as a purely secular phenomenon, or as a simply literary one either.

She might find even more to agree with in Georges Bataille's idea of writing as transgression, an incendiary act against the logos of positivism and the means by which men may transcend words and themselves in the contemplation of an absence. Bataille is careful to differentiate this "Absence" from "nothingness." Violence is the only way of attaining the transcendental contact with it which Bataille calls "sovereignty." Where physical violence, murder, is proscribed, literary violence must take its

---

3. "La communication de l'oeuvre n'est pas dans le fait qu'elle est devenue communicable, par la lecture, à un lecteur. L'oeuvre est elle-même communication, intimité en lutte entre l'exigence de lire et l'exigence d'écrire, entre la mesure de l'oeuvre qui se fait pouvoir et la démesure de l'oeuvre qui tend à l'impossibilité, entre la forme où elle se saisit et l'illimité où elle se refuse, entre la décision qui est l'être du commencement et l'indécision qui est l'être du recommencement. Cette violence dure aussi longtemps que l'oeuvre est oeuvre, violence jamais pacifiée, mais qui est aussi le calme d'un accord, contestation qui est le mouvement de l'entente, entente qui périt dès qu'elle cesse d'être l'approche de ce qui est sans entente" [emphasis mine]. Maurice Blanchot, *L'Espace littéraire* (Paris, 1955), 265–66.

place. "Literature (fiction)," writes Bataille, "has replaced what used to be the life of the spirit, while poetry (the disorder of words) has replaced the state of actual trance." "My tension resembles, in a sense, a mad desire to laugh, it differs little from the passions with which the heroes of Sade burn, and yet it is very near the passions of martyrs or saints."[4]

I evoke Blanchot and Bataille not to argue that O'Connor or Proust ever read or would have read or approved of them. O'Connor would probably have been horrified to find herself quoted in the same paragraph with them, as she was at John Hawkes' statement that "her muse is the Devil." Still, though she was bound to deny the letter of his thesis, she was willing to admit that Hawkes' intuition in stating it was correct. Her kinship with Hawkes, with Bataille, with Blanchot, with Proust, and with the mythic Satan as well lies in the idea of transgression, literature as a hostile, aggressive gesture towards an overweening and distortedly positivistic status quo. Positivism is just as despotic and corrosive for O'Connor as for Bataille. Where Bataille would assimilate the church to that positivism, Miss O'Connor does just the opposite. She sees the modern church as forced to adopt a stance of violent dissidence; the truths of the spirit are mines, timebombs occulted in all the most apparently safe and unspiritual places and persons—many an O'Connor character turns out to be an unwitting guerrilla, sacrificing him or herself for a spirit and a spiritual truth repeatedly and assiduously denied.

Indeed, O'Connor was more than willing to concur with Hawkes that the devil, patron spirit of violence and destruction, occupied a major, perhaps the major role in her fiction. She was also careful to point out that evil cannot but serve good by forcing man to apprehend his own spirit, catalyzing that corrosive demesmerizement which she calls grace. Bataille would doubtless prefer to describe it as the contemplation of an absence. But there is nothing implicitly incompatible about the terminologies—provided one does not happen to be a dogmatic Catholic. John Hawkes has made a similar point:

4. "La littérature (la fiction) s'est substituée à ce qu'était précédémment la vie spirituelle, la poésie (le désordre des *mots*) aux états de transe réels." "Ma tension ressemble, en un sens, à une folle envie de rire, elle diffère peu des passions dont brûlent les héros de Sade, et pourtant, elle est proche de celle des martyrs ou des saints." Georges Bataille, *Sur Nietzsche, volonté de chance* (Paris, 1945), 31, 12.

Since I have mentioned that Flannery O'Connor does not agree with my no-tion of her central fictional allegiance, it is only right to say that our disagree-ment may not be so extensive after all, and that she has written that, "Those moments (involving awareness of the Holy) are prepared for—by me any-way—by the intensity of evil circumstances." She also writes, "I suppose the devil teaches most of the lessons that lead to self-knowledge." And further that "her" devil is the one who goes about "piercing pretensions, not the devil who goes about seeking whom he may devour." If Flannery O'Connor were asked where she would locate the center of her creative impulse, she might reply "in the indication of Grace." But then again she might not. And I suspect that she would not reply at all to such a question. It may be, too, that I have been giving undue stress to the darker side of her imaginative constructions, and that the devil I have been speaking of is only a metaphor, a way of refer-ring to a temperament strong enough and sympathetic enough to sustain the work of piercing pretension.[5]

"Piercing pretension," "Grace," "devil," are finally all weak and insuffi-cient figurative names for something much less prosaic and domesticable than a "temperament," literary or criminal, something too horrifically and unnervingly negative, unnameable, for even as hardy a soul as Hawkes to contemplate. For John Hawkes finally takes refuge in the very positiv-ism his fiction confounds, in reducing the devil to a metaphor—rather than considering that the Evil One might represent an effort to name, and so domesticate, through mythical narrative, that which defies nom-ination. If Flannery O'Connor would remain silent rather than "locate the center of her creative impulse," as I with Hawkes believe she would have, it is because, a stronger writer than Hawkes, she knew the ques-tion's answer could not be said.

II.   The Grotesqueness of Unbelief, or, The Sacred as a Negation of a Negation

O'Connor sees "the man of our time" as having created the dualistic world which he occupies in her stories. His darkness, ignorance, distance from the Holy are consequences of his own unbelief. His spiritual velle-ity and intellectual agnosticism put modern man in the very state of gro-tesque decrepitude in which gnostic theology would place him. The nat-

---

5. John Hawkes, "Flannery O'Connor's Devil," *Sewanee Review*, LXX (Summer, 1962), 406.

ural world is good because it emanates from God. This is a Catholic, not a gnostic sentiment. Evil, however, in O'Connor's universe, has made the natural world and the human beings in it grotesque; it has distorted and occluded their goodness. Evil can only come into being as a negation of the world, the Holy. It is derivative and can only deny, vitiate. It can only become intelligible as a destructive force and a necessary consequence of our moral freedom.[6] Evil is what blinds us to the Holy and it is the state of blindness. But we have blinded ourselves. For O'Connor, man has been his own demiurge, the author of his own fall, the keeper of his own cell. Which is not to say that evil has no physical reality. It is just as physically real as good. Believing a thing, choosing freely to believe it, does indeed make it so. Choices freely made, convictions freely held, are for O'Connor moral acts with ferociously physical, as well as spiritual, consequences.

Her fictions can be read as a catalog of the unbeliever in his many incarnations. In addition to the simple atheist, there is the one "who recognizes a divine being not himself, but who does not believe that this being can be known anagogically or defined dogmatically or received sacramentally. Spirit and matter are separated for him."[7] Again, she sees this type as a self-made gnostic. Finally, there is the sort which holds the greatest interest for her, the "modern man who can neither believe nor contain himself in unbelief and who searches desperately, feeling about in all experience for the lost God."[8] This is the archetype of the gnostic, a seeker after a knowledge that cannot be known.

The chief consequence of this partly willful, partly inherited alienation from the sacred is that the sacred can only intrude upon human perception as a violence, a rending of the fabric of daily life, a negation of the negation which is evil (albeit a passive, quiescent evil). It bruises both the spirit and the body which have based themselves in unbelief.

For Proust, it is time and space which have made monsters of men, made them grotesque. "At least, if enough force was left me to accomplish my work, I would not fail firstly to describe men (even were it necessary to make them resemble monstrous beings) as occupying such

6. O'Connor, *Mystery and Manners*, 157.
7. *Ibid.*, 159.
8. *Ibid.*

a considerable place, next to the very restricted one reserved for them in space, a place on the contrary prolonged beyond measure—since they touch, simultaneously, like giants immersed in the years, epochs so distant, between which so many many days have intervened—in Time."[9] O'Connor says much the same thing, that she has no choice but to describe men as freaks because they live in a world bereft of belief—"which doubts both fact and value," so that "instead of reflecting a balance from the world around him, the novelist now has to achieve one from felt balance inside *himself*."[10] The novelist cannot but see a distorted world, cannot but see men as monsters, the more so as he feels himself to be in monstrous discord with that world.

> The problem for such a novelist will be to know how far he can distort without destroying, and in order not to destroy, he will have to descend far enough into himself to reach those underground springs that give life to his work. This *descent into himself* will, at the same time, be a descent into his region. It will be *a descent through the darkness of the familiar into a world where, like the blind man cured in the gospels, he sees men as if they were trees, but walking*. This is the beginning of vision, and I feel it is a vision which we in the South must at least try to understand if we want to participate in the continuance of a vital Southern literature. I hate to think that in twenty years Southern writers too may be writing about men in gray-flannel suits and may have lost their ability to see that these gentlemen are even greater freaks than what we are writing about now. I hate to think of the day when the Southern writer will satisfy the tired reader.[11]

The work of the novelist is not meant, or ought not to be meant to soothe or satisfy, but to upset and perturb. The writer's vision is a violence wreaked on the world, the violence of perception, the brutality of the sacred bursting into the lives and senses of self-anesthetized men and giving them visions which reveal the world and the people in it as strange players in a hugely terrible mystery.

9. "Du moins, si elle m'était laissée assez longtemps pour accomplir mon oeuvre, ne manquerais-je pas d'abord d'y décrire les hommes (cela dût-il les faire ressembler à des êtres monstrueux) comme occupant une place si considérable, à côté de celle si restreinte qui leur est réservée dans l'espace, une place au contraire prolongée sans mesure—puisqu'ils touchent simultanément, comme des géants plongés dans les années, à des époques si distantes, entre lesquelles tant de jours sont venus se placer—dans le Temps." III, 1048.

10. O'Connor, *Mystery and Manners*, 49.

11. *Ibid.*, 50 [emphasis mine].

III.   The "Taint" of Vision: The Artist as Criminal and Leper

The impact of that apprehension of the ineffable ravages the writer more than his characters, for it isolates him, estranges him, deforms him in the eyes of the world. It infects him like love, which Proust called an agony to be cultivated to the point at which disease and sufferer are indistinguishable. The writer and the lover (for Proust) and the seer, the believer (for O'Connor) are untouchables, a "citizen of an unknown country," as Proust describes the composer Vinteuil, inhabiting "a closed realm, with impenetrable borders," as he said of the painter Elstir.[12] The business of all these visionaries is to wreak havoc on their own perceptions, and the perceptions of others. In both ways they rend the world, as the conduit through which the Holy enters and transforms it. This—their art—is a curative, redemptive gesture. It may not appear so, but this is because the advanced state of the malady makes it impossible to treat the patient without maiming him.

The para-Freudian interpretation of Proust's artistic stance which I tried to make in the last chapter would seem to hold true for O'Connor as well, notwithstanding her protestations of Christian orthodoxy. If her work does not structurally resemble Proust's in almost any way—it is rather linear than circular; it can by no stretch of the imagination be read as autobiographical, though it must inevitably be involved in a specular relation with the subject who made it as it is with the subject who reads it—her work reflects a fascination with sickness, with disabilities of mind, spirit, and matter. Both Proust and O'Connor were invalids for most of their adult lives. This is bound to have something to do with their sense of the sacred as physically destructive.

The "lines" traced by O'Connor's narratives end so often in death that she has been criticized for resorting too frequently and facilely to destruction of her characters as a way of ending her stories. This sort of criticism ignores the internal necessity of death, the intense desire for it

12. "citoyen d'une patrie inconnue"; "un royaume clos, aux frontières infranchissables." III, 257, II, 125. Marcel describes the greatness of Elstir's mature work as the distortion it works on conventional perceptions: "Et l'atelier d'Elstir m'apparut comme le laboratoire d'une sorte de nouvelle création du monde." I, 834. "je me retrouvai dans un monde inconnu . . . ce monde était un de ceux que je n'avais même pu concevoir que Vinteuil eût créés." III, 249. "j'avais pensé aux autres mondes qu'avait pu créer Vinteuil comme à des univers clos comme avait été chacun de mes amours." III, 252.

in so many of her characters. Death, or maiming, a step in the direction of death, is askesis, a movement towards the Holy. In her stories, her world, death is the force which invades and undoes the negation of unbelief. Death appears as a negative force only because we see it from an already negatively defined context, which is our own unbelief. The unbeliever—which describes most of her critics—reads O'Connor's stories much as the atheist Mr. Paradise watches the boy Bevel drown himself in "The River." Paradise's unbelief is emblemized in the cancer over his ear which he pointedly displays before the faithful to mock the alleged healing powers of their minister; his name casts a grim irony over his own positivistic attitudes, throwing the corruption of his physical body into relief. He tries to rescue Harry/Bevel from "the rich red river of Jesus' Blood," the river "that was made to carry sin," "a River full of pain itself, pain itself."[13] But the boy—who in baptism has taken the name of the preacher who baptized him—has discovered in his immersion a calling, "the calling": "to Baptize himself and to keep on going this time until he found the kingdom of Christ in the river." This discovery, from Mr. Paradise's vantage point, looks like death. But Bevel in fact leaves Mr. Paradise behind "like some ancient water-monster"; leaves him in place and spirit.[14]

The criminals of Miss O'Connor's world, monsters remarkable in their reality, doers of violence not to themselves directly but to the unbelieving world which offers no other issue to the striving of their spirits, destroy and torment for the pleasure of spite, which is no pleasure at all ("Shut up Bobby Lee, it's no real pleasure in life"). They destroy in desperation and rage at their own unbelief. Unwittingly, though, as ministers of violence they are instruments of good. So, ironically, does the Devil undo his own designs. The Misfit, or the Bible salesman of "Good Country People," brings about a spiritual askesis in the people whose lives he invades and upsets. The force of his intrusion ferrets individuals out of their elaborately articulated despair and philistinism, out of the pettiness in which they have sought refuge from the horrible burden of believing, communicating with the Holy. Bringing death, the Misfit brings the

13. Flannery O'Connor, "The River," *A Good Man Is Hard to Find*, reprinted in *Three by Flannery O'Connor* (New York, 1962), 151.
14. *Ibid.*, 159.

grandmother of "A Good Man Is Hard to Find" to a searing intuition of the sacred, out of the old-womanly selfishness which has defined her character throughout the story. "'Jesus!' the old lady cried. 'You've got good blood! I know you wouldn't shoot a lady! I know you come from nice people! Pray! Jesus, you ought not to shoot a lady. I'll give you all the money I've got.'"[15] She reaches such a clarity of vision that she is able to recognize what she and the Misfit have in common, and to pity his hopelessness: "the grandmother's head cleared for an instant. . . . She murmured, 'Why you're one of my own babies. You're one of my own children.'"[16] For the instant before she dies, the sacred takes hold of this old lady and for perhaps the first time in her life she is filled with charity. The Misfit has been the instrument of her salvation, and not entirely unwittingly. He says that "she would of been a good woman if it had of been somebody there to shoot her every minute of her life."[17] He knows that he is sending the old woman off to heaven. This is why he finds no pleasure in killing and destruction. He knows that evil can have no positive impact, cannot redound to its own benefit. If it has any impact, it is as the unwitting servant of the good it despises—and secretly longs for. Evil, for O'Connor as for Milton, is comical. All its violent antics are, in the long view, so much futile slapstick. It cannot affect the ultimate outcome of things. But evil for O'Connor bears a greater dignity than mere unbelief, because there is some force of will and spirit behind it, and deliberate choice—and because genuine evil knows perfectly well that it cannot but serve the good. The preacher of "The River" admonishes his audience to "believe Jesus or the Devil . . . Testify to one or the other!"[18]

Those who choose Jesus and deliberately minister to others who would choose him are hardly more benign than the Misfit himself. The Reverend Bevel Summers cautions his congregation in "The River" that "you can't leave your pain in the river." "The River of Life, made out of Jesus' Blood" is "a River full of pain itself." To be saved, one must enter that

---

15. O'Connor, "A Good Man Is Hard to Find," *Three by Flannery O'Connor*, 142.
16. *Ibid.*, 143.
17. *Ibid.*
18. O'Connor, "The River," *Three by Flannery O'Connor*, 152.

river and be part of it. Only the river of pain and trouble and blood moves towards the Kingdom of Christ. "'If it's this River of Life you want to lay your pain in, then come up,' the preacher said, 'and lay your sorrow here. But don't be thinking this is the last of it because this old red river don't end here. This old red suffering stream goes on, you people, slow to the Kingdom of Christ. This old red river is good to Baptize in, good to lay your faith in, good to lay your pain in, but it ain't this muddy water here that saves you.'"[19] "You won't be the same again," he warns the boy Harry, whom he is about to baptize Bevel "in the river of suffering." Nor—such at least must have been her hope—nor will the reader who deeply feels O'Connor's fiction be the same after reading it. It might seem at first a joke, as the river seems to Harry-Bevel. But it is no joke. Her story means, like the river, to make us "count," even if it does so by forcing us to "swallow some dirt," to feel what it's like to "tread on nothing," to suffer literally the experience of death by drowning.

> He stopped and thought suddenly: it's another joke, it's just another joke! He thought how far he had come for nothing and he began to hit and splash and kick the filthy river. His feet were already treading on nothing. He gave one low cry of pain and indignation. Then he heard a shout and turned his head and saw something like a giant pig bounding after him, shaking a red and white club and shouting. He plunged under once and this time, the waiting current caught him like a long gentle hand and pulled him forward and down. For an instant he was overcome with surprise; then since he was moving quickly and knew that he was getting somewhere, all his fury and fear left him.[20]

The monstrous figure of Mr. Paradise ("like a giant pig") strikes a discordantly comical note in this hauntingly severe vignette. It is not Bevel-Harry's death which is comic, but Mr. Paradise's failure to understand its significance.

IV. *Epiphanies and the Underworld*

The fury and fearsomeness of O'Connor's work is meant to submerge us in an epiphany more consciously religious than Proust's, but just as firmly based on an aesthetic principle of madness, violence, and what James

19. *Ibid.*
20. *Ibid.*, 159.

Hillman calls a fall into the underworld, the world of death, dreams, and the Holy.[21] Hillman finds it useful to speak of our active, wakeful selves as Herculean, and of the persona in which we dream and otherwise enter the deathworld as Orphean. Hercules puts aside all action to enter the kingdom of death—as Orpheus, he must submit to death's authority to gain entry. Proust had his own, remarkably similar language for these faces of the personality:

> The being who was reborn in me when, with such a shudder of happiness, I heard that noise common to both the spoon touching the dish and the hammer striking the wheel, to the unevenness of step of the flagstones in the Guermantes courtyard and of the baptistery of Saint Mark's, etc., that being is nourished only by the essences of things, in them only does it find its sustenance, its delight. It languishes in the observation of the present where the senses cannot bring it this essence, in the consideration of a past which the intelligence dries up, in the anticipation of a future which the will constructs out of fragments of the present and past from which it has withdrawn still more of their reality, retaining of them only that which serves the utilitarian and narrowly human end which it assigns them. But if a noise, an odor, heard or smelled before, should happen to be heard or smelled again, at once in the present and the past, real without being contemporaneous, ideal without being abstract, then the permanent and habitually hidden essence of things is liberated, and our true self which, sometimes for very long, had seemed dead but was not entirely, awakens, stirs itself, receiving the celestial nourishment which is brought to it. One minute free from the order of time has re-created in us, by the perception of it, the man liberated from the order of time. And we understand this man's confidence in his joy, even if the mere taste of a madeleine cake does not logically appear to contain the reasons for that joy, we understand that the word "dead" has no meaning for him; situated outside of time, what can he fear from the future?[22]

---

21. Hillman, *The Dream and the Underworld*, see particularly 23–67.

22. "L'être qui était rené en moi quand, avec un tel frémissement de bonheur, j'avais entendu le bruit commun à la fois à la cuiller qui touche l'assiette et au marteau qui frappe sur la roue, à l'inégalité pour les pas des pavés de la cour Guermantes et du baptistère de Saint-Marc, etc., cet être-là ne se nourrit que de l'essence des choses, en elle seulement il trouve sa subsistance, ses délices. Il languit dans l'observation du présent où les sens ne peuvent la lui apporter, dans la considération d'un passé que l'intelligence lui dessèche, dans l'attente d'un avenir que la volonté construit avec des fragments du présent et du passé auxquels elle retire encore de leur réalité en ne conservant d'eux que ce qui convient à la fin utilitaire, étroitement humaine, qu'elle leur assigne. Mais qu'un bruit, qu'une odeur, déjà entendu ou respirée jadis, le soient de nouveau, à la fois dans le présent et dans le passé, réels sans être actuels, idéaux sans être abstraits, aussitôt l'essence permanente et habituellement cachée des choses se trouve liberée, et notre vrai moi qui, parfois depuis longtemps,

This *être de mort* can only be nourished by concealed essences, a comestible lode situated somewhere beyond the laws of time, outside the day-world—in the realm of Pluto, then, Hades. Hillman has some interesting things to say about the mythology and etymology of death and its god.

Hades' name was rarely used. At times he was referred to as "the unseen one," more often as Pluto ("wealth," "riches") or as Trophonios ("nourishing"). These disguises of Hades have been taken by some interpreters to be covering euphemisms for the fear of death, but then why this particular euphemism and not some other? Perhaps Pluto is a description of Hades, much as Plato understood this God. Then, Pluto refers to the hidden wealth or the riches of the invisible. Hence, we can understand one reason why there was no cult and no sacrifice to him—Hades was the wealthy one, the giver of nourishment to the soul. Sometimes, he was fused with Thanatos ("Death") of whom Aeschylus wrote, "Death is the only God who loves not gifts and cares not for sacrifices or libation, who has no altars and receives no hymns . . . " (frg. *Niobe*). On vase paintings when Hades is shown, he may have his face averted, as if he were not even characterized by a specific physiognomy. All this "negative" evidence does coalesce to form a definite image of a void, an interiority or depth that is unknown but nameable, there and felt even if not seen. Hades is not an absence, but a hidden presence—even an invisible fullness.

Etymological investigations into the root word for *death demon* show it to mean "hider." To grasp better the ways in which Hades hides invisibly in things, let us take apart this concept, listening for the hidden connections, the metaphors, within the word *hidden* itself: (1) buried, shrouded, concealed from eyesight, whether a corpse or a *mysterium*; (2) occult, esoteric, concealed in the sense of secret; (3) that which per se cannot be seen: non-visible as non-spatial, non-extended; (4) without light: dark, black; (5) that which cannot be seen on inspection, i.e., blocked, censored, forbidden, or obscured; (6) hidden, as contained within (interior) or as contained below (inferior), where the Latin *cella* ("subterranean storeroom") is cognate with the Old Irish *cuile* ("cellar") and *cel* ("death"), again cognate with our *hell*; (7) that which is experienced with dread and terror, a void, a nothing; (8) that which is experienced as hiding, e.g., withdrawing, turning away from life; (9) stealth, surreptitiousness, deceit, such as the hidden motives and unseen connections of

---

semblait mort, mais ne l'était pas entièrement, s'éveille, s'anime en recevant la céleste nourriture qui lui est apportée. Une minute affranchie de l'ordre du temps a recréé en nous, pour la sentir, l'homme affranchi de l'ordre du temps. Et celui-là, on comprend qu'il soit confiant dans sa joie, même si le simple goût d'une madeleine ne semble pas contenir logiquement les raisons de cette joie, on comprend que le mot de 'mort' n'ait pas de sens pour lui; situé hors du temps, que pourrait-il craindre de l'avenir?" III, 872–73.

Hermes. In short, Hades, the hidden hider, presides over both the crypt and cryptic, which gives to Heraclitus' phrase (frg. 123): "Nature loves to hide" (*physis kryptesthai philei*), a subtle and multiple implication indeed.[23]

Ancient myth and modern psychology agree that there is no time in the underworld. So it makes no sense to think of the underworld as the setting of the afterlife. It is rather "the afterthoughts within life."[24] "It is not a far-off place of judgment over our actions but provides that place of judging now, and within, the inhibiting reflection interior to our actions."[25]

The underworld is contiguous and simultaneous with the dayworld. Hades is a mirror image, a negative image of Zeus. Every event in the upper world is reflected in, has a reflection in the lower world, the difference between the two being a difference of perspective rather than of substance.[26] The spiritual perspective is the one which is without time or light. The epiphanic moment, for Proust and for O'Connor, is that moment at which a sudden breach in the upper world occurs, dropping both reader and character—and writer, for that matter—into the occulted underworld, the moment at which the supernatural, the invisible, the spiritual, erupts into the consciousness of reader or writer or character, not necessarily taking hold but reminding us that it exists. O'Connor's stories frequently end with a literal sinking: Harry-Bevel's drowning in "The River" ("treading on nothing"), the grandmother collapsing in a ditch after the Misfit shoots her; or with a rejection of the world and its light such as Haze Motes' self-inflicted blindness. Sometimes the netherworld creeps rather than bursts into the picture, as at the end of "A Stroke of Good Fortune"—a fine story to which both Miss O'Connor and her critics have been unkind, perhaps because it is more dramatically subtle and moves more slowly than her other fictions. The only movement in the story is that of a woman climbing a flight of stairs. Her painful ascent is accompanied by the gradual realization that she is pregnant, something which she has taken every precaution to avoid and which she has always dreaded fiercely.

23. Hillman, *The Dream and the Underworld*, 28.
24. *Ibid.*, 30.
25. *Ibid.*
26. *Ibid.*

She sat on the step, clutching the banister spoke while the breath came back into her a thimbleful at a time and the stairs stopped seesawing. She opened her eyes and gazed down into the dark hold, down to the very bottom where she had started up so long ago. "Good Fortune," she said in a hollow voice that echoed along all the levels of the cavern, "Baby." "Good Fortune, Baby," the three echoes leered. Then she recognized the feeling again, a little roll. It was as if it were not in her stomach. It was as if it were out nowhere in nothing, out nowhere, resting and waiting, with plenty of time.[27]

Hillman, in a brilliant and radical revision of Freudian theory, redefines Thanatos so that the pathology of this aesthetic which I tried to elaborate in the last chapter is rendered moot by being established as not at all pathological but perfectly normal. "Because his realm was conceived as the final end of each soul, Hades is the final cause, the purpose, the very *telos* of every soul and every soul process. If so, then *all* psychic events have a Hades aspect, and not merely the sadistic or destructive events that Freud attributed to Thanatos. All soul processes, everything in the psyche, moves towards Hades."[28] Hillman has a point here, but one that would seem more apt in some cases than in others. Which is to say that I remain convinced that the gnostic aesthetic, absorbed as it is with what Hillman calls Hades, does represent a deviation from the norm— though I would be as hard pressed as anyone to say what that "norm" might be. Hillman himself admits that this reflective, oneiric mode of consciousness affects some individuals much more than it does others. For those whom it does affect, says Hillman, it is accompanied by a profound sense of loss—another observation which agrees entirely with my readings of Proust and O'Connor. "The movement from three-dimensional physical perception to the two dimensions of psychical reflection is first felt as a loss: *thymos* gone, we hunger, bewailing, paralyzed, repetitive. We want blood. Loss does characterize underworld experiences, from mourning to the dream, with its peculiar feeling of incompleteness, as if there is still more to come that we didn't get, always a concealment within it, a lost bit. A life that is lived in close connection with the psyche does indeed have an ongoing feeling of loss."[29] Whether

27. O'Connor, "A Stroke of Good Fortune," *Three by Flannery O'Connor*, 181–82.
28. Hillman, *The Dream and the Underworld*, 30.
29. *Ibid.*, 52–53.

the sense of loss—which is also the sense of "the presence of the void"—
is cause or effect of a "close connection with the psyche" is impossible
to say.

What O'Connor shares with Proust is the use of the written word as
a dark glass, to bring us into contact with our underworld selves, our
"dead" selves. Literature and every literary activity, reading or writing, is
innately reflective and introspective. As Proust said, "In reality, every
reader is, when he reads, reading himself. The work of the writer is only
a sort of optical instrument which he offers to the reader that the latter
may discern that which, without the book, he might not have seen in
himself."[30] Proust and O'Connor use this innate property of literature to
bring us into contact with a part of ourselves which many of us might
prefer to ignore. Their fictions are elaborately constructed chutes through
which we are supposed, if not to fall into the underworld, to gain some
sense of its reality. It is entirely appropriate that the images by which we
make that transition should be violent, even repugnant—what is being
represented is "the collapse of the corporeal."[31]

The reader's willingness to subject himself to unpleasant imagery, or
simply to undertake the task of reading, must in some sense derive from
the sense of loss which Hillman, O'Connor, and Proust have all pointed
to as a crucial part of their work. We enter the realm of death to recover
something, as Orpheus entered it to bring back Eurydice. He failed to
bring her into the dayworld by forgetting to observe the rules set down
by Pluto; he reverted to the rules of the upper world before he was in it,
and so lost what he had gone to find. Absence, loss, lack, have substance
only in the place of the dead. We can go there and "see" it, but we cannot
bring it out. The sense of loss is far greater as we come out than it was
before our descent. So it drives us back into the underworld. Surely Miss
O'Connor never conceived that her fictions would precipitate the kind
of extreme and physical rejection of the world that Haze Motes experiences; it must be safe to say that she neither wanted nor expected readers

30. "En réalité, chaque lecteur est, quand il lit, le propre lecteur de soi-même. L'ouvrage
de l'écrivain n'est qu'une espèce d'instrument optique qu'il offre au lecteur afin de lui per-
mettre de discerner ce que, sans ce livre, il n'eût peut-être pas vu en soi-même." III, 911.
31. Hillman, *The Dream and the Underworld*, 54.

to blind themselves with lye. More probably she wanted us to have some sense, like Ruby Hill, of staring down a black stairwell, hearing a voice at once ours and not ours, some part of us speaking from "the very bottom where she had started up so long ago," "out nowhere in nothing, out nowhere, resting and waiting, with plenty of time."[32]

32. O'Connor, "A Stroke of Good Fortune," *Three by Flannery O'Connor*, 181–82.

CHAPTER 7

Art, Delusion, Disease, and Reality: The Apotheosis of Asbury Fox in "The Enduring Chill"

I thought and thought about a sentence to introduce it with but to no avail. I can only write stories. However, I think I should prefer: "A wretched young man arrives at the point where his artistic delusions come face to face with reality." What I really mean is *arty* delusions, but you can maybe make it better. Why not just have an arrow or a hand on the left side of the page, pointing downward, indicating that the story is below. Those ladies under the dryer all consider themselves intelligent.

—F. O'Connor to Alice Morris, February 28, 1958

"The Enduring Chill" first appeared in *Harper's Bazaar* in 1958. O'Connor had read *Swann's Way* (in English) before, and was to read all of *A la recherche* before her death in 1964, when she was still revising and rewriting the story.[1] Its protagonist, one Asbury Fox, *artiste manqué*, is the closest thing in all of her work to a Charles Swann, an individual of creative temperament but who produces nothing. He also bears strong resemblance to Marcel who, after all, is a failure until the end of his story, which is also a story of "arty delusions" lost. Another reason for dealing with this story of all the ones O'Connor produced in her short lifetime is that this one is the only one which identifies literary, artistic violence explicitly with physical violence. It is unlike many of her better-known stories in the subtlety of its violence. No one is maimed, no one dies, no one is even robbed or beaten. But the violence is no less violent for all its sublimation. What I propose to do is to treat it in much the same fashion as I treated Proust's *La Prisonnière*—to tell the story of my reading it, hoping to squeeze from it some greater understanding of what "art," "delusion" and "reality" mean, to Flannery O'Connor, to Proust, and to me.

1. Flannery O'Connor, *The Habit of Being*, ed. Sally Fitzgerald (New York, 1979), 150, 490.

I. *Asbury as a Reader of Proust*

Asbury Fox might be taken as a prototype of those who would read Proust as a celebration of the vocation of art, effete Horatio Algers, and set out in their lives to reenact the same happy ending. The awfulness of what Marcel discovers escapes them. By assuming what Jacques Maritain called "the habit of art," though, they may come to appreciate the violent nature of art even if they never produce any work worthy of the experience.[2] It is not necessary to write or paint or to be an artist in any practical sense to experience the violence of art, and if there is anything exalted about the artist or what he does, there is no more than in the act of reading, knowledgeably (gnostically) executed. Cultivating the habit of art will not lead everyone to produce art. It can lead anyone to participate in it.

Flannery O'Connor seems to have been particularly horrified by those individuals who want "to have written," to live in what appears noble subservience to beauty and the Muse, winning the praise of book club editorial boards without "suffering" very much, if at all. Art, for Proust and O'Connor, is a disease which, to have any positive outcome, needs to be made chronic and irreversible. And which, in the context of the world as we know it, is less noble than ludicrous and pitiful. It is Asbury Fox's farcically tragic destiny to discover, too late for renunciation, that he has got what he wanted—to see the world and himself with an artist's eyes.

II. *Asbury's Homecoming: The Mirrors of Home and Family*

Asbury is returning home not because he wants to but because he has to—he is sick and has lost his job in New York. Home is a small southern town called Timberboro where he is confronted by a mother and sister to whom he believes himself infinitely superior. Asbury vehemently refuses to acknowledge any physical or spiritual kinship between himself and his family or the place of his birth. In fact, he is estranged even from his own body, for which it would be difficult to blame him. "Mrs. Fox observed that his left eye was bloodshot. He was puffy and pale and his hair had receded tragically for a boy of twenty-five. The thin reddish

2. Jacques Maritain, *Art et scolastique* (Paris, 1920), *passim.*

wedge of it left on top bore down in a point that seemed to lengthen his nose and give him an irritable expression that matched his tone of voice when he spoke to her."[3] There is a brief moment in which Asbury seems to anticipate a Proustian transmogrification of the primal landscape, aborted by his satisfaction at his own appallingly bleak appearance and its impact on his mother. "Asbury felt that he was about to witness a majestic transformation, that the flat of roofs might at any moment turn into the mounting turrets of some exotic *temple for a god he didn't know*. The illusion lasted only a moment before his attention was drawn back to his mother" (82; emphasis mine). What Asbury wants is to do violence to his mother's perceptions, to upset her tranquillity without disturbing his own. "She had given a little cry; she looked aghast. He was pleased that she should see death in his face at once. His mother, at the age of sixty, was going to be introduced to reality and he supposed that if the experience didn't kill her, it would assist her in the process of growing up" (83). Asbury has got things precisely backwards. He sees in the specula of his mother and home exactly what is going to happen to him eventually, an "introduction to reality," a confrontation with "the god he doesn't know." Denial and projection, these are Asbury's defenses against the epiphanic moment towards which he is already moving.

He aims to have the Misfit's pleasure in destruction without the Misfit's awful knowledge and despair, that "it's no real pleasure in life." This way, he has the artist/criminal's power and glory without their trouble. Asbury wants to *be* artistic perception and what it perceives, to embody the experience of artistic violence. This is his disease and his ignorance, that Asbury conceives the artist as superior to his audience, a more noble and significant being. He does not understand what his author took as a fundamental truth, that the writer must endure his product even more intimately and wrenchingly than his reader if it is to have any value. That involvement would produce a passiveness, a humility, a sense of spiritual and physical infirmity and dissolution of which Asbury is willfully ignorant.

Just as he believes that the artist has nothing in common with his

3. Flannery O'Connor, "The Enduring Chill," *Everything That Rises Must Converge* (New York, 1978), 83. Hereinafter page references to this collection are given parenthetically in the text.

audience, so Asbury believes that he has nothing in common with his home or family, "irked that he had allowed himself, even for an instant, to see an imaginary temple in this collapsing country junction" (83). But his return home belies his superiority and power. There is no place he would less like to be than Timberboro. He has been forced to return there by a literal exhaustion of physical and economic resources. Sick and penniless, he has no place else to go.

III. Death as Deification

Asbury takes his physical decline to mean that he is going to die very soon. This is how he manages to turn his helplessness into power. He envisions death, in typically maudlin fashion, as a transfiguration of himself, a vengeance upon his mother in particular. He has stayed away from home at great physical and fiscal expense, expense which has debilitated him to the point that he can go nowhere but home. Destitution and disease, however, will only consecrate his life the more to art, render him more admirable in the eyes of its acolytes. But this sort of scenario demands an audience devoted to the mysteries and rites of art, and this Asbury left behind in New York. "He had become entirely accustomed to the thought of death, but he had not become accustomed to the thought of death *here*" (83).

Art in the gnostic mode does not partake of Cartesian dualism, does not acknowledge subjects distinct from objects, does not recognize objects at all, and sees subjectivities as mere mirages, trick pictures made with mirrors. Gnostic art is a reflective, a specular activity, an involvement of images and subjectivities that dissolves the notion of subjectivity as autonomous and distinct. Now Asbury, like many of the "acolytes" of art—call them *joueurs de flûte*, as Norpois does in *A la recherche*, or those who wish to "have written"—does not understand this. He wants to be the only subject and the only object around, to define everyone else's perceptions according to his own. Mesmerizing them by the spectacle of his superior knowledge and being, eclipsing all other objects in their view, he means in this fashion to deprive them of their autonomy, their subjective powers of perception. He is not so wrong in thinking that art derives its strength from death. What he does not know is that the strength, if it can be called that, belongs to art, not to the artist. He understands death as a positive entity, rather than as the entropic unthing it is. His trouble is that he does not understand what Proust and O'Connor and the journalist Marshall Frady, in this passage about a writer of fiction (Jesse Hill Ford), do, that "it is a writer's peculiar unease that while potentially any number of people he is finally none of them, belongs in the end to none of their worlds, but hangs in an endless abeyance among them all. He lives in a kind of anarchy. Beyond whatever order and intelligence takes form in his work, he is without any real sense of himself. And in this would lie the last and most fearsome loneliness—a suspicion sometimes that, passing before a mirror, he will see nothing but an empty room."[4]

In fact, Asbury must not really feel so comfortable about dying, for after all, he could have hastened his death by staying in New York. Cold, disease, and starvation would have sacrificed him sooner rather than later, and in the very bosom of sophistication. He has returned home to avoid suffering, to forestall death, sacrificed "his last connection with a larger world" in order to live longer and to impose the spectacle of his death on the only audience to whom it would make the slightest difference, his family. Clearly, Asbury does not like the idea of death and suffering. What he likes is the authority and power which he thinks impending death will give him.

IV. Body and Spirit, Doctors and Priests

Asbury insists to his mother that doctors, especially the cretinous (to Asbury) Dr. Block, can do him no good, his malady being of the spirit. "What's wrong with me is way beyond Block" (85). He finds himself unable, however, as his friend Goetz had advised, to see the town "as illusion," to dissociate himself from it. It asserts a firm grip on his senses, and he recoils in vain, as from his sister whom, though he affects to despise, he resembles startlingly. The major dissimilarity between them is Mary George's larger bulk. The usual ratio of sibling sexual resemblance is reversed, turning their kinship into a parodic reflection. Asbury is really just a frail and shrunken effigy of his robust sister. She is a school principal, the equation which has made her larger and sloppier having

4. Marshall Frady, "The Judgment of Jesse Hill Ford," *Southerners: A Journalist's Odyssey* (New York, 1980), 210.

metamorphosed Asbury's pretensions to art into grammar school peda-
gogy. True to her travesty of masculinity, Mary George wears a black suit
and Girl Scout shoes. Asbury has no choice but to give her "a revolted
look of recognition" (84)—this despite his contention that no student of
the physical, no doctor, could diagnose, much less cure, his ailment. His
family holds up physical mirrors to Asbury, subverting his gropings for
power, showing him himself as he would rather not be seen. Dr. Block
is a custodian, trustee of these resemblances, and Asbury wants nothing
to do with him.

There follows a short analepsis recounting Asbury's late encounter with
a priest, at a lecture on the Vedanta to which his friend Goetz had invited
him. Asbury had searched out the priest in the crowd and identified with
his demeanor of superiority and reserve, his spiritual segregation of himself from the rest of the crowd. Later, he was impressed by the priest's
calm disdain for the pronouncements of Goetz and the others in the
audience. The priest, like Asbury, had participated from a distance, as if
vicariously, from a higher plane. He and Asbury had smiled at one another "over the heads of the others." The priest attracted Asbury as the
perfect spectator of his demise, his self-sacrifice on the altar of art. "The
priest appealed to him as a man of the world, someone who would have
understood the unique tragedy of his death, a death whose meaning had
been far beyond the twittering group around them." Remembering this
in the car with his mother and sister, Asbury repeats his contempt for
the medical profession which would trivialize his dysfunction as the purely
physical symptom of a purely physical breakdown. " 'What's wrong with
me,' he repeated, 'is way beyond Block' " (86–87).

V. The Maternal Perspective

Asbury's mother interprets all of this to mean that he is headed for a
nervous breakdown. All of her son's problems seem to her to come down
to two things: being "smart" and having an "artistic temperament," both
highly undesirable. His feet are "not on the ground"; he refuses to take
his place as part of a physically real town and family. Dr. Block is Mrs.
Fox's champion, the man of Cartesian sensibility, who reduces everything
to cause and effect. The nearest Asbury has ever come to dealing physically with the physical world was working in her dairy, which did him

no good because he did it to provide himself with insight into the Negroes, about whom he was writing a play. Even when he acts, works, Asbury only observes, only looks for "insight." When physical reality intrudes upon his observations in rudely material and neurological fashion, as when a cow kicks him, he quickly retreats. "If he would get in there now, or get out and fix fences, or do any kind of work—real work, not writing— . . . he might avoid this nervous breakdown" (88).

Mrs. Fox's and Asbury's are not simply symmetrical points of view, however. She denies the noumenal as he denies the physical. She hides from the spiritual in trivialities, in a simple-minded preoccupation with mundane realities. She is ridiculous, too, though less so than Asbury, who admits the noumenal only as an aesthetic principle. Asbury is the ultimate fool. Not only does he reject material reality but reduces the spiritual to the purely aesthetic, to his own—failed—vocation.

VI. *Contrapuntal Comedy*

The source of much humor in O'Connor is just this sort of grotesquely miscarried intersubjectivity—grotesque, and comical, because the characters act as though it were not going on. Like the unstable relations among Proust's characters, her protagonists distort each other as they distort their own perceptions and lives. Each character presents a freakishly warped speculum to every other; each exaggerates the monstrousness of the others. The shifting of point of view, as from Asbury to his mother, accentuates the distortion and its comic effect. The friction between characters is the result of their mutual distortion and the source of comedy. Their images of each other provide shocks of recognition from which most recoil in horror, wishing to preserve fictions of uniqueness, superiority, autonomy. In O'Connor's view it is these fictions which have given rise to modern obsessions with the self.[5] The typical twentieth-century man wants, like Asbury, to be both subject and object, to dominate his world completely, objectively and subjectively, while in fact he is already lost in a perpetual ricochet of subjectivities, images, impressions.

Asbury, like Proust's Marcel, wants to arrest this play, freeze the flickering light on himself; like Marcel, he wants to write in a mimetic uni-

5. "The Teaching of Literature," *passim*, and "Novelist and Believer," 158–60 and *passim*, both in O'Connor, *Mystery and Manners*.

verse, where narrative and life are linear, punctuated by an ending, where the equivalency of signifier and signified is guaranteed by death as closure.[6] But death does not, in O'Connor's narrative world any more than in Proust's, mean closure but rather the absence of it. Asbury does not die in this story, just as Marcel does not. His literal death is displaced outside the limits of the story, yet death invests every word of it. This story works towards its own beginning, towards a knowledge which is its point of departure: the consummation of what Asbury has glimpsed in the dark glass of his home and mother, illumination and consecration, knowledge of an unknown god. As this lack of closure gives rise to Marcel's anguish in love, so it is the possibility of a new kind of comedy—Asbury cannot define himself, his mother, his home, any more than Marcel can get a fix on Albertine.

VII. *Asbury's Saving Grace and Tragic Flaw*

Asbury is special, like Marcel, because he has some intuition of this himself. His first visions of his home and mother are like Marcel's taste of madeleine—incomplete, not understood or pursued to the limit, but premonitory. Asbury would have aborted the visions himself if the visions had not aborted themselves, such is his horror at the thought that he might be seeing something of himself in Timberboro. Not only people but animals threaten to reveal some terrible resemblance. "A small, wall-eyed Guernsey was watching him steadily as if she sensed some bond between them. 'Good God!' he cried in an agonized voice, 'can't we go on? It's six o'clock in the morning!'" (88). His sister Mary George, whose miscarried femininity is suggested by her name, chimes in "'What's that cry of deadly pain?'" and of course Asbury is in ontological pain because his identity is threatened. He and all the other characters are funny insofar as they experience these glimmerings of resemblance as threats, as pain, insofar as they struggle vainly to prop up their shambling identities. Asbury's refusal of kinship, in which the physical must emblemize the spiritual, is the primal distortion. Preserving it against epiphanies, such as Asbury's on seeing his sister, gives rise to further, more extreme distortions. The encroachments of resemblance (in the nomenclature of the

---

6. Consult the conclusion of Chapter 5 herein for a detailed development of this thesis.

Derridean critic, this, again, is what would be known as a "differential phenomenon") upon distinction are fearful and provoke more and more radical distortions.

Asbury, however, is too perceptive to carry this out for very long. If his visions do not tell him everything yet, they have already told him too much. The collapse of his identity is set in motion by the first act of distortion, the first repression of resemblance. This progress is funny because it is futile, but it is also dramatic and tragic in the classical sense. Asbury's horror of his home and family, of a cow, of the possibility that he may be merely ill rather than a martyr to art, his shrilly defensive reactions, project the implosion of his carefully constructed identity, towards which the story is already moving.

The irony of his behavior is that, in his insistence on his uniqueness, his vocation as an artist (if a sterile one), he has set in motion the series of askeses which will cause his pretensions to collapse. His mother and sister, though they cling to ridiculous masks, are not horrified by resemblances as Asbury is. They lack his "artistic temperament": they are not "smart" like Asbury. They either accept, at some level, the falseness of their own social selves, or are blissfully ignorant of it. Asbury's struggles to have the affliction of art, on the other hand, have made him sick, and that disease will force the knowledge of the artist on him as surely and awfully as if he had understood what he was doing.

VIII.   The Artist in the Gas Chamber: Asbury and Flannery

Mary George provides an apt caption for the vignette of Asbury's first look at the farmhouse where he grew up: "'The artist arrives at the gas chamber,' Mary George said in her nasal voice" (90). The first thing he sees in the house is himself, in a mirror, "pale and broken." He staggers to his room and, refusing to look at anything else, falls "face down on his own bed." Another indication of the fragility of his sense of himself as superior is Asbury's revulsion at his own physical self. His mother, sister, the cow, his home, all revolt him because he sees himself in them, his creaturely, physical self. It is crucial to Asbury's "gnostic" attitude that his own flesh disgusts him. His flesh represents an obstacle to happiness, to seeing himself as he would like to be seen, to satisfactory relations with the world and with other humans. Asbury's superego imposes such constraints on his relations with the world, with himself, that it strangles desire altogether. Requital, just as I supposed in the case of Proust,[7] means embracing interdiction, Thanatos, death—a union both desired and dreaded. This is probably the one psychic characteristic common to every (potentially) gnostic writer. Asbury cannot attain satisfaction, yet he desires it to the point of near lunacy. *He desires and mourns at the same time.*

Asbury cannot find anyone—a listener, spectator—who would see him as he wishes to be seen, an object which would embody his idealized self. Only such a person could he love, for only such an idealized double would let him satisfy his superego's exorbitant demands, let him be his own subject and object. He has wondered if a priest, a Jesuit, might do, might serve as a suitable replacement for the father he affects to despise and whose absence (he died when Asbury was five), whose identification with death, must have a great deal to do with Asbury's identification of the ego-ideal and death, his sense that death will give him what he wants and needs, make him powerful. "Death was coming to him legitimately, as a justification, as a gift from life" (99). Death is what he desires and dreads, and no priest could be an adequate substitute. For Asbury, as for Marcel, there is to be no Odette de Crécy as there was for Swann, no real person who can meet his needs.

Flannery O'Connor was an invalid most of her adult life. It would be hard for anyone as ill as she was not to dislike her physical self, to be frustrated by it and even at times to be repulsed by it. The similarities between Asbury's return home and her own forced return to Andalusia, her family's farm outside Milledgeville, Georgia, are impossible to ignore. In her letters there is powerful evidence that she too had had to identify mourning with desire. In 1956 she wrote to a friend that "needing people badly and not getting them may turn you in a creative direction, provided you have the other requirements." Her father had written "speeches and local political stuff" because, she speculated, "He needed the people and got them. Or rather wanted them and got them. I wanted them and didn't." She added finally, and most revealingly, "We are all rather blessed in our deprivations if we let ourselves be, I suppose."[8] It

---

7. See the conclusion of Chapter 5 herein.
8. O'Connor, *The Habit of Being*, 169.

is also significant that she should mention her father in this respect. Edward Francis O'Connor died when Flannery was fifteen, after a prolonged struggle with lupus erythematosus, the same disease that was to afflict his daughter. He was one of the people she had needed and been denied, just as Asbury's father, in her story, died during his son's childhood. In the last year of her life, Flannery wrote, in response to a query as to what poetry she liked, that one of her favorite poems was this one by Gerard Manley Hopkins.[9] Its theme is the same as that of this study.

> *Spring and Fall, to a Young Child*
>
> Margaret, are you grieving
> Over Goldengrove unleaving?
> Leaves, like the things of man, you
> With your fresh thoughts care for, can you?
> Ah! as the heart grows older
> It will come to such sights colder
> By and by, nor spare a sigh
> Though worlds of wanwood leafmeal lie;
> And yet you will weep and know why.
> Now no matter, child, the name:
> Sorrow's springs are the same.
> Nor mouth had, no nor mind, expressed
> What heart heard of, ghost guessed:
> It is the blight man was born for,
> It is Margaret you mourn for.[10]

IX. *Polemic Versus Art: Asbury's Testament*

If Asbury has never succeeded in producing any decent fiction or poetry, he has, or thinks he has, succeeded in writing a "political" document. The story contains excerpts from this, his "letter to his mother, which filled two notebooks. It was such a letter as Kafka addressed to his father" (91). It is such writing as Flannery's own father had done, expository, with persuasion in mind; the kind of writing most often done, in Flannery's words, by those who want people and get them. Asbury is trying to masquerade as one of those people. He would have preferred to address it to his father, who like Flannery's was something of a politician,

---

9. *Ibid.*, 586.
10. Gerard Manley Hopkins, "Spring and Fall, to a Young Child," *The Norton Anthology of English Literature* (New York, 1968), 2239.

"one of the courthouse gang" (87, 91), and probably wrote tracts and speeches as well—at the very least spoke them out loud. The letter might even represent a dim attempt to emulate the late Mr. Fox as something other than a dead man, other than death, to substitute something for death as superego, ego-ideal. This would align it with Asbury's efforts to locate a suitable spectator to his martyrdom, attempts doomed of course by the fact that his father *is* dead and that he can't address the letter to him, was never able to address anything to him, even to know him.

The letter is an outcry against that absence, no confession but a wail of frustration. It is Fox *fils'* private gnostic gospel. As such it is unique in O'Connor's fiction and worth close study. Its ostensible purpose is to make his mother fully aware of all the harm he thinks she has inflicted on him. Not merely for the sake of recrimination, because "he forgave her," but because "a painful realization" was "the only thing of value he had to leave her" (91). Composing the instrument of that epiphany has been an agony for him "because in order to face her, *he had had to face himself*" (91; emphasis mine). It reveals his greatest discovery as that of his own spiritual and imaginative immobility:

> "I came here to escape the slave's atmosphere of home," he had written, "to find freedom, to liberate my imagination, to take it like a hawk from its cage and set it 'whirling off into the widening gyre' (Yeats) and what did I find? It was incapable of flight. It was some bird you had domesticated, sitting huffy in its pen, refusing to come out!" The next words were underscored twice. "I have no imagination. I have no talent. I can't create. I have nothing but the desire for these things. Why didn't you kill that too? Woman, why did you pinion me?" (91–92)

Of course his failure has been in trying to appease death, to stabilize and define himself, and it is death, not his mother, which has pinioned him. He blames his mother because he has not been able to cover that dark speculum with her, and she represents his most prolonged and intense effort to block it out.

The letter is the only one of many works he has conserved. He held onto it because he believed it would give his mother "an enduring chill and perhaps in time lead her to see herself as she was." Again, he tries vainly to project his own fate onto his mother by making her "understand him," to transplant his distortions of vision onto her and make her into his ideal audience/object. But art cannot do this, at least not gnostic art; only polemic can. Asbury aspires to make his mother see him as he wants to see himself and so to acknowledge both complicity in his failure and his superiority, but he does not want to involve himself in trying to understand her. He does not want to risk any crack in his own armor of distorted vision.

In composing this letter, Asbury is fleeing the awful shades of art (death, absence, mourning) for the safe ground of polemic, exactly what he reviles his father for having done. He is behaving like the social activists of whom his author was so disdainful ("Don't know which is worse, CORE or Young Republicans for Goldwater").[11] To one conscience-stricken liberal she wrote: "I have a plan for you. Come South at your own expense & let the White Citizens Council send you back. You could tell them that you was a little light but a guaranteed nigger. This would cut your expenses in half and give you a nice vacation in the land of sin and guilt. You could even go to Hyannisport."[12] What Asbury wants is to wield power, specifically over his mother, but any number of others would do. In this he is a model for most all activists, those who would change the world, do to a society or a culture or a people what Asbury would do to his mother. They treat words as a weapon, bludgeon or lever, so that language doesn't reveal but only describes. Language becomes a kind of flypaper, holding them down to things, the secular world. So that in rejecting his physical person for some intellectual ideal, Asbury only mires himself the more in matter, in his own flesh, in Timberboro; the more he runs from them, the more they horrify him. The more he tries to be an *artiste*, the more he fails. The more he tries to put off the moment of his illumination, the nearer he is to it.

In this letter, Asbury has tried to make a reflective surface to show a particular image to a particular individual. He thinks that what matters is the image reflected in the words, rather than the phenomenon of specularity itself. This is a "polemical" attitude. It sees the written word as a way of making readers see themselves and others in particular ways. It valorizes the image seen by the reader in the text and the writer's power to manipulate it.

11. O'Connor, *The Habit of Being*, 562.
12. *Ibid.*, 475.

Another, not quite as fallacious (from a gnostic point of view), but still incomplete, is the rhetorical or "deconstructive" approach, which is concerned with reader and text as mutually specular, mutual "contaminants," but denies the *demonic* nature of human form and language, denies literature the pathos of desire and mourning.

X. *In Deprivation, Salvation?*

Asbury's predicament is defined by lack, depletion of health and pocketbook, which lead in turn (he thinks) to intellectual depletion. All of these are preceded by the physical, emotional lacuna left by his father. Asbury is anxious to believe that he is grateful for his father's early death. Grateful because it has spared him having to confront the most proximate likeness of himself, freed him from the formative influence of "a rural worthy." But in fact his father's death has left a gaping hole in his psyche, launched him on a life of searching for surrogates, trying to paper over that hole, a career of trying to define everyone in terms of himself. This is what he thinks art is all about—using words to make others "see themselves"—and him—as they and he "really are"—*i.e.*, as he would see himself and them.

This endows Asbury with a vampire's horror of any reflective surface, not because he doesn't see himself but because he does—does see himself in a mad variety of shapes, none of which bears much resemblance to his prototype of the noble, suffering *artiste*. He wants to arrogate all "speculation," all specularity, to himself, and impose opacity on everyone and everything else. The trouble with this, and the comedy of it, is that, if Asbury is the only reflector, where is he to "see" himself? Where is any image of him to appear? He wants to interrupt the play of reflection because, dimly, he fears that it will lead him to where his father is not—and he is right. But to exist, to think, he must participate, become involved, lose himself. He is forced to admit in practice what intellectually and aesthetically he refuses to admit.

In New York, he thought to have found a specular surface he could tolerate, identify with. His hometown, however, he sees as black, flat, opaque, in contrast with the "white-gold sun." He is careful not to grant any depth to its darkness, wills opacity on Timberboro lest it show him anything he doesn't want to see. But he cannot avoid seeing that the light of the sky invests the town: it "cast a strange light over the single block of one-story brick and wooden shacks." The effect of this near admission that the town does reflect is nearly to complete the circuit of specularity, mirror facing mirror, *mise en abîme* of Asbury, fall into self, underworld. Asbury postpones all of this by tarring it with the epithet "illusion" (82).

Asbury identifies this "completion of the circuit" with death, which he invokes and yet dreads. Consummating his artistic aspiration in a specular union with his mother, sister, with Timberboro, seems worse than failure, yet circumstances, his various lacks, have drawn him back into their midst, where his idealized vision of himself is assailed by cretinously prosaic reflection. His hope to discover a perfect "double," to become the original of himself instead of the simulacrum of some lost original (his father), is beset by real resemblances and differences. By branding the town, its physical reality and that of his family, as "illusion," Asbury seeks refuge in narcissism—an equally dangerous proposition since, contemplating himself, he must sooner or later arrive at the black hole at his center.

XI. *A Symmetry of Specula*

In this narcissistic strategy, Asbury is trying to be his own father, which always places him between a pair of reflective subjectivities, in the middle, trying to block, interrupt, define, freeze the play of perceptions. He steps off the train and finds himself between the cloud-staunched sky and the bleak shacks of Timberboro, refusing to let either intrude fully on his senses. He has a mother on one side and a sister on the other. And there are cows on all sides, gazing at him pregnantly: "the dry cows were on one side and the milk herd on the other" (88). On the one hand doctors, on the other priests: these provide a symmetry of men to complement his mother and sister.

Asbury falls asleep, to open his eyes on the dreaded Dr. Block (what better name for the voice of materiality, in contrast with the over-sly Asbury, too foxy for his own good). The priest already mentioned and Dr. Block, together with another Jesuit yet to appear, are paternal synecdoches, fatherly speculi, representing two approaches to man, not necessarily contradictory, man as body and man as body and spirit. Dr. Block fits in best with a juvenile's simplistic grasp of reality. "Block was irresist-ible to children. For miles around they vomited and went into fevers to have a visit from him. Mrs. Fox was standing behind him, smiling ra-diantly. 'Here's Doctor Block!' she said as if she had captured this angel on the rooftop and brought him in for her little boy" (93). Asbury sees him as a grossly secular trinity: "a pink open-mouthed face hanging over him," "two large familiar ears," and "the black tubes of Block's stetho-scope" which "extended down to his exposed chest" (93). This is a par-ody of physical man, the social self in its communicative mode: ears for listening, mouth for speaking, a rubber connection to someone else's beating heart.

But make no mistake, Dr. Block is not the villain here. Quite the op-posite, his diagnosis will catalyze Asbury's askesis at the end of the story. The point is still made that natural science and natural man at their best are ridiculous. Dr. Block is a buffoon. "The doctor, seeing he was awake, made a face like a Chinaman, rolled his eyes almost out of his head and cried 'Say AHHHH!'" (93). Here is the social self speaking in its *lingua franca*, at its best and worst: the body making idiotic gestures and noises to elicit the same from another, from which responsive gestures and noises the first party draws certain conclusions, makes certain conjectures as to the second party's physical well-being. "Blood don't lie," Block says to Asbury (95). But at least there is no pretense to know anything besides the hue of a throat or the number of heartbeats per minute.

To Asbury this is small comfort. "'Get him out of here,' Asbury mut-tered. He looked at the asinine face *from what seemed the bottom of a black hole*" (94; emphasis mine). The difference between Asbury's perceptions and Block's could not be clearer. Block is a logical positivist, has "two cold clinical nickel-colored eyes" filled "with a motionless curiosity," "a drill-like gaze" (94), and unswerving faith in the veracity of flesh, "symp-toms," blood. Asbury, for all his pretenses to social activism (concern for the welfare of Negroes), cannot see his exchange with Block as one body addressing another, two fixed images facing one another. He does not want, on the other hand, to see himself and Block as two mutually re-flective bodies, two "black holes" throwing dark light down one another. Asbury wants his polemical way. He must be the shapeless shaper, the giver of shapes, and Block must be nothing but his object, audience, reader. What frustrates Asbury here as always is his sense that he is failing to shape the images he shows Block, that he is not in control. He can't control the phenomenon, and he is afraid to participate in it if he can't control it.

And yet Dr. Block is a wise man. His faith in blood comes with a *caveat* which is probably unusual among doctors, certainly among "city doctors." Block believes in his knowledge and his instruments as far as they go, but he knows that they are a *pis-aller*, no key to understanding. Even if he could exhaust the possibilities of physical knowledge, he would still not understand. " 'Most things are beyond me,' Block said. 'I ain't found anything yet that I thoroughly understood,' and he sighed and got up. His eyes seemed to glitter at Asbury as if from a great distance" (95). As so often in Proust's fiction, the *eyes* are the focal point of social intercourse, where all the mirrors concentrate their light. This is an anxious moment for Asbury. Dr. Block is asserting his own diaphanousness; his eyes refuse to be opaque, they glitter and their volume threatens to belie an appalling depth. Asbury turns his own eyes flat in defense—"Asbury's eyes were a fierce glaring violet" (95). He is spared any askesis by his mother's simple-mindedness, which drenches the whole scene dim again—her faith in "blood" is unadulterated by any sense of mystery. " 'He wouldn't act so ugly,' Mrs. Fox explained, 'if he weren't really sick. And I want you to come back every day until you get him well' " (95).

There are other, more dangerous threats of translumination than Dr. Block. Asbury cloaks them vainly in images of his own invention, like some monk fearful of his virtue, stripping himself to cover a nude seducer. Leaks, everywhere leaks assail Asbury's intellectual makeshift. He patches them as best he can, but all he can do is postpone—not death, but a knowledge of the nature of death.

> Descending from the top moulding, long icicle shapes had been etched by leaks and, directly over his bed on the ceiling, another leak made a fierce bird with spread wings. It had an icicle crosswise in its beak and there were smaller icicles depending from its wings and tail. It had been there since his childhood and had always irritated him and sometimes had frightened him. He had often had the illusion that it was in motion and about to descend mysteriously and set the icicle on his head. He closed his eyes and thought: I won't have to look at it for many more days. (93)

XII. Asbury's Hemlock

In an analeptic episode, we get to the source of Asbury's physical debility, which turns out to be a direct result of his "polemical" behavior. The year before, Asbury had been working on a play about Negroes—a dramatic sermon addressed to such oppressors as his mother. To acquaint himself with the misery of his dark brethren, he had gone to work with them in his mother's dairy.

The two Negroes employed in the dairy, Randall and Morgan, are exemplars of the kind of passivity, fluid contemplation, which gnostic art demands. "He had wanted to be around them for a while to see how they really felt about their condition, but the two who worked for her had lost all initiative over the years. They didn't talk" (96). But they *do* talk. They just don't say what Asbury wants them to. They don't address themselves to Asbury proper, to Asbury as Asbury would have Asbury addressed. "When they said anything to him, it was as if they were speaking to an invisible body located to the right or left of where he actually was" (96). Asbury attributes this to cowardice, fear of white people generally and of his mother in particular. In fact, Randall and Morgan are amusedly contemptuous of Asbury. Refusing to let Asbury be where he wants to be, refusing to address him, they refuse the image he would force on them, the image of themselves as poor indolent broken spirits. They do not think of themselves as poor, indolent, or broken but then they do not appear to think of themselves in any particular fashion. They look askance at everything, themselves no less than Asbury. They see and are seen, reflect and are reflected in a perfectly passive way. By their passivity, they get along, they make the best of a situation which does not favor them but which sooner or later favors no one, which reduces everyone to "an invisible body located to the right or left of where he actually is."

The presence of the Negroes, and Asbury's attitude towards them— *i.e.*, his interpretation of their sidelong glances as fear compounded by ignorance, a minstrel shuck and jive, in which his mother would doubtless concur—introduces the thematic of color. The question, faced with these Negroes, is how to perceive their blackness, how to "read," or not "read" their lack of pigment. Are they just benignly opaque, posing no reflective threat to Asbury and aptly hued to see themselves as he would have them see themselves? Are they blank slates, an ideal audience? Flat opacity or infinite depth of absence, which is also represented as black? Asbury chooses to read them as surfeit rather than lack, just as he turns away from the glitter and depth of Dr. Block's eyes. Asbury wants the world neatly segregated into black and white, opaque and specular. He wants to arrogate all the reflexivity, the whiteness, unto himself, and make all the world look to him to see itself.

To seduce the Negroes, bring them under his power, Asbury discovers the necessity of an object, an inanimate, pleasure-giving intermediary. The first one he chooses is a cigarette. His mother has forbidden the smoking of cigarettes in the dairy, so that the cigarette subverts her authority, brings the Negroes (apparently) under Asbury's yoke, transforming them into an "audience." Asbury is so intent on gaining intellectual ascendancy over the two that he is oblivious to the danger of fire to which he exposes them all. The cigarette, a "lure," a kind of standard of exchange, establishes an economic bond among them. In so doing it is remarkably analogous to the written word as described by Bataille and Blanchot. These cigarettes represent an assault on the constituted authority *and* on the distinctions prescribed and recognized by that authority. It does not merely replace Mrs. Fox's authority with Asbury's. It dissolves authority. It violates the distinction which that authority exists to enforce, between black and white, speaker and listener, writer and reader. This is just what a text is supposed to do, as O'Connor knew very well. She writes, in indirect discourse, quoting Asbury's inadvertently keen thoughts with grave irony, "It was one of those moments of communion when the difference between black and white is absorbed into nothing" (97).

That the communion in no way exalts him above the Negroes is completely lost on Asbury. He tries to cement his "hold" on them by taking responsibility for a can of milk returned on account of contamination with the odor of cigarette smoke. His exhilaration in the experience is justified, however, for he has tasted the violence of gnostic perception, the ritualized loss of gnostic art. "The experience had so exhilarated him that he had been determined to repeat it in some other way" (97).

The "text" which he chooses the second time, however, is such a dangerous one that the Negroes, more versed in such mysteries and respectful of the risk involved, refuse to "read" it. Randall and Morgan take refuge in the pretended authority of Mrs. Fox. They acquiesce in her authority just because it offers this makeshift shelter. By accepting Asbury's cigarettes, they showed how little they let it determine what they think and do. Randall and Morgan understand, without being consciously or articulately aware of it, that within the passivity of reflection there is considerable room for manipulation and self-protection, even self-aggrandizement. It is all a matter of acting "as if" one believed in this or that distinction, this or that locus of authority.

> The next afternoon when he and Randall were in the milk house pouring fresh milk into the cans, he had picked up the jelly glass the Negroes drank out of and, inspired, had poured himself a glassful of the warm milk and drained it down. Randall had stopped pouring and had remained, half-bent, over the can, watching him. "She don't 'low that," he said. "That *the* thing she don't 'low."
> Asbury poured out another glassful and handed it to him.
> "She don't 'low it," he repeated.
> "Listen," Asbury said hoarsely, "the world is changing. There's no reason I shouldn't drink after you or you after me!"
> "She don't 'low noner us to drink noner this here milk," Randall said.
> Asbury continued to hold the glass out to him. "You took the cigarette," he said. "Take the milk. It's not going to hurt my mother to lose two or three glasses of milk a day. We've got to think free if we want to live free!"
> The other one had come up and was standing in the door.
> "Don't want noner that milk," Randall said.
> Asbury swung around and held the glass out to Morgan. "Here boy, have a drink of this," he said.
> Morgan stared at him; then his face took on a decided look of cunning. "I ain't seen you drink none of it yourself," he said.
> Asbury despised milk. The first warm glassful had turned his stomach. He drank half of what he was holding and handed the rest to the Negro, who took it and *gazed down inside the glass as if it contained some great mystery*; then he set it on the floor by the cooler. (97–98; emphasis mine)

The milk, in its unremarkable pallor, does contain a great mystery, which does not in any way derive from Asbury—and over which he has no control. The "as if" describes Asbury's reading of Morgan's behavior. Morgan knows what Asbury does not. He is not pretending. This milk dissolves differences in such a way that there can be no pretense to authority by anyone, no sense of distinction, no clear separation of white man from black man, speaker from listener, writer from reader. Asbury does not know it yet, but his physical decline dates from his drinking those two glasses of unpasteurized milk. The milk, which emblemized an effort to assert authorial privilege over the Negroes and the larger world of his home, has made Asbury's return home and ultimate askesis, fall into the underworld, inevitable. It won't bring death as Asbury wants death, the sort of end which would freeze everything with him at the specular center: "Death was coming to him legitimately, as a justification, as a gift from life. That was his greatest triumph" (99). So he thinks.

But of course it is not to be. Asbury has witlessly quaffed the liquefied *lapis philosophorum*. The milk he poured down his scrawny throat has commenced to dissolve him. It has hastened the moment "when the difference between black and white is absorbed into nothing," the covering veil of flesh and words is permanently rent, and life and death are revealed as two faces of one body, both uninterruptible, invisible processes—the same process and the one which subsumes all others: aging, perception, recollecting, forgetting. If the terminology is pretentious (*lapis philosophorum*), it should not be allowed to distract us from the point, from the homeliness and the banality of the thing described—some unpasteurized milk, a cigarette—anything can serve as "art." The "text" and the name we give it matter infinitely less than what they do, the process they catalyze and make us see. The black and white, the print and the page, the object, dissolve in the act of reading.

Asbury, however, holds fast to his identity and his ignorance. He will, he thinks, be the author of his own end. It will be his one great legacy. It will force everyone to see themselves as he sees them, to see him as he would be seen, and most important, it will show him himself as he wants so badly to see himself. He believes with the ferocity of a wounded and cornered animal that he is the sole arbiter of his own ending. " 'Mother,' he said, 'I AM going to die,' and he tried to make each word like a hammer blow on top of her head. She paled slightly but did not blink. 'Do you think for one minute,' she said angrily, 'that I intend to sit here and let you die?' Her eyes were as hard as two old mountain ranges seen in the distance. He felt the first distinct stroke of doubt. 'Do you?' she asked fiercely. 'I don't think you have anything to do with it,' he said in a shaken voice" (101–102).

XIII. *Asbury's Unbeatific Vision*

Asbury has a dream fairly bloated with significance, all of which is completely lost on him. He interprets it as it suits him, according to his wish to believe that "he had failed his god, Art, but he had been a faithful servant and Art was sending him Death. He had seen this from the first with a kind of mystical clarity." Asbury dreams of his own burial, presided over by a Jesuit in whose "mysteriously saturnine face . . . was a subtle blend of asceticism and corruption" (103). The Jesuit disappears and Asbury awakes to find himself between two perfectly symmetrical specula: the moon and stars overhead, and a "black pond . . . speckled with little nickel-colored stars" below, with cows "spread out grazing." "One large white one, violently spotted," identified as "Art come to wake him," "was softly licking his head as if it were a block of salt." The white on black of the sky above and below (in the pond) is turned inside out in this cow, stupidly, mechanically, bovinely, reflexively, passively slobbering on Asbury's head as if it were something soluble, an inanimate mineral chunk—a *block*, as Block, doctor and scientist, might view it. In death, Asbury will be absorbed by art, into complete passivity, reflexivity. Though he refuses to understand the dream, it terrifies him. "He awoke with a shudder and discovered that his bed was soaking from a night sweat and as he sat shivering in the dark, he realized that the end was not many days distant. *He gazed down into the crater of death and fell back dizzy* on his pillow" (104; emphasis mine).

Asbury is confronting and refusing to comprehend that death is not death, a thing among other things (the corollary of course being that there are not any ineluctable "things" at all), not the ending which gives sense and shape to the story but pure negativity. Death, as Marcel discovers, is not death anymore, but life-in-death and death-in-life, a dizzying and perpetual dislocation, loss, sweet and stifling and nauseating as the reek of a million periwinkle flowers in a summer-hot room packed with humid air. It cripples, paralyzes, mesmerizes; the one thing it does not ever do is bring relief. Marcel's narrative, which displaces death outside its monolithic circumference, reflects this gnostic verity and so will Asbury's.

Asbury is like Swann in his failure to produce any written art. But he is very unlike Swann in the way that matters, in what he finally knows, and knows he does not know. Death comes to Swann in the prosaic and conceivable way. He knows he is going to die, he dies, he is dead, we hear no more of him except as others remember him. Bergotte's death is somewhat different, catalyzed and consumed by and indistinguishable from his contemplation of Vermeer's *View of Delft*, but it does neatly conclude his active role in the novel. So the deaths of Swann and Bergotte transcribe a progression towards a new idea of death and so of life; they point toward Marcel's perpetual recommencement, the alchemist's dragon swallowing its tail. Asbury's non-demise is like Marcel's even though he fails, like Swann, to produce any written art. Gnostic art needs no paint, canvas, pen, paper, print. It is a sense of losing, of a loss never finished and always in progress. Death, as Marcel and Proust both knew, is an ongoing process, present in the most vital instances of life.

XIV.   *Father Finn from Purgatory*

The peculiar and incidental personage of Father Finn demands comment because he exemplifies and in some measure explains O'Connor's fusion, or confusion, of Catholic dogma with gnostic theology. He disappoints Asbury deeply, proving physically as well as intellectually a speculum flawed far beyond the purpose which Asbury had designed for him, "blind in one eye and deaf in one ear" (105). He has never heard of James Joyce. He tries to make Asbury recite the catechism, Asbury responding that "the artist prays by creating" (106), an ominously ironic statement which he quickly belies. "I'm dying," he tells the priest, again attempting to wield death as an instrument of authority. Father Finn pierces cleanly through his pretensions: "But you're not dead yet!" You are dying, Asbury, not dead, which could be said of any newborn child. Asbury is distinguished because he very nearly knows it, knows what it means.

Not dead but dying, and what Asbury needs to do, according to Father Finn, is "Ask Him to send the Holy Ghost." Now, of course, the Holy Ghost is what O'Connor herself saw in the waterstain bird on the ceiling of Asbury's bedroom, the Catholic reading of it. But this naming, all naming, is a reflective process, a dialectic of image and language in the one mind of the perceiver—seer and namer. "Holy Ghost" is the nominative veil O'Connor drapes over that bird with the icicle in its beak, just as the image of a bird and an icicle are Asbury's own projected pictures. This "Holy Ghost" epitomizes the perpetual defensive posture of the psyche, draping layer after layer of word and image, interpretation, over encroaching emptiness. "The Holy Ghost," Asbury says, "is the last thing I'm looking for!" The priest replies, with a strange irony of which even O'Connor may have been only vaguely aware: "'Do you want to suffer the most terrible pain, greater than fire, the pain of loss? Do you want to suffer the pain of loss for all eternity?' Asbury moved his arms and legs helplessly as if he were pinned to the bed by the terrible eye" (107). This is just what he must do before he can "meet God face to face"; he must suffer loss and displacement of himself. He *is* lost, already being displaced and misplaced and reinterpreted and misinterpreted all the time. What he has to do is acknowledge this, see it, feel it, and give himself up to it. This is why Father Finn says that "the Holy Ghost will not come until you see yourself as you are." The divine will not be accessible to Asbury until he has felt "the most terrible pain, the pain of loss, for all eternity."

XV. Last Inklings

He is making marked progress in that direction. The day after Father Finn's visit, "He felt as if he were a shell that had to be filled with something but he did not know what." Asbury inches toward the debilitating admission that he has no authority to define himself or anyone else, that he is intellectually and spiritually null. "He even looked at the fierce bird with the icicle in its beak and felt that it was there for some purpose that he could not divine" (108). Once he has accepted his own mental implosion, himself as a shell, then Asbury will be near the passivity of art. But he still resists the suction of that black hole at his center, growing "more and more frantic for fear he would die without making some last meaningful experience for himself." Illumination, however, is inevitable. He works weird transubstantiations on the elements of his small world, absence becoming palpable to him, opacity and clarity, light and dark turning back and forth, each emerging from its opposite number. "The light in the room was beginning to have an odd quality, almost as if it were taking on presence. In a darkened form it entered and seemed to wait. Outside it appeared to move no farther than the edge of the faded tree-line, which he could see a few inches over the sill of his window" (109). He remembers smoking with Randall and Morgan in the dairy, another "experience of communion" in which distinctions seemed to come un-done. He wonders if perhaps he can't re-create that communion by re-convening the Negroes and passing out cigarettes.

He sends for Randall and Morgan, but the two refuse to play Asbury's game. Their passiveness, if not "art," is strong enough to spare them the pathos and embarrassment of "telling Asbury goodbye," of confronting his decline and having a "last smoke" with him. All they want is to extract themselves from this uncomfortable and potentially damaging situation without offending Asbury or his mother, without contributing to either's potential or actual authority over them, having let themselves be ushered into the sanctum of the white power structure and into the middle of a struggle between two of its prime movers, with Asbury on the one side, his every word pregnant with death's looming finality, and his mother on the other, their more accustomed, but no less vengeful and jealous dic-tatress. Asbury wants to use them to gain the advantage against his mother. Their passiveness, a chameleonlike aptitude for disappearing into the white man's expectations, into "niggerness," lets Randall and Morgan over-come Asbury's home-court advantage. They spare themselves having to reenact the pretentious defiance of smoking with him, this time in plain view of his mother. At the same time, they manage to make off with the cigarettes.

> The two of them came in grinning and shuffled to the side of the bed. They stood there, Randall in front and Morgan behind. "You sho do look well," Randall said. "You looks very well."
> "You looks well," the other one said. "Yessuh, you looks fine."
> "I ain't ever seen you looking so well before," Randall said.
> "Yes, doesn't he look well?" his mother said. "I think he looks just fine."
> "Yessuh," Randall said, "I speck you ain't even sick."
> "Mother," Asbury said in a forced voice. "I'd like to talk to them alone."
> His mother stiffened; then she marched out. She walked across the hall and into the room on the other side and sat down. Through the open doors he

could see her begin to rock in little short jerks. *The two Negroes looked as if their
last protection had dropped away.*

Asbury's head was so heavy he could not think what he had been going to
do. "I'm dying," he said.

Both their grins became gelid. "You looks fine," Randall said.

"I'm going to die," Asbury repeated. Then with relief he remembered that
they were going to smoke together. He reached for the package on the table
and held it out to Randall, forgetting to shake out the cigarettes.

The Negro took the package and put it in his pocket. "I thank you," he
said. "I certainly do prechate it."

Asbury stared as if he had forgotten again. After a second he became aware
that the other Negro's face had turned infinitely sad; then he realized that it
was not sad but sullen. He fumbled in the drawer of the table and pulled out
an unopened package and thrust it at Morgan.

"I thanks you, Mist Asbury," Morgan said, brightening. "You certly does
look well."

"I'm about to die," Asbury said irritably.

"You looks fine," Randall said.

"You be up and around in a few days," Morgan predicted. Neither of them
seemed to find a suitable place to rest his gaze. (110–11; emphasis mine)

They shuffle, stammer, grin toothily, act so much like white man's niggers
that they are immune to the white man's will. This passiveness is the only
escape possible. To contest Asbury they would have to emulate him, and
this, under the circumstances, would only confirm his advantage. So they
refuse to rest their gaze, to let Asbury cast himself on their retinas. They
have turned the tables on him. His only concern now is how to get rid
of them.

> Asbury looked wildly across the hall where his mother had her rocker turned
> so that her back faced him. It was apparent she had no intention of getting
> rid of them for him.
>
> "I speck you might have a little cold," Randall said after a time.
>
> "I takes a little turpentine and sugar when I has a cold," Morgan said.
>
> "Shut your mouth," Randall said, turning on him.
>
> "Shut your own mouth," Morgan said. "I know what I takes."
>
> "He don't take what you take," Randall growled.
>
> "Mother!" Asbury cried in a shaking voice. (111)

The *artiste* is reduced to nothing more than his mother's child.

He has exhausted not only every avenue of apotheosis but his own capacity for credence in the effort. No point in not seeing his mother for what she is, his blood reflection, fleshly mirror and matrix. That acceptance gives him a new perspective. "He sank into a heavy sleep from which he awoke about five o'clock to see her white face, very small, at the end of a well of darkness." His passiveness and hopelessness have given him distance. Mrs. Fox reflects him only across a dark warp of years and accommodation with various and ineffable adversaries.

> He awoke a little after six to hear Block's car stop below in the driveway. The sound was like a summons, bringing him rapidly and with a clear head out of his sleep. He had a sudden terrible foreboding that the fate awaiting him was going to be more shattering than any he could have reckoned on. He lay motionless, as still as an animal the instant before an earthquake.
>
> . . . The doctor came in making faces; his mother was smiling. "Guess what you've got, Sugarpie!" she cried. Her voice broke in on him with the force of a gunshot.
>
> "Found theter ol' bug, did ol' Block," Block said, sinking down into the chair by the bed. He raised his hands over his head in the gesture of a victorious prize fighter and let them collapse in his lap as if the effort had exhausted him. Then he removed a red bandanna handkerchief that he carried to be funny with and wiped his face thoroughly, having a different expression on it every time it appeared from behind the rag.
>
> "I think you're just as smart as you can be!" Mrs. Fox said. "Asbury," she said, "you have undulant fever. It'll keep coming back but it won't kill you!" Her smile was as bright and intense as a lightbulb without a shade. "I'm so relieved," she said.
>
> Asbury sat up slowly, his face expressionless; then he fell back down again.
>
> Block leaned over him and smiled. "You ain't going to die," he said, with deep satisfaction.
>
> Nothing about Asbury stirred except his eyes. They did not appear to move on the surface but somewhere in their blurred depths there was an almost imperceptible motion as if something were struggling feebly. *Block's gaze seemed to reach down like a steel pin and hold whatever it was until the life was out of it.* "Undulant fever ain't so bad, Azzberry," he murmured. "It's the same as Bang's in a cow." (112–13; emphasis mine)

"It will keep coming back, but it won't kill you." Asbury has been diagnosed. His condition is ludicrous, not terminal, or no more terminal than anyone else's. Asbury has got his wish: he is both Misfit and Grandmother, the author of his violence and its object. The milk he drank in the vain attempt to lure Randall and Morgan into "one of those moments of communion when the difference between black and white is absorbed into nothing" has dissolved his existence into an endless repetition of decline and recovery, contraction and dilation, an endlessly prolonged and rehearsed helplessness, neither life nor death for long ascendant: a roller-coaster limbo not unlike O'Connor's own ordeal with lupus. Asbury's will to power has condemned him to an eternity of contemplation, the most sublime, noble, and appalling of occupations, that of the highest of angelic orders, the Seraphim, whose duty it is to bear still and silent witness to the Deity.

To spend his life still and staring into the face of God Asbury must live in the contemplation of something not in front of him or anywhere else in the mortal world. The world and Asbury, each dissolved in reflection on the other, cannot see God as they see each other. Asbury looks in the mirror now and sees his eyes changed, turned inward, prepared to accept their own image, their own reflexivity.

> The eyes that stared back at him were the same that had returned his gaze every day from that mirror but it seemed to him that they were paler. They looked shocked clean as if they had been prepared for some awful vision about to come down on him. He shuddered and turned his head quickly the other way and stared out the window. A blinding red-gold sun moved serenely from under a purple cloud. Below it the tree-line was black against the crimson sky. It formed a brittle wall, standing as if it were the frail defense he had set up in his mind to protect him from what was coming. The boy fell back on his pillow and stared at the ceiling. His limbs that had been racked for so many weeks by fever and chill were numb now. The old life in him was exhausted. He awaited the beginning of a chill, a chill so peculiar, so light, that it was like a warm ripple across a deeper sea of cold. His breath came short. The fierce bird which through the years of his childhood and the days of his illness had been poised over his head, waiting mysteriously, appeared all at once to be in motion. Asbury blanched and the last film of illusion was torn as if by a whirlwind from his eyes. He saw that for the rest of his days, frail, racked, but enduring, he would live in the face of a purifying terror. A feeble cry, a last impossible protest escaped him. But the Holy Ghost, emblazoned in ice instead of fire, continued, implacable, to descend. (114)

XVI. The "Holy Ghost"

O'Connor gives this moment to the Holy Ghost. But that is another name, and so antithetical to the moment. It *is* the last film of illusion, the final covering veil, for the Catholic mind. The last veil is always there, always covering, so long as we are encumbered by mortality and words; it is only through the name, the veil, the print on the page, that we intimate its antithesis, *our* antithesis. The Holy Ghost is like Zeno's arrow: like death, like life, always descending, reaching, never attaining, never being finished. It has always already been where it is going and always going there again. Asbury discovers, as does Marcel, that art does not bring death per se, as ending, justification or anything else. Death has been misplaced, lost, cast outside the circle of Proust's novel, past the unbounded line of O'Connor's story, punctuated as it is by the mathematician's broken line and arrow connoting only direction, pointing off the page, out of the room. The ending is everywhere and nowhere, a reduction, a descent, the most subtle and cataclysmic implosion, continuing, "implacable." So Asbury, "sunk low, but mounted high," endures in the unpunctuated chill of contemplation, contemplation of a thing not there.

PART III

CHAPTER 8

François Villon, the Misfit

Nous cognoissons que ce monde est prison
(We know this world to be a prison)
        —Villon, translated by Galway Kinnell

So far I have considered the work of a writer who would probably have had no particular objection to being called gnostic, and one who would have objected strenuously (and did). Now I come to one who would probably not have been able to make up his mind how to respond. The common gnostic "taint" binding them together is violence. Proust's province was psychological violence, O'Connor's physical—both as emblems of the spiritual. And as every reader of Freud knows, it is the sexual which links the psychological and the physical. Hence it is for Villon, one of the most erotic of poets in any language, to complete the circle.

I. The Genre of Le Lais

Villon is best known for two long poems, *Le Lais* and *Le Testament*, in both of which a dying narrator makes bequests to friends and enemies. The latter poem is larger, more mature, and therefore richer, but the *Lais* contains all of Villon's obsessions in a limited volume of words, and for that reason I will use a close reading of it to gain entry to the other works. Mock testaments were a literary commonplace of the time. The form reflects the fusion which medieval theology had effected of the moment of death and the moment of judgment, death as the moment at which the good and evil of a lifetime were tallied up, weighed in the balance. In the fifteenth century, it was believed that an individual's destiny in the afterlife depended on his state of mind at the time of this inventory. The drama of salvation or perdition was concurrent with the individual's shedding his possessions, singling out others for reward or retribution, his last look back at his life, works, and goods.

> God and his court are there to observe how the dying man conducts himself during this trial—a trial he must endure before he breathes his last and which will determine his fate in eternity. This test consists of a final temptation. The dying man will see his entire life as it is contained in the book, and he will be tempted either by despair over his sins, by the vainglory of his good deeds, or by the passionate love for things and persons. His attitude during this fleeting moment will erase at once all the sins of his life if he wards off temptation or, on the contrary, will cancel out all his good deeds if he gives way. The final test has replaced the Last Judgment.[1]

A will, as a record of a man's reflections on his goods, friends, enemies, the accumulated detritus of a life, became a highly significant document, in a spiritual sense, one notarized by death itself.

The usual testament-poem was satirical and obscene. The anonymous "Pig's Testament" bequeaths the porker's "bones to the dicemaker, his feet to the errand runner, and his penis to the priest."[2] Villon's tone, however, is one of both pathos and fierce sarcasm. All in all, he takes the form very seriously and in a manner consistent with the popular idea that the moment of death gave meaning to an individual's life, that death shaped life into a clear, complete narration, with beginning, middle, and end. Death revealed the sense, the form which life had obscured. In all his poetry, Villon seeks to make sense of himself, to puzzle out his life, using the authority of death. Of course, he was not really dying when he wrote them. It is virtually certain, however, that he was, when he wrote the longer *Testament*, all the things he says he was—sick, impotent, in pain, hoarse, prematurely old. In the *Lais*, dying is rather a metaphor for having been spurned in love, for loss, then, and the ensuing work of mourning, detachment of libido from the lost love object. The poem is a legal metaphor for a psychic process.

II. *Stanza One: "In Harness"*

> In the year fourteen fifty-six
> I the scholar François Villon
> Sound of mind, in harness

1. Philippe Ariès, *Western Attitudes Toward Death from the Middle Ages to the Present,* trans. Patricia M. Ranum (Baltimore, 1974), 36–37.
2. Galway Kinnell, *The Poems of François Villon* (Boston, 1977), xiv.

Champing the bit, believing
As Vegetius the wise Roman
And great counselor advises
We must think out our works
Or else miscalculate.[3]

The first figure of the *Lais* compares the narrator to a beast of burden. As David Kuhn has demonstrated, Villon characteristically deals not in metaphor or simile—both "integrating" sorts of figure—so much as in *équivoques*, descriptive evasions of figurative language which point to a property or properties common to two or several things, in this case the *frain* and the *collier* common to the narrator and a prototypical work-horse or ox. We might suppose this to be an exception to Villon's usual practice, for the speaker does not actually sport bridle or harness. But there is really no periphrastic simile here at all; the equivocation, "doubling" of sense is simply linguistic rather than physical, having to do with actual shared physical properties. Such a linguistic "scattering" of meaning is most characteristic of Villon, most evidently in his jargon poems but throughout all his work.[4]

The word *frain* comes from the Latin *frenum*, meaning bridle, reins, bit, curb, that which restrains, a restraining object or force. No less a rhetorician than Cicero uses the expression *frenum mordere* just as Villon

3. L'an quatre cens cinquante six/ Je Françoys Villon escollier/ Considerant, de sens rassis/ Le frain aux dens, franc au collier/ Qu'on doit ses oeuvres conseillier/ Comme Vegece le raconte/ Sage Rommain, grant conseillier/ Ou autrement on se mesconte [Kinnell, 2]. I have used the translation, with French text, by Galway Kinnell, for two important reasons. First, because the translations have had the advantage of a close reading, and suggestions for revision, by David Kuhn. Kuhn, to my mind, and to Kinnell's, has done more to advance our understanding of Villon's work than any recent critic, and arguably, than any critic ever. Second, because Kinnell's volume reproduces the most reliable French text possible, the Longnon-Foulet edition of 1932, with some readings from the Neri edition of 1923, from the 1974 Rychner-Henry edition of the *Testament* (their 1977 edition of *Le Lais Villon et les poèmes variés* is also very useful), and some variants, where scholarship has determined these more reliable. Any text is necessarily problematic, for we have only four manuscripts on which to base them, along with the printed edition of 1489; none of the manuscripts is in Villon's hand and there are frequent and significant differences among the texts. The translation of Anthony Bonner (*The Complete Works of François Villon* [New York, 1960]) is also very useful.

Kinnell's book, however, does not include the text of the poems in jargon—translating these would be impossible. The best study of them is Pierre Guiraud, *Le Jargon de Villon, ou le gai savoir de la Coquille* (Paris, 1968), to which I am much indebted. André Burger's *Lexique de la langue de Villon* (Geneva, 1957), has also been indispensable.

4. See Guiraud, *Le Jargon de Villon*.

does, as meaning, "to chafe against restraint."[5] Two closely related words are the verb *frenare*, to hold in, and *frendare*, to gnash the teeth or simply to crush. Phonemically, all these are related to *fremere*, which may mean to grumble or complain, something done with the mouth and which might be accompanied by a gnashing of teeth. *Fremere* in French becomes *frémir*: "to be agitated by a slight movement of oscillation or vibration, producing a slight, obscure sound."[6] All of these evoke another French word of fairly recent coinage in Villon's time: *frénésie*, "a violent delirium brought on by acute cerebral ailment."[7] In this one word, there is layer upon layer of "sense," a discomposure and perturbation of sense suggested by all its phonic and epigrammatic strata: restraint, containment, crushing, *repression*, madness, trembling, vibration, productive of a low sound, a tremor which might be a plaint, a groaning.

All of which jars with *de sens rassis*, the legalistic statement of mental competency. *Rassis* itself adds interesting connotations. Its first known use was to describe lead which had cooled and hardened, resolidified, returned to a physical equilibrium. *Frain, rassis*: there is a tension drawn by both words, within and between them, a movement of pacification, which is a movement towards solidness, heaviness, weightiness, a stolid and palpable equipoise, containment, restraint, but the restraint is producing a tension, an audible vibration, a low tremor which might well be madness.

Franc au collier evokes the same tension, within itself and in contrast with *de sens rassis* and *le frain aux dens*. A horse which is *franc du collier* is one which works well in harness, pulls with great energy. We may suppose that the substitution of *au* for *du* is not intended to change the meaning. The expression *franc du collier* means, by figurative extension, "to act freely and boldly."[8] The expression is severely oxymoronic due to an ambiguity immanent in the word *franc*. What began as meaning a good, strong, energetic beast of burden, one which pulls in the harness as if free of it, as if the harness were not there, winds up meaning simply,

5. See *Cassell's Latin Dictionary* (New York, 1977), 255.
6. *Le Petit Robert, dictionnaire de la langue française* (Paris, 1976), 147: "être agité d'un faible mouvement d'oscillation ou de vibration qui produit un son léger, confus."
7. *Ibid.*, 747: "délire violent provoqué par une affection cérébrale aiguë."
8. *Ibid.*, 743–44.

to act boldly and freely. "Free in the collar" has become "free of the collar." But it is crucial that the latter meaning is the metaphorical one. *Franc du collier*, in its metaphorical sense (as applied to men), really means "acting as though free when in fact not free at all but strapped in, encumbered."

Franc comes from the Germanic tribe which gave France its name. Metonymically, it came to refer to the "free" status of the members of that tribe. Later it comes to mean "metaphysically, morally free," "honest, open," "simple, pure," and finally, "of unmistakable authenticity"—"that which is truly such."[9] It is the antonym of *douteux, équivoque*. The word also, by metonymic derivation from the Frankish people, means a unit of monetary exchange originally equal to a pound. Freedom is allied with economy, exchange, and these are always for Villon code words for sexuality. In the fourth stanza for instance he will speak of the necessity of *"autres complans," "*new fields to plow,*" "et frapper en ung autre coing," "*and a new die for striking coins." These expressions are literal *équivoques*, pointing to physical properties in which several acts overlap: breaking earth, pouring molten metal into a mold to form a coin, and coitus. Remember that *rassis* originally meant "hardened," lead which had been cooled and solidified. The expression *franc au collier*, signifying free and yet not free, encircled, bound, evokes the image of a piece of money in a necklace, or any setting, a band around its circumference or even a die. A bit of liquid gold, *lapis philosophorum*, poured and set, trapped in a shape.

Villon would be identifying himself as the coin then, but he must also be the one who pours it—sexually, it is the male who plows, strikes the coin. He is coin and coiner, act and actor, dance and dancer, written and writer. The gold in the die is solid, but in its molecular structure liquefaction is latent, immanent. And though occulted in the iron or sand of the die, it is still gold, gold though coated with base metal, liquid though solid, free though bound. It will not declare itself "purely, simply," yet it is pure and simple, the purest and simplest of substances. It cannot be named, described; it is none of the things it has been, and all of them. The only container, "die," which may give it "free rein"—contain it and

9. *Ibid.*, 744, "qui est véritablement tel."

liberate it at once—is language. So there is great irony in saying that "We must think out our works/ Or else miscalculate." We may think them out all we please; when it comes to what truly matters, we are "bound" to miscalculate anyway. Thinking out, indeed, is a protracted miscalculation, a failure to reduce, contain. It is, or should be, an uncalculation, an unraveling. If coin and coiner are the same, neither can contemplate the other as a totalized thing. A thing cannot calculate itself when it is not itself, but both itself and something else, always becoming something else.

It is also worthy of note that after giving the date, the first stanza brings up the matter of identity: *"Je Françoys Villon escollier."* *Escollier*, in the context, is equivocal indeed, containing "collar" and the contraction *es, en* + *les*—in harness or collar. The harness is allied with the egoistic *Je*, then, which is identified as the learned, the writerly *ego faber*, the plodding, careful thinker-out of things. The first stanza rhymes *escollier*, *collier*, and *conseillier*, the latter occurring twice. *Conseillier* splits the two syllables of *collier* and interjects a third. *Seille* means simply bucket, a wooden hollow receptacle for water. *Con* is a vulgar name for the female sexual organ, Villon's "die" for coining, also a hollow, for containing, receiving, and shaping the male essence. *Ciller*, which can be phonetically obtained by dropping one letter (an orthographic liberty which medieval scribes would have thought quite negligible and minor), means to blink, to close the eyes quickly, conjuring the image of a cavity by turns open and closed. The irony of the stanza's last line is again underscored: *conseillier ses oeuvres* implies an oscillating movement, a closing which immediately comes undone, reopens. It implies an always incomplete movement towards closure. Short of closure, of course, we always must miscalculate. There are too many variables for the equation to admit a solution.

III.   Stanza Two: *"The Prison of Great Love"*

> In the year above mentioned
> Near Christmas, the dead time
> When wolves live on the wind
> And men stick to their houses
> Against the frost, close by the blaze

> A desire came to me to break out
> Of the prison of great love
> That was breaking my heart.[10]

Christmas time, "the dead season," the season of death, when "wolves
live on the wind," "and men stick to their houses/ Against the frost, close
by the blaze." *Devant*, in the first line, becomes *du vent* in the third, a
word connoting time and space metamorphosed into a meteorological
phenomenon. Again, rather than the obvious conclusion, that here is a
periphrastic statement that the wolves are starving, it is true to the spirit
of Villon to wonder what more equivocal figuration might be occurring.
Wind is displaced air; it often implies noise, vibration of air concurrent
with displacement, as in wind instruments. Again the motif of vibration
is visible, a low noise, perhaps a plaintive one. The noise made by wind
is often characterized as whining or groaning, and the image of a man at
home by the fire in the dead of winter calls up memories of such sounds.

Vivre, in the meantime ("*se vivent du vent*"), can have a transitive meaning. To "live" something is to experience it deeply, intimately, as in Proust's
saying, "My loves, I have lived them, I have felt them"/ "*Mes amours, je
les ai vécus, je les ai sentis*," or Sartre's, "A feeling is a defined way of living
our connection with the world around us"/ "*Un sentiment est une manière
définie de vivre notre rapport au monde qui nous entoure*."[11] So the vibration, grinding of the teeth on the bit, the *frénésie* of the *frain aux dens* is
partly a phenomenon of wind (inhaling/exhaling). In the season of death,
survival, for *les loups*, is a matter of perceiving the wind's music very
acutely, feeling and hearing the *va-et-vient* of air very carefully. That music is the play of ambiguity itself, the uncertainty of direction and identity, and language, already introduced in the first stanza.

The most interesting word here, though, is *loup*. An archaic meaning
of it is a lesion, a wound, by metonymic connection with the wolf who
would make it with his teeth—biting the flesh as if it were a bit. Add a
mute 'e' and *loupe* is obtained, from the Frankish *luppa*, "large unformed

---

10. "En ce temps que j'ay dit devant/ Sur le Noel, morte saison/ Que les loups se vivent
du vent/ Et qu'on se tient en sa maison/ Pour le frimas, pres du tison/ Me vint ung vouloir
de brisier/ La tres amoureuse prison/ Qui souloit mon cuer debrisier" [Kinnell, 2].

11. *Petit Robert*, 1915.

mass of a clotted matter."[12] More specifically, it refers to a pearl or precious stone with an imperfection. So that the motif of a "hollow," a cavity, is repeated, this time with the connotation of pain, an emptiness made by the violent removal of flesh, and consequent clotting, the formation of an imperfection, a scar, such as that in an "imperfectly crystallized stone," which keeps it from being transparent, causes it to refract or reflect or obstruct the passage of light. There is also the common adjectival use of the word *wolf* in French to mean extreme, as in *une faim de loup* or *un froid de loup* (wolfishly hungry, wolfishly cold). An open wound feels extremes of cold and wind more acutely than whole flesh. It "lives" it more vividly.

This fourth line throws the second two into relief: "And men stick to their houses/ Against the frost, close by the blaze." Men protect their wounds from the searing of the wind; men hide from the howling elements and stay close to the fire so that they don't "live" the cold, so that the wind doesn't score their wounds and make them groan and howl. A *tison* is the remains of a log, most of which has been burnt up. The contrast drawn is between an enveloping, vast, windy, noisy cold, inhabited by animals, or, more abstractly, brutish beings, the brutish aspect of life, and the enclosed, narrow space of the house, lit and warmed by the tiny, expiring flames.

This tableau gives a specific topography of the figure which follows, of breaking out "Of the prison of great love." A prison is an enclosure like a house, offers a small space in which warmth and light may survive in an atmosphere of cold and dark, in which the howling of the wind may be more or less ignored. But it also implies forced confinement, "collaring." Breaking out of the prison means freedom, unbinding, release of the repressed, but also madness, frenzy, the screaming, biting cold wind. It means that the wound, filling like a die with blood, will harden, the blood dry, set (*rassis*) in the cavity and in so doing feel the blows of the elements. Freedom means pain. It also means revelation, the emergence from concealment of the flaws which make the living matter distort, twist light—cavities in which the wind makes odd, "unnatural" noises. The prison is the house of *great* love, and the confinement it

12. *Ibid.*, 1010, "grosse masse informe d'une matière caillée."

imposed "Was breaking my heart." The heart of the prison, of course, is the *tison*, and in this sense the breaking heart is the prison's own. The prison, its warmth and light, feed on their own heart, gradually consume and "break" it. So life feeds on itself, "breaks" itself, in its subservience to death, its dependence on death.

Villon's desire, in writing this poem, is to break out of the prison of love, which is the prison of life, with all that implies. He wants to break out in order to escape death—the core/*cuer* of the prison which feeds it and drags it down. His project is to escape love, life, and thereby death as well.

IV. *Stanza Three: "Celle devant mes yeulx/ Consentant à ma desfaçon"*

> I came to this point
> By watching her before my eyes
> Agreeing to my undoing
> Without even profiting from it
> Which is why I groan and cry to heaven
> And ask every god of love
> To give me revenge upon her
> And ease from love's pain.[13]

Death was in the fifteenth century a conventional metaphor for lost love, and here Villon introduces, without naming her or giving any particulars as to her identity, the author of his unhappiness, the one who consents to his "undoing" (*desfaçon*) apparently out of sheer malice, without "gaining" anything from it. As David Kuhn has pointed out, woman is like snow (*"Mais où sont les neiges d'antan?"*) in Villon's work, an emblem and an agent of the instability and ambiguousness of the self and its world. For the poet, "she," abstract woman, is a living *équivoque*, a winking wound, blinking cavity, the undoing (death) immanent in life. *Celle* has no clear antecedent and there is no development of the character forthcoming. "She" remains pronominal, hypothetical, unnamed and unnameable. The poem circles her, this blank center, like an empty har-

---

13. "Je le feis en telle façon/ Voyant celle devant mes yeulx/ Consentant à ma desfaçon/ Sans que ja luy en fust mieulx/ Dont je me dueil et plains aux cieulx/ En requerant d'elle venjance/ A tous les dieux venerieux/ Et du grief d'amours all'ejance" [Kinnell, 2].

ness or an unfilled die, a house whose embers have expired or a prison with no prisoners inside, a wound without blood; one long circumlocutionary lament of its absent locus.

There are three feminine nouns in the preceding stanza: *maison, saison,* and *prison.* All have to do with physical and temporal limitation, confinement and duration, the passage of time, parameters enforced by laws and men or the elements of the physical world (and, any good gnostic would add, its gods, the evil archons, the shock troops of time and space). The desire to escape these confinements, to break out of the prison of love and life, has come from the spectacle of "her" rejection of the narrator. Yet she is life, love, the house, the prison, the season of love. Love's, life's treachery have made Villon want to break out of them. They are melting him down, un-making (*des-façon*) him, consuming the ember of his heart "without even profiting from it." Finally, the motif of groaning, the almost inaudible lament, breaks through the surface of the language and becomes overt: "Which is why I groan and cry to heaven" ("Dont je me dueil et plains aux cieulx"). He is not mourning "her" but what she has agreed to, *his* unmaking, his own self. Tautologically, he calls on all the gods "of Venus" to avenge this, his loss of himself, on "her," who is love, his prisonkeeper, who in his pantheon is Venus. He wants to turn the goddess' own dogs on her.

Venereus in Latin often refers specifically to sexual love, as in *res Venereae*, when it doesn't mean simply, "of Venus." But does Villon mean the gods subservient to Venus or the gods superior to her? He is not clear, and perhaps it doesn't matter. What would seem to matter very much is the contrast drawn between these gods of *sexual* desire (venereal gods) and the poet's *grief d'amours, amor* being desire in its more emotional, less physical aspect, personified not as Venus but as Cupid. But "Cupid" in Villon's pantheon is feminine, "celle." Villon's project then would be to set sex against love. Love (*amor*) is his prison (*celle/cellule*) and he is calling on lust to loose him from the grip of more emotional attachment.

The most significant word in this stanza, for me, is *dueil*—it appears in the fifth line. This is from the Latin *dolere,* to suffer pain, mentally or bodily. In French, the noun *deuil* has always had the specific connotation of loss by death of a loved one. Villon is mourning his loss of himself. His use of the word is reflexive. His grief emanates from his "coming undone." The hole at the center of this poem, "*celle*," the absence un-nameable, is himself. The love he is talking about is, in one sense at least, self-love. The love object he has lost personifies this emptiness inside him, the death immanent in all life, and which is the principle of life, the possibility of it. The negativity of death is always at the heart of life, precedes life, fuels it and gradually extinguishes it just as combustion causes wood to give off warmth and light and to reduce itself to its chemical origins, to undo. The harness begins empty and ends empty, plenitude is temporary and illusory, a "miscalculation." Death (*La Morte Saison/ Saison de la Mort/ Saison de la Celle-ule*) is the prison and the guard, life and love. How can we break out of "her" harness? Of course, we might have guessed that the unspecified center of a poem written as a will would be death.

V. Rhetorical Death and Psychological Death

Villon, like Freud much later, sees death as *desfaçon*. This allies it with his favorite figure, the *équivoque*, which scatters, dissembles, and disassembles, deconstructs its own pretense to sense, or in the case of Villon's poems in jargon, which appear willfully nonsensical, act like palimpsests, meanings layered as richly and carefully as the multicolored strata of some fantastic torte, creating fault lines on the surface: one layer's ambiguity causes the whole to quiver, symptom of a poetic schizophrenia. This immanent negativity is death, scatterer, undoer, but also revealer of secrets, Proserpine. When Villon implores the *dieux venerieux* to avenge the perfidy of love, he is calling on the deities of flesh, of *carrion*, to overthrow the supposed gods of love, those hypocrites and deceivers. Cupid's arrows drug humans into ignorance of the nature of their own flesh, let them see beauty in (soon-to-be) rotting flesh, *including their own*. Here is a testimonial from *Le Testament.*

> This is what human beauty comes to
> The arms short, the hands shriveled
> The shoulders all hunched up
> The breasts? Shrunk in again
> The buttocks gone the way of the tits
> The quim? aagh! As for the thighs
> They aren't thighs now but sticks
> Speckled all over like sausages.

> This is how we lament the good old days
> Among ourselves, poor silly crones
> Dumped down on our hunkers
> In little heaps like so many skeins
> Around a tiny hempstalk fire
> That's soon lit and soon gone out
> And once we were so adorable
> So it goes for men and women.[14]

We need to keep in mind the hypothetical situation of a dying man who, by his attitude at the moment of death, will either save or damn his soul. He is faced with the problem of how to confront the loss of all he never really owned at all, the loss which is always implicit in possession (an illusion created by the "vapours" of amour) and precedes it. His body, his loved one(s), his possessions, his identity. This is a constant theme in all of Villon's work, reflected in his fondness for acrostics spelling out his name, but perhaps most visible in the ballade every line of which contains the words *"je congnois,"* I know.

> Prince, I know all things
> I know the rosy-cheeked and the pale
> I know Death who devours all
> I know everything but myself.[15]

He cannot concretize himself, totalize himself. Only death can do this. The problem is first a psychological one. Freud tells us that the self is constituted through its first love objects, usually parents. The ego comes into being to cathect and to emulate these object-choices, to internalize them as the superego. Objects might be projected or internalized—it is impossible to know which comes first—but suffice to say that the investment of libido in the self and investment of libido in objects are both necessary to what Freud called "love-attachment."

---

14. "C'est d'umaine beauté l'issue/ Les bras cours et les mains contraites/ Les espaulles toutes bossues/ Mamelles, quoy? toutes retraites/ Telles les hanches que les tetes/ Du sadinet, fy! quant des cuisses/ Cuisses ne sont plus mais cuissetes/ Grivelees comme saulcisses./ / Ainsi le bon temps regretons/ Entre nous, povres vielles sotes/ Assises bas a croupetons/ Tout en ung tas comme pelotes/ A petit feu de chenevotes/ Tost allumees, tost estaintes/ Et jadis fusmes si mignotes/ Ainsi en prent a mains et maintes" [Kinnell, 58].

15. "Prince, je congnois tout en somme/ Je congnois coulourez et blesmes/ Je congnois Mort quit tout consomme/ Je congnois tout fors que moy mesmes" [Kinnell, 166].

In cases of melancholia, when the ego perceives that it has lost something dear, whether the loss is real or whether the object was ever in any sense "possessed," the loss is felt as a real deficit of the ego's own substance, of libido; the ego makes no distinction between self-love and object-love. What it loves in others is projected; what it loves in itself are the introjected features of others. No distinction between the two is possible. If the object of love turns out to be death, a synecdochal figure of death, carrion, the self turns out to be the very same thing.

The ego cannot love carrion, death, once it recognizes them, once it is no longer so drugged by desire. It can love neither itself nor anyone else. Freud makes a distinction between simple mourning and melancholia, which he expressed as the difference between perceiving the world as empty and perceiving the self (and the world) as empty. Mourning is the "normal" process. In it the self remains in love with itself; its structure, subtended by libido (self-love), is not threatened. The melancholic, however, is afflicted by a pathological clarity. He sees his own shortcomings with a brutal lucidity.[16] This is Villon's state. He has realized the immanence of death in himself, in his lover, in love, in life. How can he love, others or himself, without loving death? His inability to love himself turns the scaffolding of the self to jelly, scatters sense, meaning, the normative structure which is the self's constitution, the psychic *modus operandi* of every human, soldered with libido. Like Proust, like O'Connor, Villon cannot bring himself to kiss life because it looks to him like a rotting corpse. This means he cannot bear to see himself in the mirror. Jean Laplanche has shown that this same notion, this inkling that Thanatos and Eros might be one and the same, is implicit, present but repressed, in Freud's own work.

Villon expresses the anxiety of this knowledge in his fondness for equivocal figurations and for antiphrasis. The best example of the latter is the famous ballade which begins with a line from Charles d'Orléans, "I die of thirst beside the fountain":

> I'm hot as fire, I'm shaking tooth on tooth . . .
>
> A white swan is a black crow
> The people who harm me think they help

16. Freud, "Mourning and Melancholia," *General Psychological Theory*, 167–68.

> Lies and truth today I see they're one
> I remember everything, my mind's a blank
> Warmly welcomed, always turned away.[17]

A more overtly psychological instance is *Le Debat de Villon et Son Cuer*. This poem is a dialogue between ego and superego, which can find no suitable milieu in which to meet. Like a homonymic *équivoque*, they are confined to one self, and yet desire and spiritual love, the lust of the id and the constraints of the superego, find no room to overlap in the ego, and the latter must swing wildly back and forth, in schizophrenic fashion, from the one to the other. One voice of the poem laments the sins of the flesh, while the other bewails the failure of the flesh, its aging. Each bemoans its incapacity to prevail over the other. Purely carnal love, embodied in *la grosse Margot* ("On filth we dote, filth is our lot"[18]) is opposed to the pure love of his mother, of his benefactor Guillaume de Villon, of the pure, "chaste" woman, always the one who rejects Villon, whom he loses before he has ever possessed her. In the self, as in the poem, layers of meaning are superimposed, various codes membraneously laminated on each other, creating oozing fissures, fault lines in the surface.

> You don't know a thing—Yes I do—What?—Flies in milk
> One's white, one's black, they're opposites—
> That's all?—How can I say it better?
> If that doesn't suit you I'll start over—
> You're lost—Well I'll go down fighting—
> I've nothing more to tell you—I'll survive without it—[19]

"I can't love, and I can't be loved," "I can't love myself, and I can't love anyone else," these formulas paraphrase the broken economy of libido suggested by the use of coinage and the casting of coins as figures of

---

17. "Je meurs de seuf aupres de la fontaine/ Chault comme feu et tremble dent a dent . . . // D'ung cigne blanc que c'est ung corbeau noir/ Et qui me nuyst croy qu'il m'ayde a povoir/ Bourde, verté, au jour d'uy m'est tout un/ Je retiens tout, rien ne sçay concepvoir/ Bien recueully, debouté de chascun" [Kinnell, 176–78].

18. "Ordure amons, ordure nous assuit" [Kinnell, 128].

19. "Rien ne congnois—Si fais—Quoy?—Mouche en let/ L'ung est blanc, l'autre est noir, c'est la distance—/ Est ce donc tout?—Que veulx tu que je tance?/ Se n'est assez je recommenceray—/ Tu es perdu—J'y mettray resistance—/ Plus ne t'en dis—Et je m'en passeray—" [Kinnell, 198].

desire, libidinal transaction: "I can't get back in circulation/ No more than cried-down money."[20]

In one passage of the *Testament*, Villon compares Narcissus' fate to Orpheus', concluding that they are the same.

> Love made the sweet minstrel Orpheus
> Playing his flutes and bagpipes
> Risk death from the murderous
> Dog four-headed Cerberus
> It made the fair-haired boy Narcissus
> Drown himself down in a well
> For love of his lovelies
> Lucky the man who has no part in it.[21]

Narcissus, of course, never knew he was in love with himself. It is impossible to separate love from self-love. Any kind of love is a descent into hell, is to die and be buried *without knowing it*. Both Orpheus and Narcissus went to their ends without any idea that that was what they were doing, drugged by love, hallucinating life where there was only death, Venus where was Proserpine.

Villon, however, is no longer deceived. He has realized the emptiness of his self, and his world. Where once he "took encouragement/ From those sweet looks and winning ways/ That seemed so sincere"[22] (his own and others'), he now sees betrayal and destruction. He proposes to replace the old deities of love, redefine love itself: "I need fresh fields to plough/ And another die for coining in."[23] To avoid the prison of life ("She" who "took me prisoner" and "wills and orders that I suffer/ Death and cease to live"[24]), he proposes to embrace death, the immanence of death in every thing: "*Sound of limb I die* . . . And become a martyred lover/ One of the saints of love."[25]

20. "je ne me puis mettre/ Ne que monnoye qu'on descrie" [Kinnell, 60].
21. "Orpheüs le doux menestrier/ Jouant de fleustes et musetes/ En fut en dangier d'un murtrier/ Chien Cerberus a quatre testes/ Et Narcisus le bel honnestes/ En ung parfont puis se noya/ Pour l'amour de ses amouretes/ Bien est eureux qui riens n'y a" [Kinnell, 66].
22. ". . . prins en ma faveur/ Ces doulx regars et beaux semblans/ De tres decevante saveur" [Kinnell, 2].
23. "Planter me fault autres complans/ Et frapper en ung autre coing" [Kinnell, 4].
24. "Veult et ordonne que j'endure/ La mort et que plus je ne dure" [Kinnell, 4].
25. "Par elle meurs les membres sains/ Au fort je suis amant martir/ Du nombre des amoureux sains" [Kinnell, 4].

What he means to "take leave of" and "put from himself" in the seventh stanza are the hallucinations which normal investment of libido makes possible. He is committing himself to a state of permanent melancholia, the pathological state of mourning occasioned, according to Freud, by the "narcissistic" sort of object-choice, by a confusion of object-love and self-love, and by a powerful ambivalence in the relation to the lost object.

> In melancholia the relation to the object is no simple one; it is complicated by the conflict of ambivalence. The latter is either constitutional, i.e. it is an element of every love-relation formed by this particular ego, or else it proceeds from precisely those experiences that involved a threat of losing the object. For this reason the exciting causes of melancholia are of a much wider range than those of grief, which is for the most part occasioned only by a real loss of the object, by its death. In melancholia, that is, countless single conflicts in which love and hate wrestle together are fought for the object; the one seeks to detach the libido from the object, the other to uphold this libido-position against assault. These single conflicts cannot be located in any system but the Ucs, the region of memory-traces of things (as contrasted with word-cathexes). The efforts to detach the libido are made in this system also during mourning; but in the latter nothing hinders these processes from proceeding in the normal way through the Pcs to consciousness. For the work of melancholia this way is blocked, owing perhaps to a number of causes or to their combined operation. Constitutional ambivalence belongs by nature to what is repressed, while traumatic experiences with the object may have stirred to activity something else that has been repressed. Thus everything to do with these conflicts of ambivalence remains excluded from consciousness, until the outcome characteristic of melancholia sets in. This, as we know, consists in the libidinal cathexis that is being menaced at last abandoning the object, only, however, to resume its occupation of that place in the ego whence it came. So by taking flight into the ego love escapes annihilation. After this regression of the libido the process can become conscious; it appears in consciousness as a conflict between one part of the ego and its self-criticizing faculty.[26]

Of course, it is just such ambivalence that conditions Villon's view of everything, himself as well as the object, an ambiguity which must finally be that of life and death, the one within the other.

This is a confusion which Freud himself, and indeed, Western culture, have never resolved. As Laplanche has made clear, Freud struggled in vain to make an effective distinction between Thanatos and Eros. For

26. Freud, "Mourning and Melancholia," *General Psychological Theory*, 177–78.

Villon, of course, this ambivalence is not the exception at all but the rule, not, as Freud has it, a neurotic symptom. Rather, melancholia is the only possible result of realizing the intrinsic perfidy of any love object, internal or external, melancholia as a sense of loss of self and loved one(s). Freud himself comes very near to admitting that the melancholic is more lucid than his mentally healthy brethren: "We only wonder why a man must become ill before he can discover truth of this kind."[27] Villon would doubtless reply that, naturally, if health is defined as a blindness to the horror of life and love, to the death within them, then clarity of vision must be considered "sick."

VI. *The Strategy: Psychic and Sexual Anarchy*

First the narrator proposes to call "her," the female locus of his poetical universe, by a more appropriate name or names than the innocent sounding "Venus" or "love"—Proserpine, or death, or prison, or prison-keeper, or perhaps most ominous and fitting of all, the transparent pronoun *she*, for she is nothing but flux. Why Villon chooses to characterize the force of death-in-life as female is a complicated issue, rendered largely moot by what "she" emblemizes: the equivocal nature of reality which obscures as well the distinction between man and woman. It undoubtedly owes something to contemporary poetic convention, which made lost love a commonplace for death, and to Villon's own personal psychic history. Her equivocal sexuality, however, is suggested by the very terms in which he takes his leave of her: "I'm sure it's best that I leave (*fouïr*)/ So Goodbye I'm off to Angers."[28] Kuhn has shown that *fouïr* plays upon the two meanings of *foutre* and *fouiller*, while *aller a Angiers* is synonymic with *ongier*, *foutre*, and *aller a Bourges*, which means "to become a pederast." Mightn't we surmise, then, that to avoid "such danger," he means to give himself up to a homosexual ardor? "Since she won't let me have/ Her favors . . . "[29] There are broad hints in his other works that Villon suffered from venereal disease, and this might be one sense in which he refers to "danger," the sense in which love, sex, literally attack the body's tissues. Evoking homosexuality, the narrator gives a clear signal as to the

27. *Ibid.*, 167–68.
28. "Mon mieulx est ce croy de fouïr/ Adieu, je m'en vois a Angiers" [Kinnell, 4].
29. "Puis qu'el ne me veult impartir/ Sa grace ne la me departir" [Kinnell, 4].

meaning of what he is really proposing: a permanent melancholia, sense of loss, and the clarity of vision, knowledge, implicit therein. He means to ignore apparent distinctions, to see through the hallucinatory conventions of "normal" behavior. He will escape danger by identifying with it, becoming indistinguishable from it.

This is of course no real escape, and he is not proposing real escape. There can be no exit from one's own self, substance. What he means to do is to join in the dance of death (sex, life) in full knowledge of what it is, to lie with death while seeing it for what it is, to infect himself deliberately, pervert himself willfully, wreak violence, above all sexual/psychic violence, which to Villon is not distinguishable from poetic violence, deliberately. He means to adapt the Misfit's (note the overlapping terminology of the two writers: Mis-fit, *des-façon*) strategy of random physical violence to sexuality and therefore, necessarily, to psychology as well; he intends to combine the doctrines of Marcel and the Misfit. His violence will be sexual, psychic and therefore literary, and physical.

VII. "Sound of Limb I Die"

This strategy is to act as if dead while still living, to possess nothing, have no center, no heart, to participate in and be part of the forces of corruption and decay. To enact it, he must strip himself of every supposed possession, as a dying man would, starting with his own body. This is precisely what he intends to do: "there's no way-station after you die/ And I go into a distant land/ So I draw up this present legacy."[30] He leaves his heart—"pale, pitiful, dead and gone"[31]—to "her." He disowns his fame, his cutlass, a pair of pants, a hauberk, books, various items of clothing, comestibles, properties which he never really owned but which are part of his memory's domain. All of these are equivocal figurations of the basic sexual theme: "tools, purses, and coins, for example, serving as symbols for the penis, and gardens, houses, shoes, hats, stockings, and so on, representing the vagina."[32]

30. "Et après mort n'y a relaiz/ Je m'en vois en pays loingtain/ Si establis ce present laiz" [Kinnell, 6].
31. "Palle, piteux, mort et transy/ Elle m'a ce mal pourchassié/ Mais Dieu luy en face mercy" [Kinnell, 6].
32. Kinnell, xviii. Kinnell is paraphrasing David Kuhn. See Kuhn, *La poétique de François Villon* (Paris, 1967).

VIII. *"Lastly as I Sat Writing"*

The great bell of the Sorbonne interrupts the inventory of dispossession, tolling nine o'clock, 3 × 3, the number of the Trinity, the hour of Angelus, prayer in remembrance of the Annunciation. The bell, metal cast in a "die," hollow itself like a die, containing a bit of metal which causes it, and the air, to vibrate, make a sound—this to recall to all who hear the resurrection of the body, defiance of death, of Jesus Christ. Villon, too, tries to believe this and take comfort from it. "I stopped and wrote no further,"[33] as if writing and prayer were antithetical, or as if one were a substitute for the other, or both. The antithesis is strongly suggested by the sudden reappearance of the heart he is supposed to have given away: "In order to pray as the heart bid,"[34] *cuer* being the locus, the centrum of which he supposedly stripped himself. The tolling of Angelus is a sound very different from a low, sad, whistling wind, or a groan— the voice of orthodox religion, as opposed to the voice of the poet/poem; the latter more subtle, more a rustling than a tolling. This moment is one of nostalgia for the heart, for the certainties, illusions of normalcy.

But in taking up his *cuer* again, the poet grows "muddled/ Not from any wine I'd taken/ But as if my spirit were bound,"[35] which is just what he ought to feel, putting on the *collier* of faith, restoring his "heart." Though a part of him yearns to go back, to leave the cold and go back inside by the dying fire, the aging heart, to go on loving "her," to take back what it has lost, it knows that this is not really possible. Whereupon *La Dame Mémoire*, Lady Memory, another avatar of "her," the lost lady, the prisonkeeper, "takes up" all the intellectual faculties, defenses, structures of normality, distinction, order, the scaffolding of the well-adjusted self. These are described as her "collateral specie, currency," "species," that is, those faculties akin to her, to memory, and which are the means of exchange, the *modus operandi*, the lubrication in the intellect's economy: the "opinionative," the "intellectual," the "estimative," the "similitative," and the "formative." The "lost one" collects these in her *aulmoire*, the drawer where *aumones*, religious or charitable donations, would be

33. "Si suspendis et mis en bonne" [Kinnell, 18].
34. "Pour prier comme le cuer dit" [Kinnell, 18].
35. "Ce faisant je m'entroublié/ Non pas par force de vin boire/ Mon esperit comme lié" [Kinnell, 18].

kept, and takes them with her. They are part of her, of what is lost, abolished by the knowledge that they were makeshift, fictive. Without them, "you can go/ Mad and lunatic."[36]

The moment of nostalgia for sanity is quickly over, though it appears in other places in Villon's work, and indeed, is an integral part of the sense of lack and loss which is melancholia. It is not, as many critics have maintained, evidence of a fidelity to Catholicism. Rather, his inability to sustain these moments, when they occur, is evidence of his distance from Catholicism. *Oubliance*, a richer word than *forgetfulness*, connoting oblivion, nothingness, non-remembrance and non-sense, is placed on the emptied throne of memory, and the sensory (*le sensitif*), the sensual, the "organs," are brought to power. The sensual and the sexual are the "currency" of *oubliance*, its "collateral species."

Of course, this is no proper ending at all. No real conclusion, closure, is possible. Death is everywhere in the poem, immanent, and cannot mean closure any more. The ink (the intellectual faculties) is frozen and the fire (the *cuer*, locus of things, distinctions) has gone out ("I couldn't have found any fire . . ."[37]). Villon is "Unable to give it another ending."[38] The final stanza, however, does suggest the poet's "diseased" state, the sickness of knowing what he knows and the pain which his loss, his lack, his perpetual melancholia/mourning, cause him: he "doesn't eat, shit or piss/ Dry and black like a furnace mop . . ."[39] In knowledge of death, in cheating death by unmasking it, seeing through its disguises and rending them, doing violence to them, exaggerating its own *danse macabre*, there is no real pleasure, no peace in this world, death's world. As O'Connor's Misfit says, "Shut up Bobby Lee, it's no real pleasure in life." And yet, in that knowledge, in that unpleasure, Villon knew there was a cruel, searing joy: "Verity, are you ready to hear it?/ In sickness alone is there joy."[40]

Perhaps that joy amounts to this, the true divine paradox: if death is

36. "Que par leur trouble homme devient/ Fol et lunatique par mois" [Kinnell, 20].
37. "De feu je n'eusse peu finer" [Kinnell, 20].
38. "Et ne peus autrement finer" [Kinnell, 20].
39. "Qui ne menjue, figue, ne date/ Sec et noir comme escouvillon" [Kinnell, 20, 22].
40. "Voulez vous que verté vous die?/ Il n'est jouer qu'en maladie" [Kinnell, 168].

not only process but, as the Middle Ages saw it, passage as well, then living so close to it would bring us into proximity with the real life to come, as close as we in this world can be—not to hell, which only prolongs death eternally, but to the crumb of gold always absent from the alchemist's alembic, the elemental distillate of uncreated life.

Conclusion

Both mourning and melancholia, in Freud's paradigm, are states of "working-through," "letting-go," in which the ego de-cathects an object which it can no longer perceive as an object. "The testing of reality, having shown that the loved object no longer exists, requires forthwith that all the libido shall be withdrawn from its attachments to this object."[1] It "works through" the cathexis, which survives the object, and gradually convinces itself of the "reality" of the loss, admits it, and so "frees" the libido to recathect a new object. This working through is a struggle; it is characterized by "a turning away from reality" and "great expense of time and cathectic energy."[2] Melancholia may result from a different sort of clash between "reality" and the self's cathexes. It may result from "a loss of a more ideal kind."[3] "One feels justified in concluding that a loss of this kind has been experienced, but one cannot see clearly what has been lost, and may the more readily suppose that the patient too cannot consciously perceive what it is he has lost. This, indeed, might be so even when the patient was aware of the loss giving rise to the melancholia, that is, when he knows whom he has lost but not what it is he has lost in them."[4] The distinction between the two processes comes to just this: the melancholic's loss is unlocatable, but seems more or less reflexive, for "in grief the world becomes poor and empty; in melancholia it is the ego itself."[5] The self's loss, while it cannot

---

1. Freud, "Mourning and Melancholia," *General Psychological Theory*, 165.
2. *Ibid.*, 166.
3. *Ibid.*
4. *Ibid.*
5. *Ibid.*, 167.

be specified, is experienced as a loss *of* self, "an impoverishment of his ego."[6] The distinction between mourning and melancholia, then, comes to the difference between the loss of the object as other and the loss of the object as self. The distinction, like so many Freud makes, does not hold up very well.

It is based on the same sort of inner/outer model as the distinction between narcissistic and anaclitic object-choices. In the former, cathexis is supposed to be based on "resemblance," whereas in the latter, the ego cathects an object which does not so much resemble it as respond to some need, contribute to its "survival." The classic Freudian example of an anaclitic choice is the infant's cathexis of its mother. Yet the distinction dissolves along with the self/other one when we consider it in the light of Lacan's "mirror-stage," the child's realization of himself as a self by the perception of his image outside of himself, as other: "The specular image seems to be the threshold of the visible world," says Jacques Lacan. The function of the mirror-stage is to "establish a relation between the organism and its reality—or, so to speak, between *Innenwelt* and *Umwelt*."[7] This relation is based on confusion, non-distinction. The child conceives, organizes itself as other, and it perceives reality, otherness, as a function of itself as otherness. But we do not even need to go to Lacan to discover that Freud's anaclitic/narcissistic distinction cannot hold up. Both types of cathexes reflect the self's wish to supplement a perceived lack: the narcissist may love what he is, was, would like to be, or "someone who was once part of himself."[8] The last possibility suggests strongly the bond between mother and child, supposedly the prototype for all anaclitic relations. The anaclist, in turn, loves what he does not have but needs for "survival." In both cases desire is defined in terms of introjection (see page 10 of my Introduction). The self wishes to possess its objects and to possess itself in its objects, to supplement its own insufficiency, to take into itself, incorporate, what it lacks. There is bound to be some narcissism and some anaclisis in any object-cathexis, some measure of identi-

6. *Ibid.*
7. "l'image speculaire semble être le seuil du monde visible"; "établir une relation de l'organisme à sa réalité—ou, comme on dit, de l'*Innenwelt* à l'*Umwelt*." Jacques Lacan, *Ecrits I* (Paris, 1966), 92, 93 [translation mine].
8. Freud, "Mourning and Melancholia," 71.

fication with the desired other (for desire *is* the wish to incorporate, introject, the object). As Laplanche and Pontalis put it, "The two types of object-choice are thus looked upon as purely ideal, and as liable to alternate or to be combined in any actual individual case." They go on: "Yet it is doubtful whether an antithesis between the narcissistic and the anaclitic object-choices even as ideal types, is tenable. It is in 'complete object-love of the attachment type' that Freud observes 'the marked sexual overvaluation which is doubtless derived from the child's original narcissism and thus corresponds to a transference of that narcissism to the sexual object'."[9]

This issue is complicated by the inevitable fact that no object is going to respond perfectly to the exigencies of the desiring subject, if for no other reason, then simply because the subject cannot succeed in possessing the object, introjecting it completely. The object asserts its autonomy by expressing its own desires, all of which cannot meet the desiring subject's demands, supplement its "insufficiencies" ideally. What this means is that ambivalence—or, more aptly, polyvalence—is bound to characterize any object-choice, a commingling of the positive desire to introject and the negative desire to project—the "ambivalent" desire to possess certain aspects of the other but not all. Insofar as the self knows itself as other, this polyvalency of desire will affect it regardless of any object-choice. Melanie Klein goes so far as to contend that "the instinct is ambivalent from the start: 'love' for the object is inseparable from its destruction, so that ambivalence becomes a quality of the object itself."[10] Thus the ambivalence which Freud wishes to ascribe to melancholic object-cathexes must be a more or less prominent characteristic of any relation, of self to self or self to other.

Mourning and melancholia follow on the self's perception that there *is* no object. In melancholia, there is the complication that the subject may not have any idea what he has lost and may never have known. Awareness of the object seems indistinguishable from awareness of loss. Not only is there no object, but there never *was* one. In the "normal"

9. Laplanche and Pontalis, *The Language of Psychoanalysis*, 259.
10. *Ibid.*, 27. See Melanie Klein, *Contributions to Psycho-Analysis* (London, 1950), and Melanie Klein, *et al.*, *Developments in Psycho-Analysis* (London, 1952); also Jacques Lacan, "L'Aggressivité en psychanalyse," *Ecrits*.

case of mourning, the self "undoes" the old cathexis so that it may finally cathect a new *accessible* (real) object. The melancholic, however, has perceived his loss as reflexive, as a loss of himself, some indeterminate part of himself. This means that the melancholic's loss breaks the economy of the self, the self's perception of itself as an object, as totalized, constituted. The loss itself would appear indistinguishable from this sense of "uncenteredness" to such an extent that it is pointless to wonder which may have come first, which "caused" the other. The multivalencies of desire (introjection and projection, Eros and Thanatos) are directed inward, but without any precise object. Paradoxically, Freud observes that this results in a strange clarity: the melancholic self sees itself and its failures, its insufficiency, with a cruel impartiality. It becomes visible to itself as a botched, incomplete totality, a would-be whole riddled with irremediable holes. Freud implies that the melancholic self, to cathect new objects, must first undo this object*less* cathexis which it directs inward, toward its own "empty," absent center. It must locate a new object *in* itself so that it may reconstitute itself *as* an object (a whole object), and so restore the economy (totalization) of its psychic constitution. This, he points out, is often achieved through a narcissistic object-choice, "identification" with a real object.[11] In any case, what occurs when the melancholic admits the loss of his hypothetical and centerless "inner" object, works through and succeeds in "undoing" the cathexis which uses up so much psychic energy "probing," "groping" after the lost object, seeking to "totalize" the object's absence, is *mania*—an ecstatic overflow of psychic energy which had been absorbed in attempting to cathect (totalize) the hypothetical object. "When mania supervenes, the ego must have surmounted the loss of the object (or the mourning over the loss, *or perhaps the object itself*), whereupon the whole amount of anticathexis which the painful suffering of melancholia drew from the ego and 'bound' has become *available*. Besides this, the maniac plainly shows us that *he has become free from the object* by whom his suffering was caused, for he runs after new object-cathexes like a starving man after bread."[12] He runs

---

11. Freud, "Mourning and Melancholia," 81. Freud also says that, in regressing from the narcissistic "object-choice" to reflexive narcissism, the melancholic "abolishes" the object; 173.

12. *Ibid.*, 175–76 [emphasis mine].

to bind the energy all over again, then, to re-totalize an object—himself and the other, himself *in* the other.

Yet we must begin to wonder if, in the context of Freud's own theory, this is possible. The multivalency of any cathexis, the tangle of introjection and projection which must inevitably characterize the subject's perception and desire of itself and the other implies that the "object-cathexis" of self or other can never be fully realized, and that any cathexis must be more or less simultaneous with a de-cathexis, a "working-through," detachment from the object as it was so as to re-cathect the object as it is becoming, in the negative space of the present, the point of the future's fall into the past. (Freud himself says that ambivalence—if not "constitutional," in which case he is excused from offering any explanation of it—must result from "those experiences that involved a threat of losing the object";[13] if we have learned anything from Proust, O'Connor, and Villon, it is that *any* experience of *any* other, including the self, is nothing but the threat of loss.) This constant dialectic of loss and possession in which neither can actually occur parallels the tension of Eros and Thanatos, the former always threatening to turn into the latter. This means that loss is not an event, but an ongoing perception, and more than that, perception itself. In the Heideggerian model of temporality, the present cannot be totalized, objectified; it is no more than the loss of the future as it turns into memory, memory in turn causing the moment (*Augenblick*) to signify by virtue of arbitrary association, as in the case of Proust's *calorifère*.[14] The "testing of reality" which is the work of mourning never reveals anything but the object constituted in terms of memory (lost time). Cathexis, desire, as phenomena of the present, must always, as Proust said of jealousy, "struggle in the void."[15] Cathexis is the perception of loss—lost time—so cathexis is remembering, which by virtue of random association causes the "object" to "mean" something, to seem to be an "object" while in fact, "imprisoned" in the present, it can exist only negatively. To desire (cathect, attempt to totalize, objectify) the otherness of the present in the otherness of the present is to lose, and the self that

13. *Ibid.*, 177.
14. Martin Heidegger, *Sein und Zeit* (7th ed.; Tubingen, 1953) and *Being and Time*, trans. John Macquarrie and Edward Robinson (New York, 1962), *passim*.
15. See note 1, Chapter 4 herein.

perceives this, that knows it, is in a state of perpetual and reflexive mourning, *unless it leaves off the last stage of the Freudian paradigm, the stage of cure, and ceases trying to totalize the other.*

What would result from such a "free-floating" cathexis, deliberately undirected desire? What but the ecstatic *mania* which results from the release of energy always bound in object-cathexes? We might call this self-conscious loss a *gnostic* ecstasy in the full sense of the word, ecstasy that is loss and beyond loss, that is constant self-displacement, desire that is "free" because it knows that it has (can have) no object. This is the violent, antithetically knowledgeable ecstasy of desire which knows that it is synonymous with loss and does not care; Marcel laughing at his loss of "time"; Asbury Fox struck dumb by the untotalizable emptiness of "grace"; Villon, wallowing in the "corruption" of his own flesh and psyche; Ruby Hill hearing her own voice rise out of the dark, "out nowhere in nothing"; Harry-Bevel ecstatically drowning in "The River of Pain," the flow and constantly displacing current of loss, an ecstasy which the logical positivist and objectifier (like unto Dr. Freud himself) Mr. Paradise can never see as anything but tragic. The self gives up on restoring some hypothetically "previous" economy—distinction and correspondence of signifier and signified, self and other, ego and superego, Eros and Thanatos—and turns loss, the eternally renewed effort to objectify, totalize, possess, into an ecstatically repetitious mania.

Reading and writing bring us into this state of (and beyond) "treading on nothing," as O'Connor put it, of "struggling in the void," as Proust put it, by refusing to let us say what we or the poem means, by receiving our desire to "make sense" (to "possess" the text) and throwing it back at us, forcing us into memory in order to "decipher," inspiring a desire for meaning which is objectless, providing *pre*texts for desire which is denied any object—gratuitous, directionless desire. We are jealous of the text's meaning. We may, as I have, enter into a work of mourning, a working through of any text in which we "test" its "reality" through any methodology we like—linguistic, biographical, thematic, rhetorical—but what we must finally discover is the projective/introjective multivalency of our readerly desire to make sense (to objectify the "object"), the fact of its constantly renewed failure to satisfy, requite us—its "mendacious flimsiness." But it is this frustration, our naming of the text, forcing it to name us, like Albertine's naming of Marcel, which pushes us beyond loss of the object and into pure loss. We must consent, as Villon puts it, to our own *desfaçon* as we consent to the text's. Death, Hades, the scatterer, is all we can know—not ourselves or the other or the text or any abstract "truth" about these things. "Lies and truth today I see they're one."[16] To perceive is to decipher and to decipher is to rend(er); the gnosis is to know one's rending even as one renders and to be glad of it, for there is nothing intrinsically good in the matter rent (the text or some Albertine).

The point of having dreams, as Proust said, is to see them fail. The effect of violence, evil, as O'Connor said, is to serve the good by "piercing pretension." The end of love, as Villon wrote, is to "undo" us until we have no choice but to put off the defensive shroud of the totalizing intellectual faculties, "bound" up as they are with the effort to possess, reify, the poet's indeterminate object—"her." If we have to die we may as well embrace death knowing it for what it is; if we must lose we may as well embrace loss in the same spirit. In that "sickness alone," as Villon tells us, "is there joy."[17]

This loss would appear to be implicit in reading and writing as it is in desire. What sets the three writers which I have discussed apart is that they are aware of the loss and celebrate it, in one guise or another, instead of struggling against it. There are surely other writers who realize this same possibility, always latent in the act of writing, but none so powerfully complementary as these, at least for me. Of course, part of my discovery, and theirs, is that any choice of which text to read (to lose) must, at the gnostic level, of self-conscious loss, be arbitrary. Any sense we make of such choices is an attempt to belie the loss of reading them. All objects of desire, whether persons or texts, serve no purpose save to make us experience desire—objectless desire. Such a statement in no way exaggerates or distorts the statements of the writers themselves. Proust tells us that the only thing any writer can do is to give us desires. O'Connor says that purpose in any serious writer must be to exhaust the "concrete," exhaust all modes of "making sense" and leave the reader with a sense of

16. Kinnell, 176–78.
17. *Ibid.*, 168.

incomprehensibility.[18] The choice of what to read or how to read it is unimportant, provided that they "exhaust the concrete," "give us desires," and reveal the identity which Villon discovered between "truth and lies."

With this in mind, one last additional author may provide a pretext for recapitulating all I have observed so far, and for a summation of the "gnostic" view of desiring, writing, and reading. Rilke wrote a poem entitled "Mourning" which contradicts the Freudian paradigm in just the way that Proust, O'Connor, and Villon do, but with just the verbal economy called for by a "conclusion."

> *Mourning* (Crying Out)
>
> Whom will you mourn (cry out to), heart?
> More and more fleetingly
> your way struggles through the unknowable
> People. All the more vainly perhaps
> since it holds to its old path,
> Holds to the path to the future,
> to the lost.
>
> Earlier. Did you mourn (cry out)? What was it?
> A fallen
> Berry of joy, unripe.
> Now my oak of joy is breaking for me
> breaking for me in the storm is my late
> Oak of joy.
> The most beautiful in my invisible
> Landscape, by which you make me knowable
> to Angels who are invisible.[19]

The poem begins by an interrogative prolepsis—"Whom?" The ques-

---

18. See Proust, *Pastiches et Mélanges*, 229; and O'Connor, *Mystery and Manners*, 38, 41–42.

19. *Klage.* "Wem willst du klage, Herz? Immer gemiedener/ ringt sich dein Weg durch die unbegreiflichen/ Menschen. Mehr noch vergebens vielleicht,/ da er die Richtung behalt,/ Richtung zur Zukunft behält,/ zu der verlorenen.// Früher. Klagtest? Was wars? Eine gefallene/ Beere des Jubels, unreife./ Jetzt aber bricht mir mein Jubel-Baum/ bricht mir im Sturme mein langsamer/ Jubel-Baum./ Schönster in meiner unsichtbaren/ Landschaft, der du mich kenntlicher/ machtest Engeln, unsichtbaren." The German text is from *Selected Poems of Rainer Maria Rilke*, bilingual text with translations and commentary by Robert Bly (New York, 1981), 162 [translation mine].

tion is never answered, simply points to something absent, the absence of an object. The "heart" itself is a metonymy of the self as object, as centered, totalized. What object can the self find, then, to reflect and so totalize its center, its desire? Where can "you" find an object that will let you be as centered as your metonymic name? In no person, the poem implies, for "your way" is through the "unknowable people," "vain" because it is the way of the present, the way of the future falling into the past, being "lost," only known in terms of memory and desire, anticipation. All the "people," perceived proleptically, are projected losses, known only as the future of the past, the anticipated moment in which the future will have become the past.

The second stanza places us at that anticipated moment, reverses the first stanza's forward motion in a metaphorical analepsis: "Earlier." The interrogative groping after an indeterminate object ("What was it?") is repeated from this reversed perspective. The loss which these questions cannot locate is implicit in the temporal reversal of the questions themselves, their backward/forward movement, situating us in the moment of reading, of questioning, of seeking to locate the poem's object— "Whom?" "What was it?" What event, what individual, precipitated this seesaw of displacement, dilation of desire? We cannot know that. All we can know is the consequence: "a fallen berry of joy." "Unripe"—the fall must have been incomplete, arbitrary, premature. A fall from whom, what, where? From some unspecified origin, primal identity with some unlocatable object, a "tree" which the poem omits. But the fallen, "lost" berry germinates, duplicates whatever it fell away from, "imitates" it. At least, in becoming a tree, it leads us to suppose that the absence from which it fell was also a tree with which, in its germination (work of mourning?), it "identifies," losing itself in the image(lessness) of the invisible tree, its response to the two unanswerable questions of the poem, future and past. Now the image, figure, mimesis of that misplaced tree is "breaking" in "storm." What can the storm be but the "mourning," crying out, work of mourning, the identification with and duplication of loss, absence, which is the work of mourning, the fallen berry's "effort" to displace itself, like Proust's furnace with its disagreeable noises, towards some object lost in memory? It is simultaneous and synonymous with my effort to reproduce the poet's and the poem's "image," the present of my reading the poem, "breaking" the duplicated "tree" of Rilke's loss in my reduplication of it, refiguration of it, its renewed fall in my reading. (Fall from where? the page? the future? In either case, from some unspecifiable absent origin, ahead of and behind me, which I may only infer by the shape, the sort of "tree" which the poem makes in my eye, my present memory of reading it, made possible by all my memories of other poems, words, "shapes" of trees, real and rhetorical.) My act of reconstituting, "regerminating" the tree, is an act of identification with the poet's initial (but hypothetical, imagined, lost) act of writing the poem, its "falling" from his pen.

The tree becomes a "tree of joy" by the endlessly renewed storm and breakage of reading and losing. The obvious sexual reading of the poem would provide another emblem of this readerly desire, always breaking, losing itself outwards, as purely physical desire also does. This repeated loss and celebration of losing situates reader and writer beyond loss, beyond the present in which loss occurs, in an "invisible," atemporal landscape of "lost" objects, repeatedly broken, and recuperated, but never as objects, never totalized, always imitating lost, original shapes. Our repeated loss of them situates us, as readers (the "you" of the poem), outside of time as well, for we identify with the poem's speaker, imitate him, as much as we identify with his hypothetical audience. We narrate the poem to ourselves. This situates us in the invisible, atemporal landscape, beyond death, presided over by atemporal beings—the invisible objects, answers to the poem's questions of "Whom?" and "What?," "invisible angels," untotalizable objects, readers lost in contemplation of the poem like the seraphim before the Deity, like Asbury, Marcel, and Villon, immobilized and lost in their contemplation of themselves, our contemplation of them, our mutual "invisibility," somewhere in between our "insufficiency" and our "anticipation."[20]

20. *"le stade du miroir* est un drame dont la poussée interne se précipite de l'insuffisance à l'anticipation"; Lacan, *Ecrits I*, 93.

Selected Bibliography

I. PROUST

A. Editions

Pastiches et Mélanges. Paris: Gallimard, 1919.
A la recherche du temps perdu. Text established by Pierre Clarac and André Ferré. 3 vols. Paris: Gallimard, Bibliothèque de la Pléiade, 1954.
Contre Sainte-Beuve. Preface by André de Fallois. Paris: Gallimard, 1954.
Contre Sainte-Beuve, preceded by *Pastiches et mélanges*, and followed by *Essais et articles*, edition established by Pierre Clarac with the collaboration of Yves Sandre. Paris: Gallimard, Bibliothèque de la Pléiade, 1971.
Jean Santeuil, preceded by *Les plaisirs et les jours*. Edition established by Pierre Clarac with the collaboration of Yves Sandre. Paris: Gallimard, Bibliothèque de la Pléiade, 1971.

B. Books and Articles in Whole or in Part About Proust

Albaret, Céleste. *Monsieur Proust: Souvenirs recueillis par Georges Belmont*. Paris: Robert Laffont, 1973.
Bardèche, Maurice. *Marcel Proust Romancier*. 2 vols. Paris: Les Sept Couleurs, 1971.
Beckett, Samuel. *Proust*. New York: Grove Press, 1957.
Benjamin, Walter. "The Image of Proust," *Illuminations*. New York: Schocken, 1969.
Bersani, Leo. *Marcel Proust: The Fictions of Life and Art*. New York: Oxford, 1965.
Blanchot, Maurice. "L'Expérience de Proust," *Le Livre à venir*. Paris: Gallimard, 1959.
Butor, Michel. "Les 'Moments' de Marcel Proust," *Répertoire*. Paris: Editions de Minuit, 1960.
Cattaui, Georges. *Marcel Proust*. Paris: Julliard, 1952.
———. *Proust et ses métamorphoses*. Paris: Nizet, 1972.
Chauffier, Louis-Martin. "Proust ou le double 'je' de quatre personnages," *Problèmes du Roman*. Paris: Confluences, n.d.

Deleuze, Gilles. *Proust et les signes*. Paris: Presses Universitaires de France, 1970.

de Man, Paul. "Semiology and Rhetoric," and "Reading (Proust)," *Allegories of Reading*. New Haven: Yale University Press, 1981.

Doubrovsky, Serge. *La Place de la madeleine*. Paris: Mercure de France, 1974.

Fowlie, Wallace. *A Reading of Proust*. 2nd ed. Chicago: University of Chicago Press, 1975.

Genette, Gérard. *Figures III*. Paris: Editions du Seuil, 1972.

Girard, René. *Deceit, Desire, and the Novel*. Baltimore: Johns Hopkins University Press, 1971.

Huyghe, René. "Vermeer et Proust." *Prométhée, Amour de l'Art*, XVII (1936), 7–15.

Joiner, Lawrence D., ed. *The Art of the Proustian Novel Reconsidered*. Rock Hill, S.C.: Winthrop College, 1979.

Levin, Harry. "Proust, Gide, and the Sexes." *PMLA*, June, 1950.

O'Brien, Justin. "Albertine the Ambiguous." *PMLA*, December, 1950.

Painter, George. *Proust: The Early Years*. Boston: Atlantic-Little-Brown, 1959.

———. *Proust: The Later Years*. Boston: Atlantic-Little-Brown, 1965.

Pasco, Allan H. *The Color-Keys to "A la recherche du temps perdu."* Genève: Droz, 1976.

Poulet, Georges. *L'espace proustien*. Paris: Gallimard, 1964.

Richard, Jean-Pierre. *Proust et le monde sensible*. Paris: Editions du Seuil, 1974.

Shattuck, Roger. *Proust's Binoculars*. New York: Random House, 1963.

———. *Marcel Proust*. New York: Viking, 1974.

Zaehner, R. C. *Mysticism, Sacred and Profane*. New York: Oxford, 1957.

II.   FLANNERY O'CONNOR

A.   Editions

Three by Flannery O'Connor. New York: Signet, 1962.

Everything That Rises Must Converge. New York: Farrar, Straus, Giroux, 1965.

Mystery and Manners. Edited by Sally and Robert Fitzgerald. New York: Farrar, Straus, Giroux, 1969.

The Habit of Being. Letters selected and introduced by Sally Fitzgerald. New York: Farrar, Straus, Giroux, 1979.

B.   Books and Articles About O'Connor

Coles, Robert. *Flannery O'Connor's South*. Baton Rouge: Louisiana State University Press, 1980.

Driskell, L. V., and J. T. Brittain. *The Eternal Crossroads*. Lexington: University of Kentucky, 1971.

Eggenschwiler, David. *The Christian Humanism of Flannery O'Connor*. Detroit: Wayne State University Press, 1972.

Friedman, Melvin J., and Lewis A. Lawson, eds. *The Added Dimension: The Art of Flannery O'Connor*. New York: Fordham University Press, 1966.

Hawkes, John. "Flannery O'Connor's Devil." *Sewanee Review*, LXX (Summer, 1962), 395–407.

Hendin, Josephine. *The World of Flannery O'Connor*. Bloomington: Indiana University Press, 1970.

Hyman, Stanley E. *Flannery O'Connor*. Minneapolis: University of Minnesota Press, 1969.

Martin, Carter. *The True Country*. Nashville: Vanderbilt University Press, 1969.

Muller, Gilbert H. *Nightmares and Visions: Flannery O'Connor and the Catholic Grotesque*. Athens: University of Georgia Press, 1972.

Orvell, Miles. *Invisible Parade*. Philadelphia: Temple University Press, 1972.

III. FRANÇOIS VILLON

A. Editions

In French

Longnon, Auguste, ed. *Oeuvres de François Villon*. *Quatrième édition revue par Lucien Foulet*. Paris: Classiques français du moyen age, 1932.

Mary, André, ed. *Oeuvres*. Paris: Garnier, 1970.

Rychner, Jean, and Albert Henry, eds. *Le Testament Villon*. Vol. I: Texte. Genève: Droz, 1974.

———. *Le Lais Villon et les poèmes variés*. Vol. I: Textes. Genève: Droz, 1977.

Thuasne, Louis, ed. *François Villon: Oeuvres*. Vol. I. Paris: Picard, 1923.

Villon, François. *Oeuvres d'après le manuscrit Coislin, texte, variantes et concordances de Rika Van Deyck, traitement automatique de Romana Zwaenepoel*. 2 vols. Saint-Aquilin-de-Pacy: Librairie Editions Mallier, 1974.

French and English

Kinnell, Galway. *The Poems of François Villon*. Boston: Houghton Mifflin, 1977.

B. Books and Articles About Villon

Brunelli, G. A. *François Villon, con bibliografia e indici a cura di P. Morabito*. Milan: Marzorati, 1961.

Burger, André. *Lexique de la langue de Villon, précédé de notes critiques pour l'établissement du texte*. Genève: Droz, 1974.

———. "l'Entroubli de Villon." *Romania*, LXXIX (1958), 485–95.

———. "La Dure prison de Meung," in *Studi in onore di Italo Siciliano*. Florence: Olschki, 1966.

Champion, Pierre. *François Villon, sa vie et son temps*. 2 vols. Paris: Champion, 1913. Second edition with a new foreword, 1933.

Demarolle, Pierre. *L'Esprit de Villon*. Paris: A. G. Nizet, 1968.

Fowlie, Wallace. *De Villon à Péguy: Grandeur de la pensée française*. Montréal: Editions de l'Arbre, 1944.

Fox, John. *The Poetry of Villon*. London: T. Nelson, 1962.

Guiraud, Pierre. *Le Jargon de Villon, ou le gai savoir de la Coquille*. Paris: Gallimard, 1968.

Kinnell, Galway. Introduction to *The Poems of François Villon*. Boston: Houghton Mifflin, 1977.

Kuhn, David. *La Poétique de François Villon*. Paris: Colin, 1967.

Longnon, Auguste. *Etude biographique sur François Villon, d'après les documents inédits conservés aux Archives Nationales*. Paris: H. Menu, 1877.

Neri, Ferdinando. *François Villon*. Turin: Chiantore, 1949.

Poirion, Daniel. Preface to *Villon: Oeuvres poétiques*. Paris: Garnier-Flammarion, 1965.

———. "Le fol et le sage auprès de la fontaine: La rencontre de François Villon et Charles d'Orléans." *Travaux de Linguistique et de Littérature de Strasbourg*, VI (No. 2), 53–68.

Rice, Winthrop H. *The European Ancestry of Villon's Satirical Testaments*. New York: Corporate Press (Syracuse University Monographs), 1941.

Rychner, Jean, and Albert Henry, eds. *Le Testament Villon*. Vol. II: Commentaire. Genève: Droz, 1974.

Siciliano, Italo. *François Villon et les thèmes poétiques du Moyen Age*. Paris: Colin, 1934.

———. *Mésaventures posthumes de Maître Françoys Villon*. Paris: A. et J. Picard, 1973.

Spitzer, Leo. "Etude a-historique d'un texte: Ballade des Dames du temps jadis." *Modern Language Quarterly*, I (1940), 7–22.

Thuasne, Louis. *François Villon: Oeuvres. Commentaire*. Vols. II and III. Paris: Picard, 1923.

Vitz, Evelyn. *The Crossroad of Intention: A Study of Symbolic Expression in the Poetry of François Villon*. The Hague: Mouton, 1974.

Yve-Plessis, R. *La Psychose de François Villon*. Paris: Schemit, 1925.

IV. BOOKS ABOUT GNOSTICISM, ALCHEMY, KABBALAH, MYSTICISM

Bloom, Harold. *Kabbalah and Criticism*. New York: Seabury, 1975.

———. *The Flight to Lucifer, a Gnostic Fantasy*. New York: Farrar, Straus, Giroux, 1979.

Burckhardt, Titus. *Alchemy, Science of the Cosmos, Science of the Soul*. Baltimore: Penguin Books, 1972.

Derola, Stanislaw K. *Alchemy: The Secret Art*. New York: Avon, 1973.

Eliade, Mircea. *The Sacred and the Profane*. New York: Harcourt, Brace, 1959.

———. *Shamanism, Archaic Techniques of Ecstasy*. Princeton: Princeton University Press, 1964.

———. *Mephistopheles and the Androgyne*. New York: Harper Torchbook, 1969.

———. *Myth of the Eternal Return*. Princeton: Princeton University Press, 1954.

Haardt, Robert. *Gnosis: Character and Testimony*. Leiden: E. J. Brill, 1971.

James, William. *The Varieties of Religious Experience*. New York: Collier-Macmillan, 1961.

Jonas, Hans. *The Gnostic Religion*. Boston: Beacon Press, 1963.

Robinson, James M., ed. *The Nag Hammadi Library*. San Francisco: Harper and Row, 1977.

Scholem, Gerschom G. *Major Trends in Jewish Mysticism*. New York: Schocken, 1954.

———. *Zohar, the Book of Splendor: Basic Readings from the Kabbalah*. New York: Schocken, 1963.

Swedenborg, Emanuel. *Angelic Wisdom Concerning the Divine Love and the Divine Wisdom*. New York: Swedenborg Society, 1885.

Zaehner, R. C. *Mysticism, Sacred and Profane*. New York: Oxford, 1957.

Zweig, Paul. *The Heresy of Self-Love*. 2nd. ed. Princeton: Princeton University Press, 1980.

V. OTHER WORKS OF HISTORICAL, PSYCHOLOGICAL, OR MISCELLANEOUS RELEVANCE

Ariès, Philippe. *Western Attitudes Toward Death from the Middle Ages to the Present*, trans. Patricia M. Ranum. Baltimore: Johns Hopkins University Press, 1974.

———. *L'Homme Devant la Mort*. Paris: Editions du Seuil, 1977. Translated by Helen Weaver. *The Hour of Our Death*. New York: Knopf, 1981.

Artz, Frederick B. *The Mind of the Middle Ages A.D. 200–1500*. New York: Knopf, 1958.

Bachelard, Gaston. *La psychanalyse du feu*. Paris: Gallimard, 1949.

Bataille, Georges. *Sur Nietzsche, volonté de chance*. Paris: Gallimard, 1945.

———. *La Part maudite*. Paris: Editions de Minuit, 1949.

———. *La Littérature et le mal*. Paris: Gallimard, 1957.

Bergson, Henri. *Oeuvres*. Texts annotated by André Robinet. Paris: Presses Universitaires de France, 1963.

Bersani, Leo. *Baudelaire and Freud*. Berkeley: University of California Press, 1977.

Blanchot, Maurice. *L'espace littéraire*. Paris: Gallimard, 1955.

———. *Le livre à venir*. Paris: Gallimard, 1959.

Bloom, Harold. *The Anxiety of Influence*. New York: Oxford, 1973.

———. *A Map of Misreading*. New York: Oxford, 1975.

———. *Poetry and Repression*. New Haven: Yale University Press, 1976.

————. "Freud and the Poetic Sublime: A Catastrophe Theory of Creativity." *Antaeus* (Spring, 1978), 355–77.

Curtius, Ernst Robert. *European Literature and the Latin Middle Ages.* Translated by Willard Trask. New York: Pantheon, 1953.

Deleuze, Gilles, and Félix Guattari. *L'Anti-Oedipe.* Paris: Editions de Minuit, 1971.

Derrida, Jacques. *L'Ecriture et la différence.* Paris: Editions du Seuil, 1967.

————. *De la Grammatologie.* Paris: Editions de Minuit, 1967.

Frady, Marshall. *Southerners: A Journalist's Odyssey.* New York: NAL/Times Mirror, 1980.

Freud, Anna. *The Ego and the Mechanisms of Defense.* New York: International University Press, 1966.

Freud, Sigmund. *Inhibitions, Symptoms, and Anxiety.* New York: Norton, 1959.

————. *The Ego and the Id.* New York: Norton, 1960.

————. *Beyond the Pleasure Principle.* New York: Norton, 1961.

————. *Character and Culture.* New York: Collier-Macmillan, 1963.

————. *General Psychological Theory.* Edited by Philip Rieff. New York: Collier-Macmillan, 1963.

————. *Sexuality and the Psychology of Love.* New York: Collier-Macmillan, 1963.

Girard, René. *Violence and the Sacred.* Baltimore: Johns Hopkins University Press, 1977.

Heidegger, Martin. *Sein und Zeit.* 7th ed. Tubingen: Niemeyer, 1953. *Being and Time.* Translated by John Macquarrie and Edward Robinson. New York: Harper and Row, 1962.

Hillman, James. *The Myth of Analysis.* Evanston: Northwestern University Press, 1972.

————. *Loose Ends.* Zurich: Spring Publications, 1975.

————. *The Dream and the Underworld.* New York: Harper and Row, 1979.

Huizinga, Johan. *The Waning of the Middle Ages.* New York: Anchor Doubleday, 1954.

Jackson, W. T. H. *The Literature of the Middle Ages.* New York: Columbia University Press, 1960.

James, William. *The Principles of Psychology.* 2 vols. New York: H. Holt and Co., 1923.

Jung, Carl J. *Memories, Dreams, Reflections.* New York: Vintage, 1965.

————, ed. *Man and His Symbols.* New York: Dell, 1968.

————. *Psychology and Alchemy.* Princeton: Princeton University Press, 1968.

Kermode, Frank. *The Sense of an Ending.* New York: Oxford, 1968.

Lacan, Jacques. *Ecrits.* Paris: Seuil, 1966.

Ladurie, Emmanuel Le Roy. *Montaillou: The Promised Land of Error.* New York: Vintage, 1979.

Laplanche, Jean. *Vie et Mort en Psychanalyse.* Paris: Flammarion, 1970.

————, and J.-B. Pontalis. *The Language of Psychoanalysis*. New York: Norton, 1973.

Lederer, Wolfgang. *The Fear of Women*. New York: Harvest, 1968.

Lewis, C. S. *The Allegory of Love*. London: Oxford, 1936.

Mallarmé, Stéphane. *Oeuvres complètes*. Text established and annotated by Henri Mondor and G. Jean-Aubry. Paris: Gallimard, Editions de la Pléiade, 1945.

Marcus, Steven. "Freud and Dora: Story, History, Case History," *Representations*. New York: Random House, 1975.

Mauron, Charles. *Introduction à la psychanalyse de Mallarmé*. Neuchatel: A La Baçonnière, 1950.

McKisack, May. *The Fourteenth Century, 1307–1399*. London: Oxford University Press, 1959.

Praz, Mario. *The Romantic Agony*. New York: Oxford, 1970.

Rank, Otto. *Art and Artist*. New York: Knopf, 1932.

————. *The Myth of the Birth of the Hero, and Other Writings*. Edited by Philip Freund. New York: Knopf, 1959.

Saulnier, V. L. *Pensée humaniste et tradition chrétienne aux XVᵉ et XVIᵉ siècles*. Paris: Boivin, 1950.

Schlegel, Friedrich. "Philosophische Lehrjahre 1796–1806," *Kritische Friedrich-Schlegel-Ausgabe*. Vol. XVIII, edited by Ernst Behler. Paderborn: Ferdinand Schoningh, 1963.

————. *Dialogue on Poetry and Literary Aphorisms*. Translated by E. Behler and R. Struc. University Park: Pennsylvania State University Press, 1968.

Singer, June. *Androgyny*. New York: Doubleday, 1976.

Starobinski, Jean. *Les mots sous les mots*. Paris: Gallimard, 1971.

Taylor, Henry Osborne. *The Medieval Mind: A History of the Development of Thought and Emotion in the Middle Ages*. 2 vols. 4th ed. Cambridge: Harvard University Press, 1959.

Thorndike, L. *History of Magic and Experimental Science*. 8 vols. New York: Columbia University Press, 1923–1958.

Trilling, Lionel. "Art and Neurosis," *The Liberal Imagination*. New York: Scribner's, 1959. Reprint, New York: Harcourt Brace Jovanovich, 1979.

The Tropology of Freud. Diacritics, 9:1 (Spring, 1979).

Tuchman, Barbara. *A Distant Mirror: The Calamitous Fourteenth Century*. New York: Alfred A. Knopf, 1978.

Valéry, Paul. *Oeuvres*. Vol. 1. Edited by Jean Hytier. Paris: Gallimard, Editions de la Pléiade, 1957.

Index